SONABAI

ANOTHER WAY OF SEEING

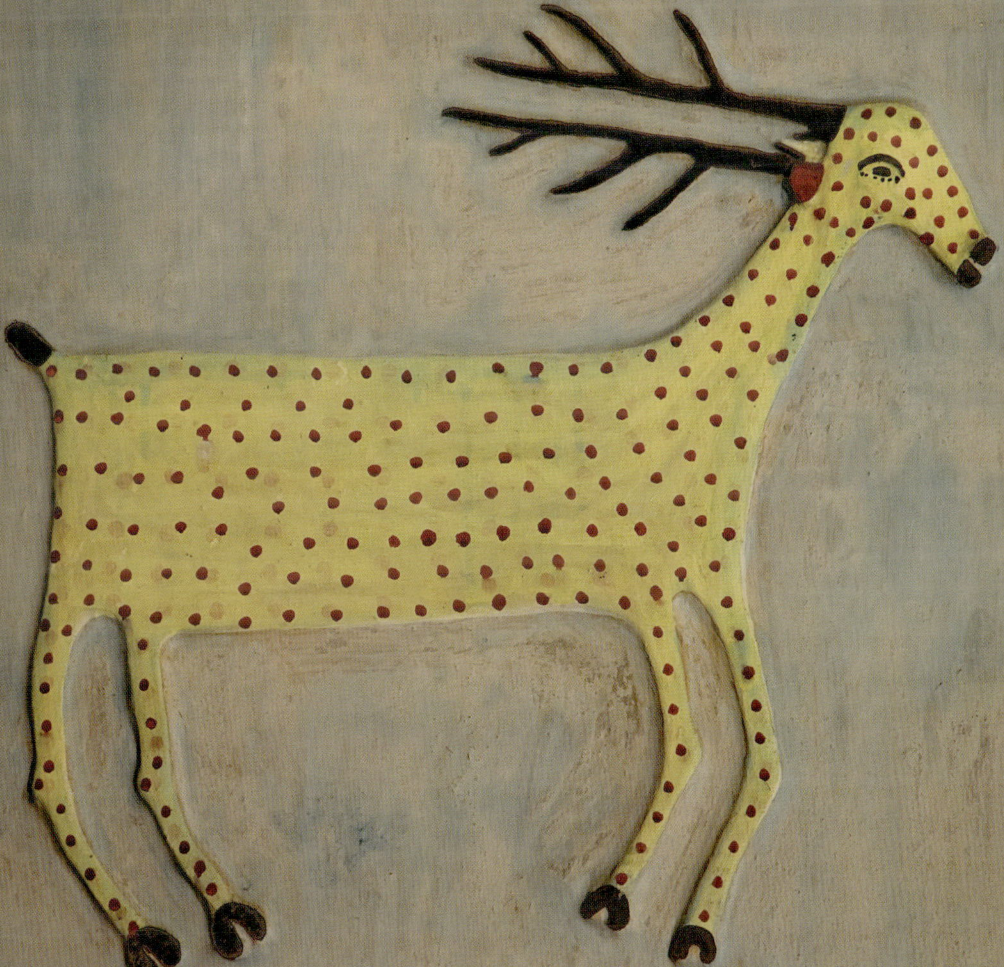

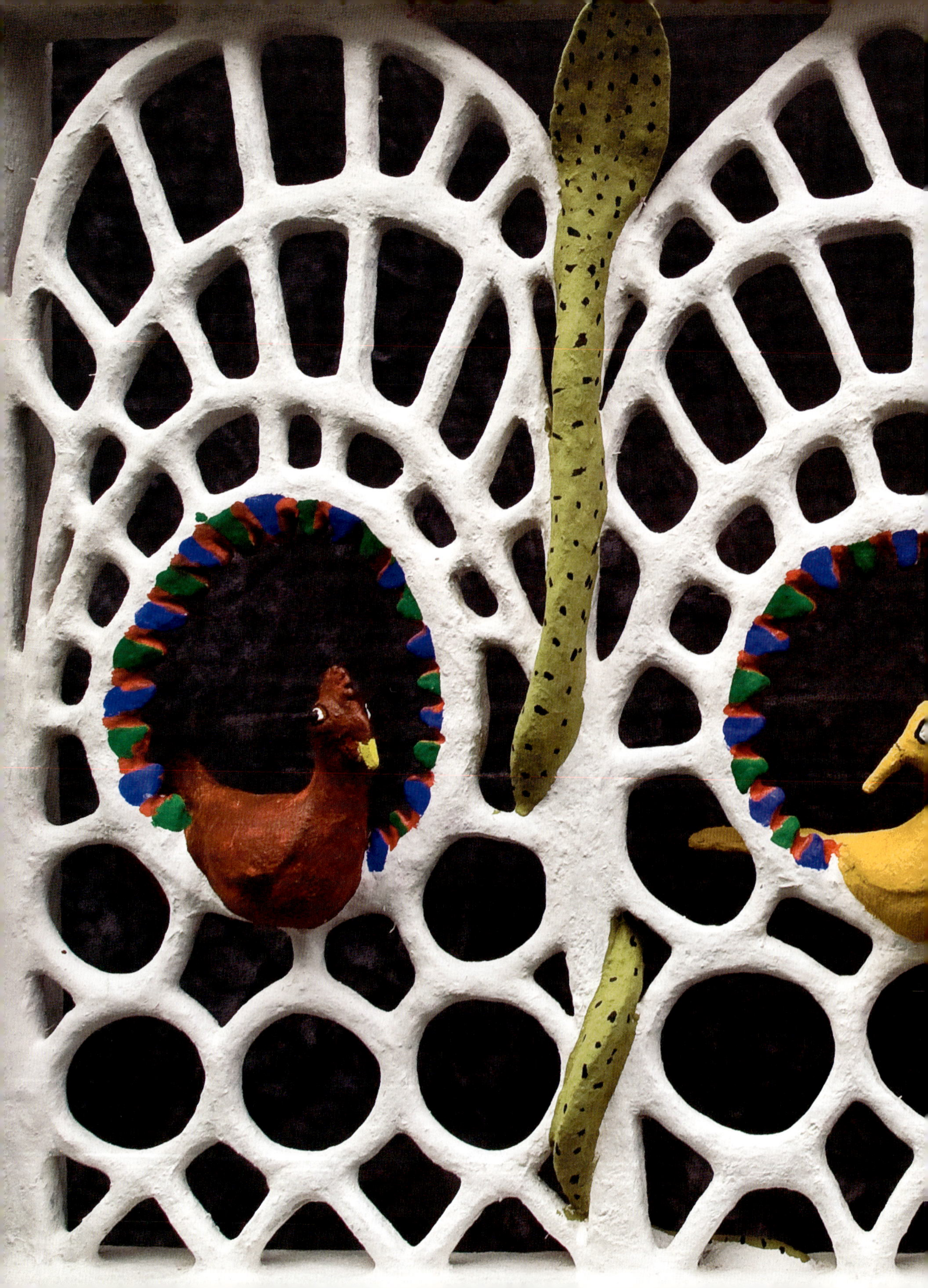

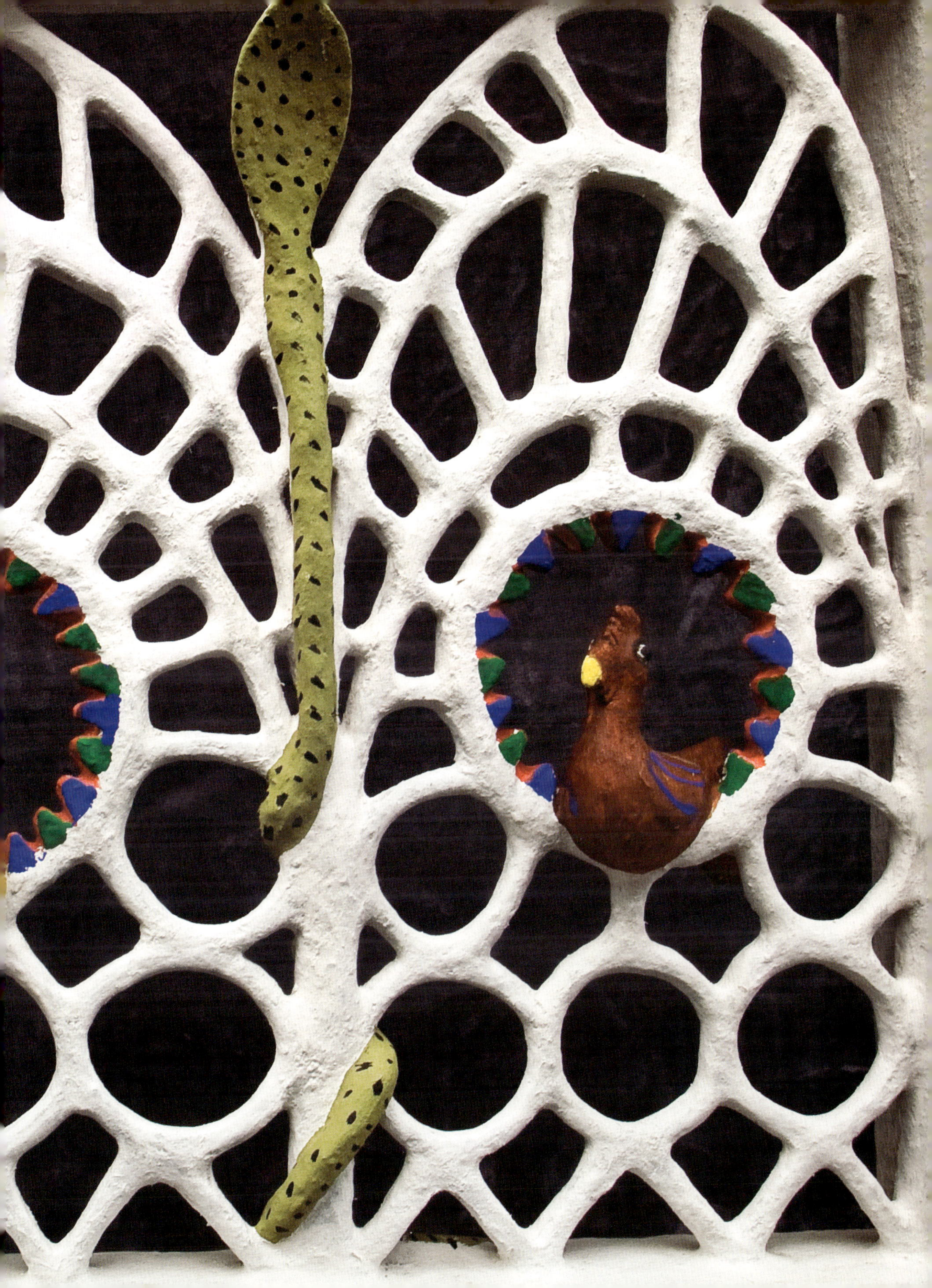

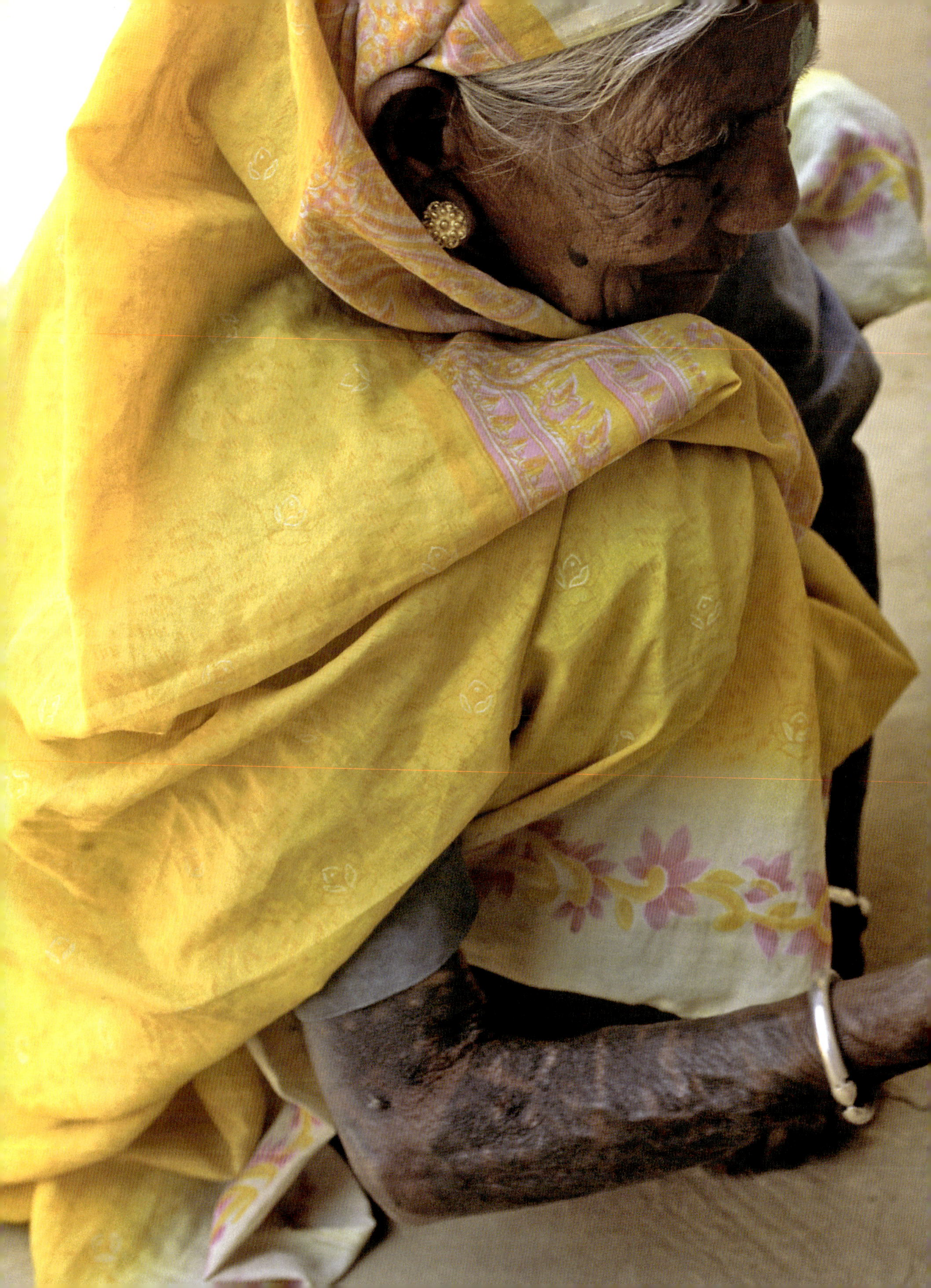

SONABAI

ANOTHER WAY OF SEEING

Stephen P. Huyler

Foreword by Leslie Umberger

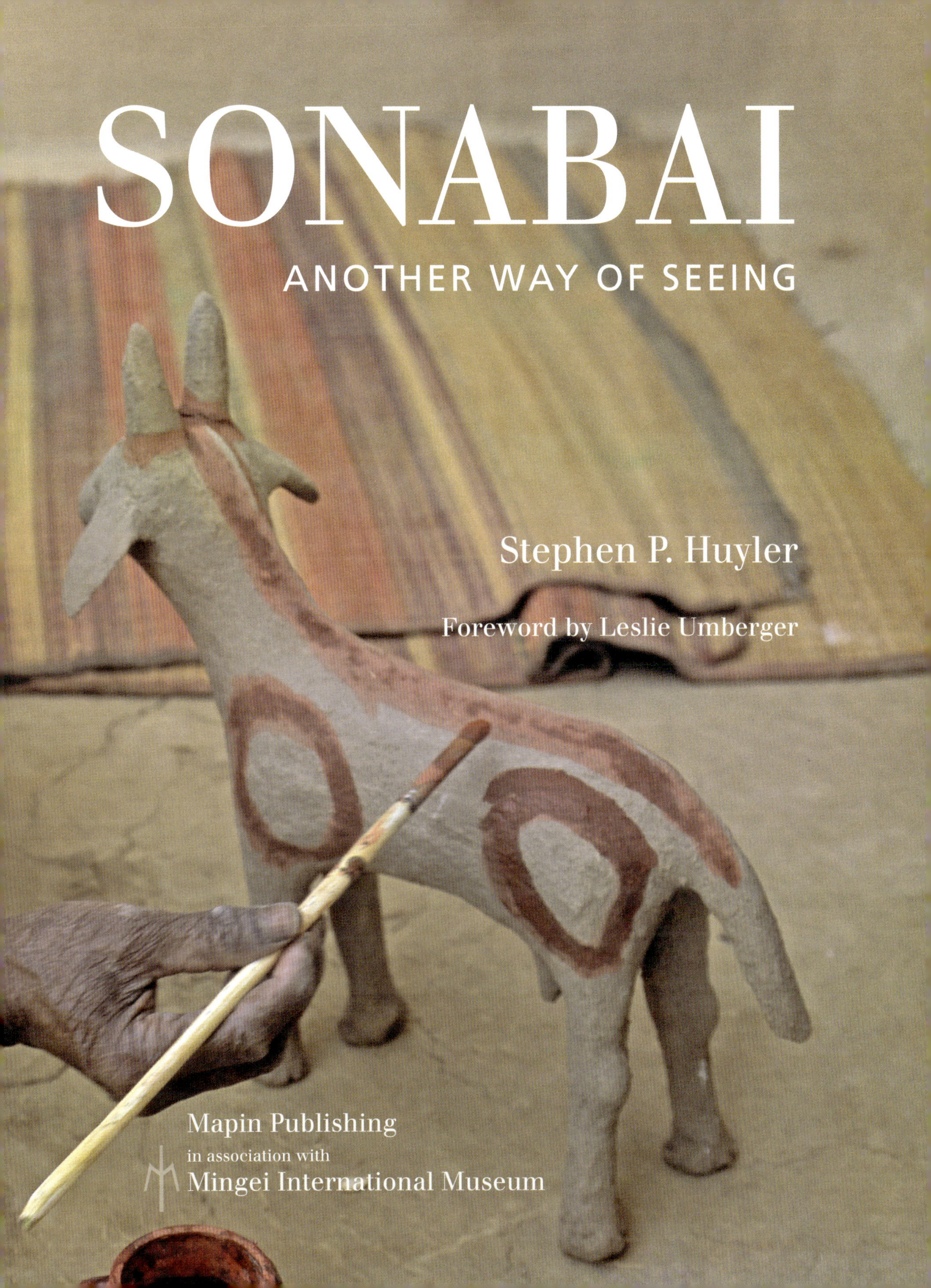

Mapin Publishing
in association with
Mingei International Museum

*For **Helene***
who is always my deepest inspiration

&

For the late Sonabai Rajawar
whose humble yet insistent creative self-expression
has enriched my vision immeasurably

This catalog is published in conjunction with the exhibition
SONABAI Another Way of Seeing
held from July 25, 2009 – September 5, 2010
at Mingei International Museum, San Diego

First published in India in 2009 by
Mapin Publishing Pvt. Ltd., Ahmedabad
in association with
Mingei International Museum, San Diego

Simultaneously published in the
United States of America in 2009 by
Grantha Corporation
77 Daniele Drive, Hidden Meadows
Ocean Township, NJ 07712
E: mapinpub@aol.com

Distributed in North America by
Antique Collectors' Club
East Works, 116 Pleasant Street, Suite 18
Easthampton, MA 01027
T: 1 800 252 5231 • F: 413 529 0862
E: info@antiquecc.com • www.antiquecollectorsclub.com

Distributed in the United Kingdom and Europe by
Marston Book Services Ltd.
160 Milton Park, Abingdon
Oxon OX14 4YN UK
T: 44 (0) 1235 465500 • F: 44 (0) 1235 465555
E: direct.orders@marston.co.uk • www.marston.co.uk

Distributed in Southeast Asia by
Paragon Asia Co. Ltd.
687 Taksin Road, Bukkalo, Thonburi
Bangkok 10600 Thailand
T: 66 2877 7755 • F: 2468 9636
E: info@paragonasia.com

Distributed in the rest of the world by
Mapin Publishing Pvt. Ltd.
10B Vidyanagar Society Part I
Usmanpura, Ahmedabad 380 014 INDIA
T: 91 79 2754 5390 / 2754 5391 • F: 2754 5392
E: mapin@mapinpub.com • www.mapinpub.com

ISBN: 978 81 89995 28 7 (Mapin)
ISBN: 978 0 944142 85 1 (Grantha)
LCCN: 2009928661

Designed by Paulomi Shah / Mapin Design Studio
Edited by Joan Phaup
Processed and printed in Malaysia

The paper used in this publication meets the minimum requirements of the American National Standards for Permanence of Paper for Printed Library Materials.

CONTENTS

FOREWORD

For most people, home is a place of sanctity, intimacy, and love; it is the heart of family life. For Sonabai Rajawar, however, such conventions were frustrated by the fact that home was also a place of imprisonment. The dwelling that Sonabai shared with her husband and child was, indeed, the seat of family life, but it was also a place of isolation, confinement, loneliness and desperation for her. Because her world was untenable as it was, Sonabai transformed her personal surroundings into a place of color, imagination, wonder and individual expression.

It is hardly uncommon for individuals to decorate their homes according to personal tastes, styles and practical living choices. Yet, when household décor gives itself over to the utter transformation of a space, it becomes a comprehensive art environment. Art environments emerge as personal responses to diverse situations and are rooted in the cultural milieu that fostered them. Sonabai is an artist who transcended the normative scope of household ornamentation and transformed her immediate surroundings into a rich world fueled by personal vision. Her project links her to a global culture of art environment builders and leaves a lasting legacy to her local community.

As Stephen Huyler so richly details, Sonabai's transformation of her home began as something simple: toys for her young son. Her resources were minimal: the soil from her yard, the whitewash used commonly to tame the dust on India's adobe houses, and the mineral, herbal, or vegetable dyes she devised in her kitchen. Maternal ingenuity served her well as she learned to extract, moisten, form, dry and paint the clay soil that would emerge as animal-shaped toys and elements of innovative and playful decoration around the house. Like Sonabai's, many art environments begin as modest home-improvement or craft projects. Ignited by the fruits of her or his labor, the maker's vision takes wing. Often such projects bloom after many decades of wage earning, when the individual is daunted by the prospect of countless unstructured days to come. Sonabai, however, was confronted with unrelenting hours of solitude when still a young woman. Coming from a large, bustling social family as a girl, the shock of isolation at the onset of her marriage was immense. Sonabai's husband cut her off from family and friends in a home that was already segregated from their small remote village. The days stretched out drearily before her. Yet, while children did not come easily to the couple, her one son brought joy into her quiet days.

Frequently, people who become environment builders do not begin with any intention of becoming any kind of an artist.

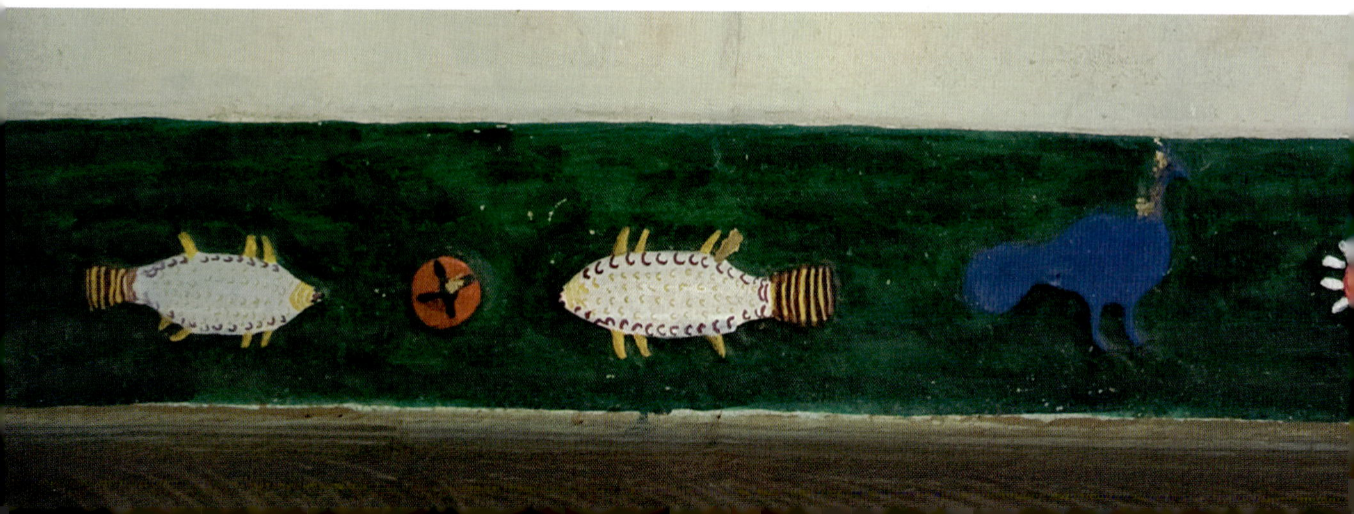

Unselfconsciously they interpret life by drawing on absorbed visual vocabularies and candidly embodying and reflecting place, era, ethnicity, culture, gender, class, physical ability and formative belief structures. The art environment is an organic response to a life lived. For example, after retiring from a career as a lumberjack around 1950, Fred Smith of Phillips, Wisconsin, felt a need to record his area's history and culture as he had known it, realizing life was changing and that unique regional customs and lore needed to be recorded. Over a period of fifteen years, Smith used concrete inlaid with glass and stones to create over 200 life-sized and over-life-sized sculptures that fuse myth, legend, local humor and history. His characters and tableaux were grounded in upper midwestern regional traditions such as religious grottos, so-called "museum bars" and roadside attractions. Exemplifying vernacular eclecticism, Smith produced—one sculpture at a time—a visual textbook on Great Lakes' regional culture.[1]

Loy Bowlin of McComb, Mississippi, created a vastly different project that spoke equally about his life. As Bowlin grew older he felt that he needed inspiration. Spurred on by the country music he so loved, he decided to reshape a world he had come to find overly drab. In the 1960s, Bowlin adopted the dazzling persona of "The Original Rhinestone Cowboy," and covered every inch of his small home with paint, rhinestones, glass ornaments, glitter, garlands, colored paper and photographs. His over-the-top bejeweled suits fit hand-in-glove with his sparkling world and he lived happily thereafter in the resplendent environs he had custom tailored. Just as Smith's iconography captured Great Lakes' regional culture, Bowlin's mirrored southern cowboy culture and country music with Mardi Gras sparkle and glamor thrown in. Their projects were highly personal, yet the vernacular culture that fostered them made a clear and indelible mark.[2]

Sonabai too embodies a vernacular culture. Although in adulthood she was isolated from her social surroundings, Sonabai had seen and apprehended much before she entered into her marriage. She indeed learned the physical aspects of creating art on her own, through trial and error—no one taught her what to do. Unarguably, however, the essence of her style draws on the folk culture of her region: colors, forms, visual styles, architecture and the images she had been immersed in for many years.

In India, figural art is taught and learned as an engagement with ritual practice. The very act of painting or sculpting a figure is a form of prayer that draws on inherited symbolic forms. At first blush, Sonabai's figurative work seems to depart from this tradition with only an

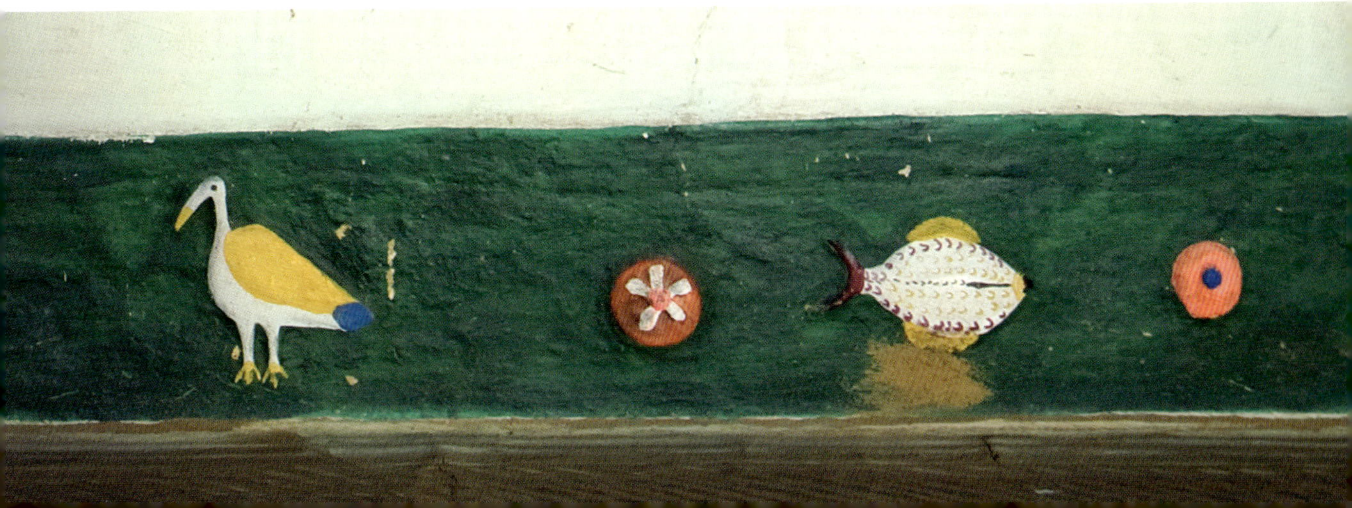

occasional reference to recognizable imagery, such as Krishna. Even Sonabai believed that her work had no ritual meaning. Yet, while Sonabai's figurative work was not responsive to specific doctrines, it became incontrovertibly an individualized form of ritual practice.

Ritual is a more subtle practice than its prescribed forms might suggest. A person put into an unusual circumstance may be more likely to abandon doctrine and inherited symbolic forms and thereby find a personal path. California artist and scholar, Amalia Mesa-Bains has described this kind of making as a survival mechanism, calling it "art for the sake of life."[3] At a base level, Sonabai—through necessity—chooses the earth itself as her medium. This engagement elicits powerful connections between the maker and the world itself; it establishes a sense of connection to the earth as spiritual mother. By shaping clay, day in and day out, Sonabai empowers herself to transform material—to shape her world—thereby engaging in a ritual practice that is self-affirming. Her creations stake her claim as a person in the world and contradict the invisibility that her enforced isolation has conferred upon her, acting as a spiritual renewal every day. Her artistic practice becomes the ritual that brings meaning to daily life.

Ritual gave meaning to another art environment builder and fellow Indian countryman, Nek Chand of Chandigarh. Deeply distressed by the strife and destruction he witnessed during and after the 1947 partition of India and Pakistan, Chand began to build an art environment in secret on a piece of regulated government land. His worries of being caught were overshadowed by his need to see growth out of destruction. Chand set out to make a garden of healing and peace by using elements drawn from sources as diverse as stones that he found inspirational and the non-biodegradable rubble from villages razed to make way for the new Punjabi capital. Creating what he referred to as an "immortal kingdom," Chand also engaged in an unconventional ritual act, one that unearthed the spirit of the Indian folk that he saw suppressed in the face of Modernism.[4] Like Sonabai, Chand worked in relative secrecy for years. Also like Sonabai, when his project was discovered, the artistic vision was so powerful that his illicit activities were set aside. The site today is a much beloved attraction.

The idea of ritual is central to Sonabai's project and, like women who build personal altars of various forms throughout the world, her practice actively delineated personal sacred space. Home altars often arise in the areas that women are able to control—sometimes limited to a small corner or closet within the heart of the domestic realm. Sonabai's husband allowed her

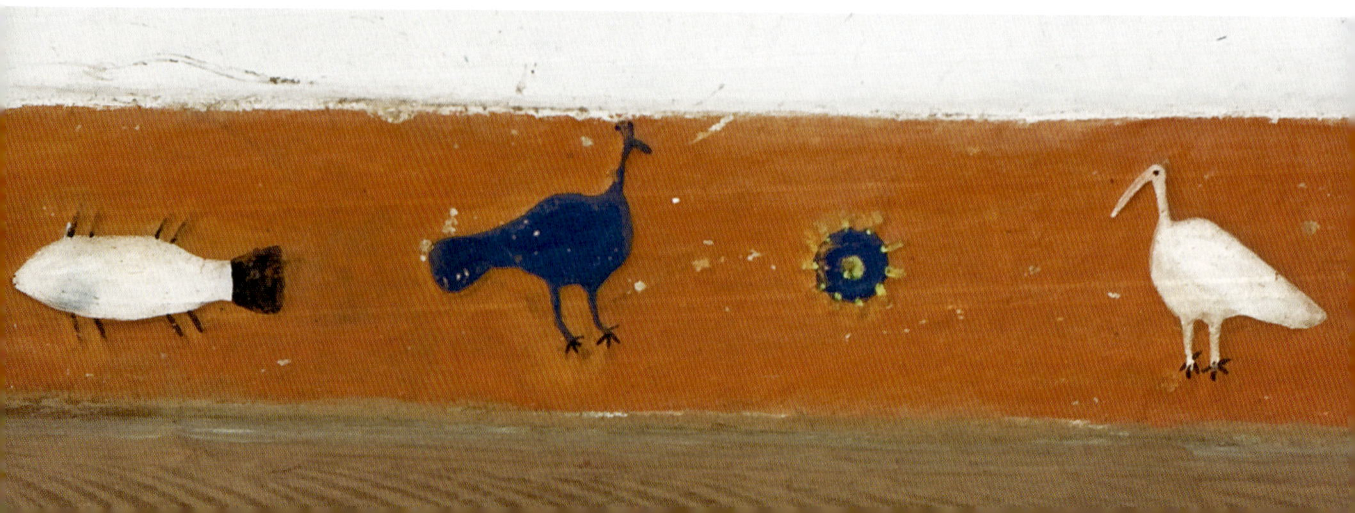

relative freedom within the home, mistakenly believing that her artistic practices were without greater meaning. By viewing her project as mere decoration, he altogether missed the covert (if unconscious) political act that was unfolding daily before his eyes. Sonabai's power to transform, redefine and ultimately amaze, circuitously opened doors that he had locked for years.

Art, such as Sonabai's, which seemingly springs from little beyond sheer will, astonishes through its ability to invent an entire world from almost nothing. It is a phenomenon that continues to place folk and self-taught artists at the epicenter of creativity and underlines the reality that true expression is not learned, but rather is mined from an underground spring that runs deep within the self.

Notes:

1 Leslie Umberger, *Sublime Spaces & Visionary Worlds: Built Environments of Vernacular Artists* (Singapore: Princeton Architectural Press and The John Michael Kohler Arts Center, 2007).

2 Ibid.

3 Amalia Mesa-Bains in Lucy R. Lippard, *Mixed Blessings: New Art in a Multicultural America* (New York: Panteheon Books; 1990), p. 58.

4 Umberger, 2007.

LESLIE UMBERGER is an art historian specializing in contemporary American art, the art of communally-, and self-trained artists, and the politics of culture and representation. Umberger is the Senior Curator of Exhibitions and Collections at the John Michael Kohler Arts Center in Sheboygan, Wisconsin. Since 1998, Umberger has curated over forty diverse exhibitions and developed the Kohler Arts Center's unique collection of the work of self-taught, folk and vernacular artists with a special focus on artist-environment builders.

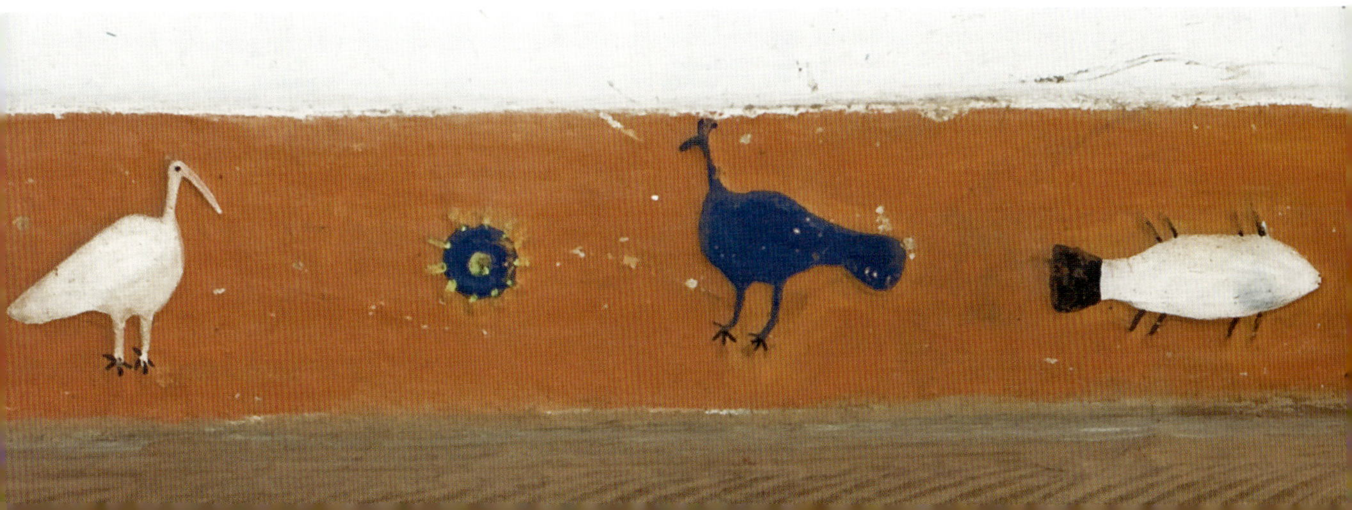

PREFACE

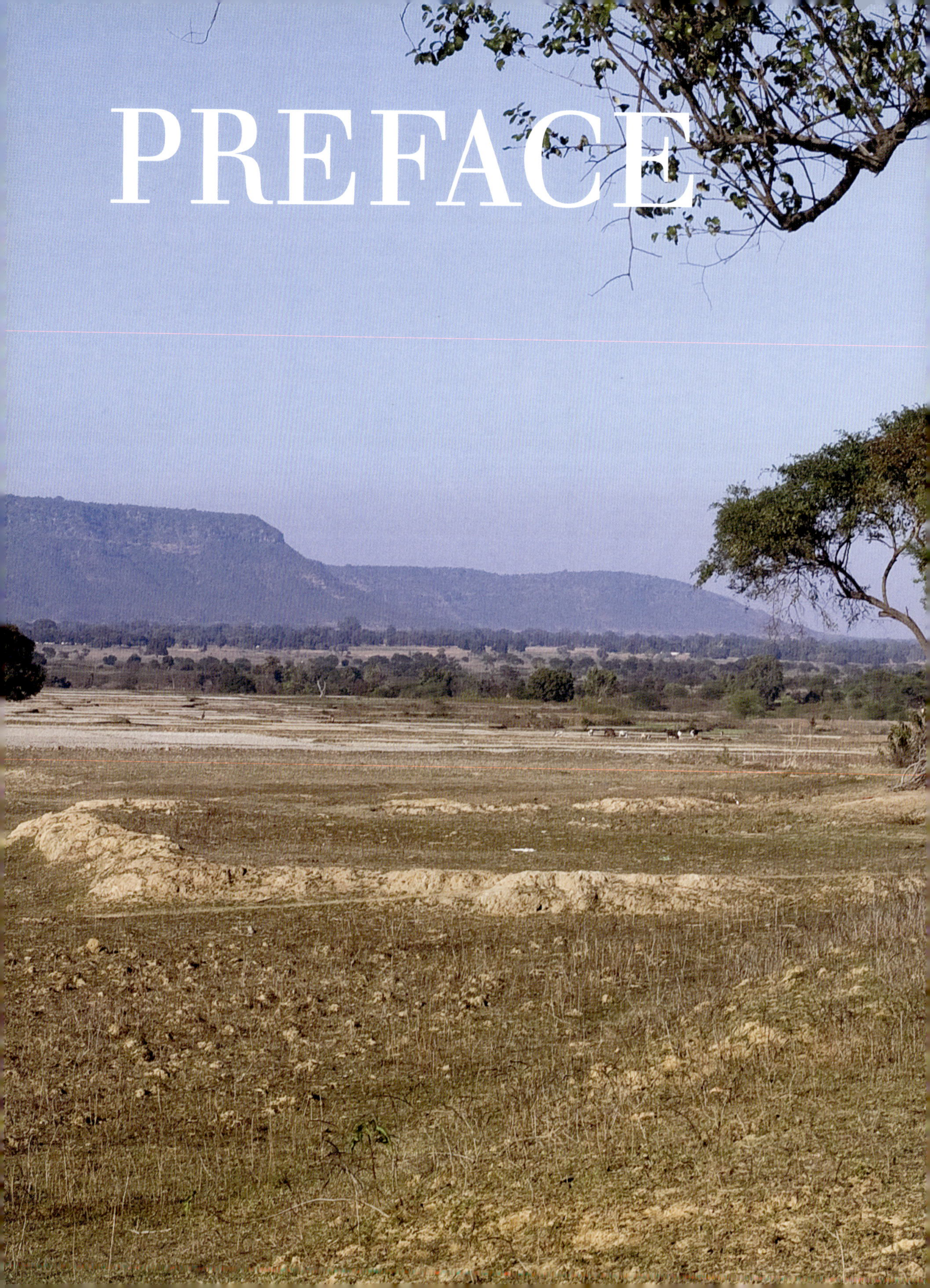

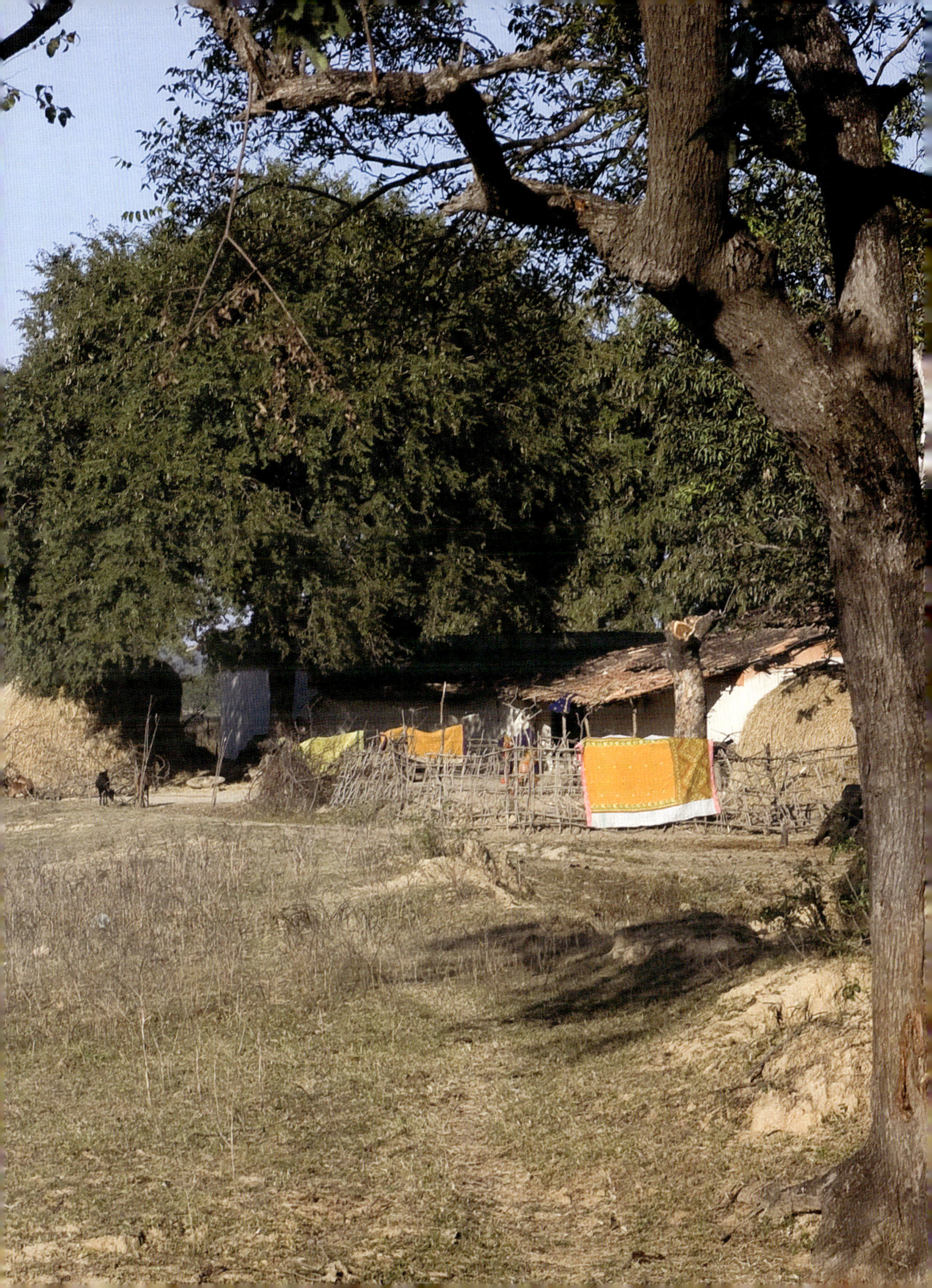

SONABAI IS ALONE. In overpopulated, noisy India, solitude is rare. She has never experienced it before. Sonabai grew up in a home full of relatives. Her father and mother, brothers and sisters, grandparents, uncles, aunts and cousins all lived in the same farmhouse in the middle of a village of similar houses brimming with people. She was always surrounded by activity and the demands of life. Children ran through the house, neighbors came and went, and her grandmother cared for the babies, while her mother and aunt sorted vegetables and cooked. When her father and uncles were not out in the fields working, they were inside mending tools, spinning rope or caring for the livestock that lived with the family.

Now, as a young wife married for ten years, all that has changed. Suddenly and unexpectedly, Sonabai has been thrust into a new home that is unlike anything she has ever imagined. No one else is there at all, only Holi Ram, her husband, and their little son, Babu. Like her father, Holi Ram is a rice farmer; he is a widower whose first wife died without having any children some years earlier. He is forty-six; through Sonabai's young twenty-five-year-old eyes, he already seems elderly. Since they have been married, Holi Ram has proved to be jealous and obsessively protective of her. For the first decade of their marriage, they lived in his village with his parents, and brothers and sisters-in-law like most other Hindu families. During all those long years while Sonabai did not get pregnant, Holi Ram became increasingly difficult, fighting with his family and neighbors and finally insisting they move out just after Babu was born.

Holi Ram decided that he didn't want to live near other people and began to build their new house in the middle of his farm far outside his community's boundaries. As is common in a rural Indian village, Sonabai helped him construct their home, aiding in carrying the timbers for the doorframes, columns and beams, packing the walls with mud, straw and cow dung, and surfacing the roof with terracotta tiles. The interior of the house is a pressed dirt courtyard surrounded by a columned verandah, off which radiates a kitchen, bedroom/storage room, and a barn. There is only one door to the outside and no windows.

Except when he lets her out to go to the well on the opposite side of the house from the village—or to the fields to help him plant, irrigate, weed or harvest—Holi Ram has made it clear that he does not want Sonabai to leave their home. He has asked her not to talk to anyone. He invites no one to visit. Her own village is only a few miles away, but Sonabai has seen none of her family since their move. She doesn't know how to read and neither does Holi Ram, and they have no books, papers or magazines anyway. They have no electricity, no radio and no outside entertainment. As they live in such a remote spot, Sonabai sees other people only at a great distance. She feels very isolated.

Sonabai Rajawar lived in almost total isolation for the first fifteen years of her marriage. Now elderly, she reminisces about the hardship of her young married years and her unusual solution to her loneliness.

One particularly hot afternoon when she is nursing Babu in their quiet, contained courtyard, Sonabai observes the way light reflects into the passageways under the eaves of the overhanging verandahs. Wouldn't there be a way to soften that light and lessen its intensity? A pile of leftover bamboo rods that had been used as construction platforms gives her an idea. Hoisting Babu into a cotton sling on her shoulder, she takes an old sari and

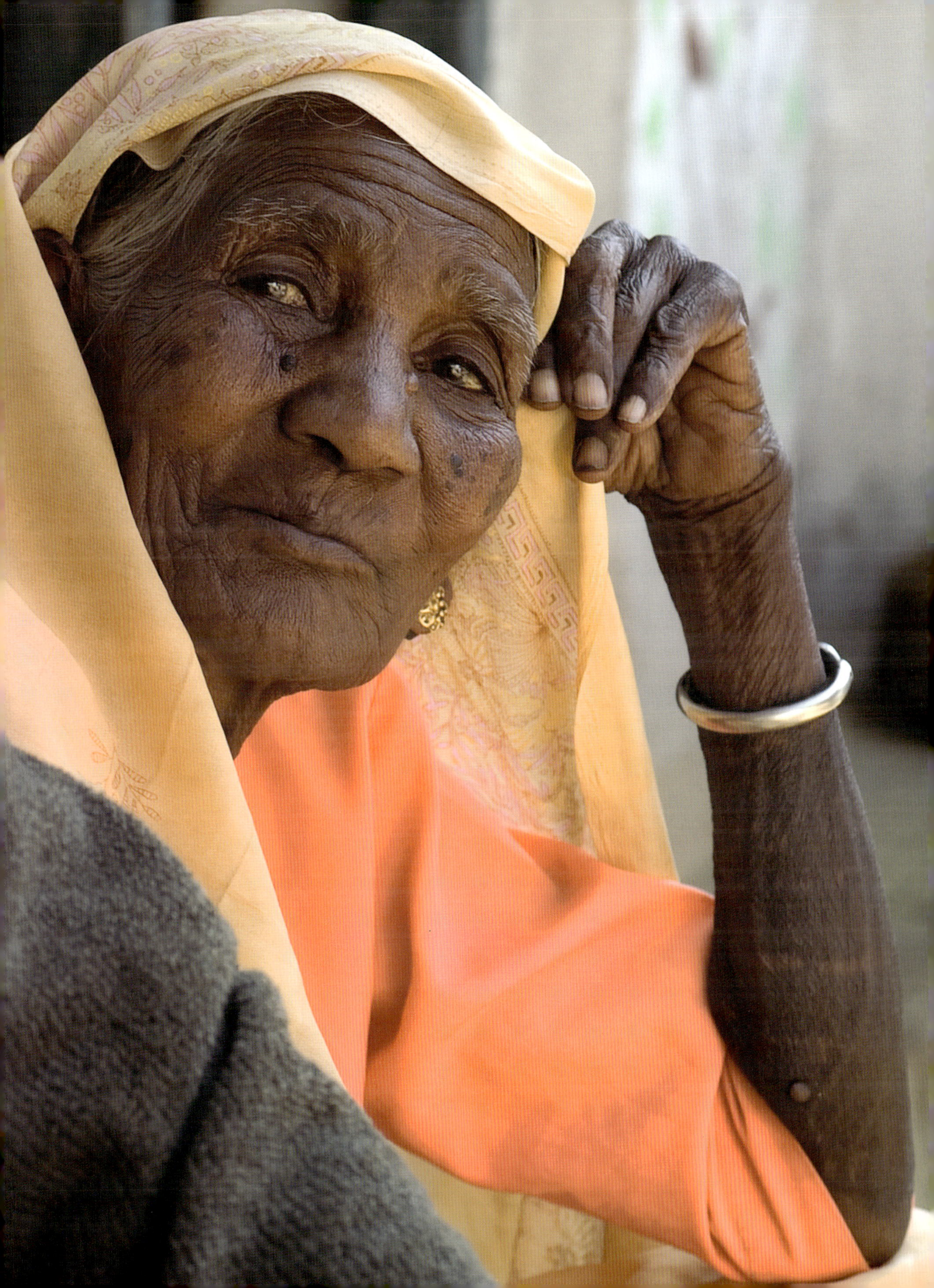

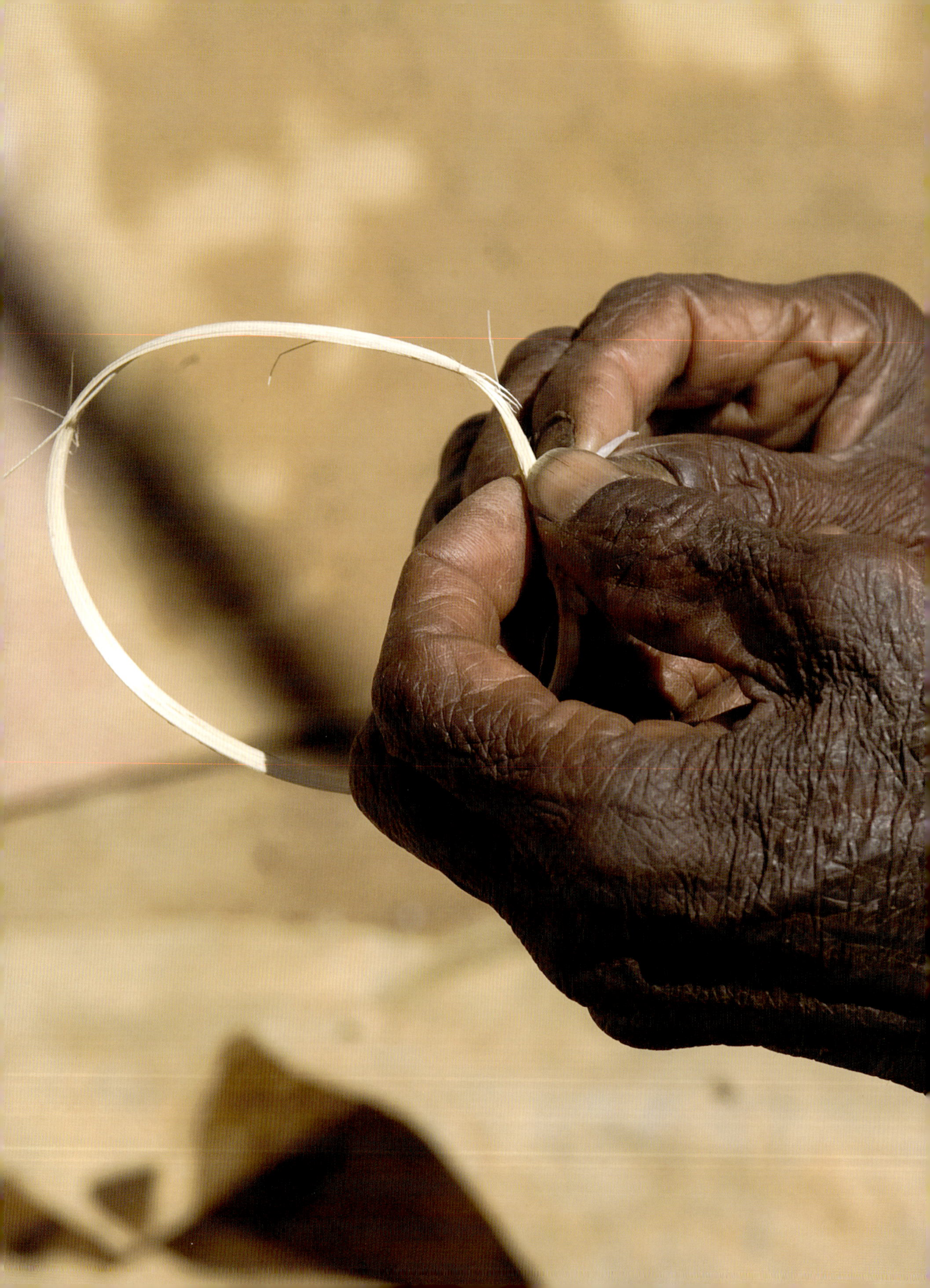

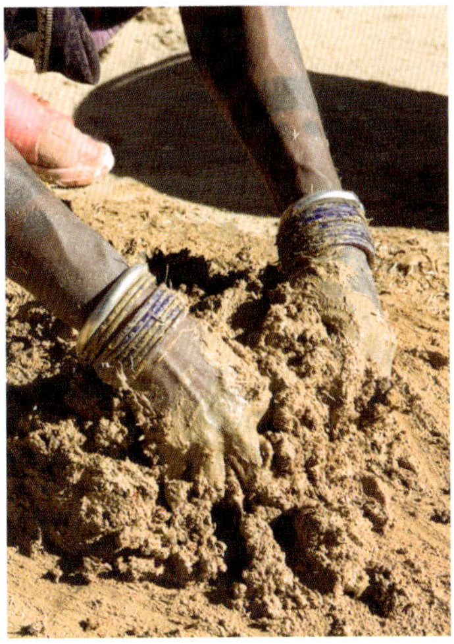

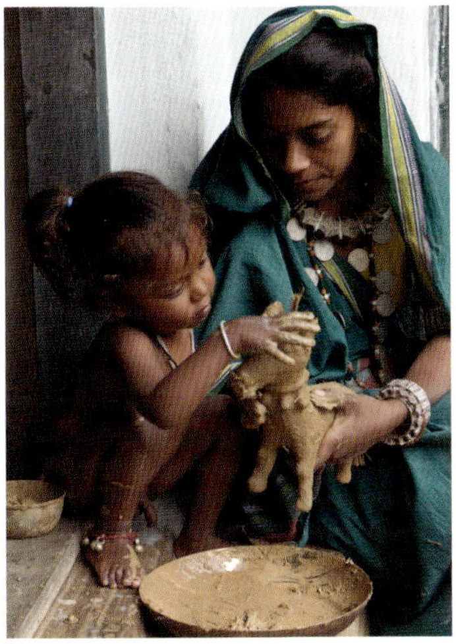

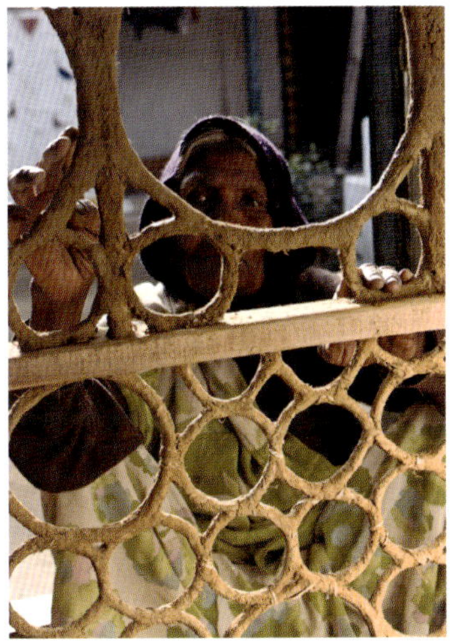

uses it to measure the width of the gap between two support pillars of the verandah and the height between the roof beam and the floor. With a sharp kitchen knife she cuts several lengths of bamboo and ties them together to build a simple grid in the space. She then pares strips from another piece of bamboo and curls these into round circles, fastening each together with a small piece of twine and joining them all within the grid. Sonabai has created a screen of sorts, but it is still insubstantial. She needs to make it last. The major building material used in her house, as in all the other dwellings in that region, is clay. Just before houses are completed, women use clay to decorate their doorways and window frames with simple designs that enhance the view from the outside. Sonabai has already sculpted a simple diamond pattern around the perimeter of her front door and painted it with yellow ochre so that it stands out against the whitewash of the walls.

Just yesterday, when washing clothes for Holi Ram next to their well, she had noticed the squishiness of the mud between her toes and realized from its texture that it is clay. Taking a sharpened stick, she returns outside and digs up several clumps. Slowly adding water as she kneads them together, she carefully removes from the clay any pebbles or leaves, creating a smooth, even ball that she carries back into the courtyard. Sonabai then takes little strips of clay from the ball, adding them to the edges and interiors of her bamboo circles, smoothing them into the rounded supports and blending the entire unit into the surface of the pillars. The result is a pleasing lattice of an organic design that refracts and softens the harsh summer sun and cools the interior spaces of her house. Even though lattices (called *jali*) are prominent architectural features in many parts of India, they are not used anywhere in Sonabai's region. She has never heard of them previously nor seen a picture of one. The concept for them came completely from within her own imagination. In her lonely life, she feels a sense of satisfaction.

Over the next months as little Babu grows into a toddler, Sonabai realizes that he has no toys, only a doll of old cloth and the little rattles she is able to make for him from bamboo. The finances of the farm are very tight and Holi Ram never takes her to the market. But her success of working with bamboo and clay has encouraged Sonabai to be inventive. Can she use clay to make toys that will not just crumble as soon as Babu begins to play with them? What will the process be?

A potter in the village where Sonabai grew up sometimes made elephants of clay that were purchased to place on rooftops in order to attract good spirits to enter the homes. But these sculptures were made of elements thrown on the wheel and fired in a kiln to make them sturdy. Sonabai has neither the tools nor the craft education to accomplish these tasks. She had, however, noticed the potter making temporary images of the Goddess Saraswati for her annual festival. He would build a substructure of sticks and straw and then cover it over with clay sculpted with the details he wanted. The images were hardened in the sun and not fired. Sonabai realizes she might be able to adapt this technique for making toys for Babu. In her tightly controlled environment, all the elements she needs are free and easily accessible. Holi Ram should not be threatened by this project. He is out in the fields. And as long as she remains at home, takes care of the house and Babu, cooks their meals and helps Holi Ram with the farm when he needs her, he leaves her alone.

In the courtyard of her house, Sonabai begins to sculpt a horse. First, she makes string by spinning rice straw in the way she was taught by her grandmother. Then she bunches a large handful of the straw and binds it tightly with the string. She secures four short bamboo sticks into the opposite edges of her bundle, making legs, and puts a longer crooked stick into one end for the horse's neck and head. Setting this substructure aside, she digs more clay next to the well, cleans it and brings it back to the house. Pulling off little bits and pieces of soft, damp clay, she adds them to the surface of her sculpture, smoothing them together, massaging them into form. Under her fingers, the horse's body is fleshed out, the sticks transform into rounded legs, the neck gains bulk, and the head materializes into a jaw, mouth, eyes and ears. Standing before her is a ten-inch-high horse! Sonabai is transfixed. It seems so easy and she loves the process. All it needs to do is dry there in the hot sun and it will be a perfect toy for Babu.

With just this one lattice and horse and no training at all, Sonabai begins her life as a sculptor. At first she is content to make horses. Then she tries sculpting bullocks and cows, then elephants and deer, goats and monkeys and snakes. Pretty soon she is sculpting images of people she knew and the Hindu gods and goddesses she has been raised to worship. As Babu begins to walk and then run all over their house, he has more toys than he knows what to do with. They are everywhere. On the edges of the courtyard, on the steps, in the verandahs, in the kitchen and bedroom and storage room—even in the barn with the real bullocks and goats! Holi Ram doesn't even seem to notice them.

And then Sonabai has another idea: what if she added the animals to her lattice?

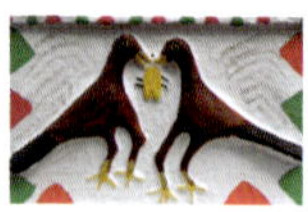

IN THE WORLD'S HISTORY, few cultures have encouraged truly innovative artistic self-expression. By and large, humanity tends to conform to the accepted norms of its specific society's standards. Perception is ingrained from infancy, informed by the cultural imperatives that define its own civilization. Consequently, the people of a given region tend to admire the creative innovation that in their view enhances and extends this vision by maintaining an accepted form, medium or technique and subtly adapting its content or expression, not by deeply challenging or disrupting it. There have always been exceptions: examples of artistic genius that sometimes signal simultaneous changes in worldview. But in traditional societies, these exceptions are particularly rare.

India is well known for its embedded cultural traditions. Take a feudal system that is naturally organized by hereditary professions. Place it in a subcontinent known throughout history for the inordinate wealth of its resources. Start with a very large indigenous population that is forced to be defensive in order to protect itself from constant invasions of its land and sea borders by foreigners wanting to share in its wealth. Sift in thousands of years of sieges, counter-sieges, cultural integrations and proudly isolated pure strains of each individual subculture, and what remains is one of the most complex groups of social organizations in the world. The caste system of India, although illegalized by the Republic of India's constitution in 1951, is still pervasive and very effective. By definition, caste refers only to the social system of the Hindus, while in reality other religions in India, including Christianity, Islam and Jainism, practise their own versions that bear strong similarities. India's social complexity is compounded by the fact that within its boundaries one-fifth of the world's population

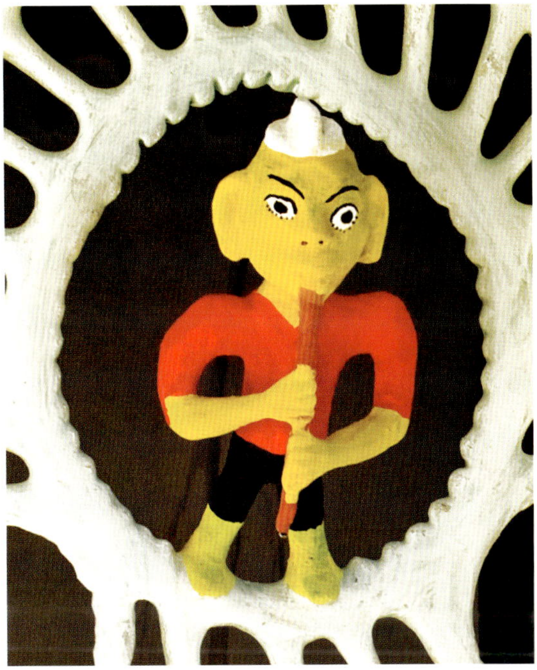

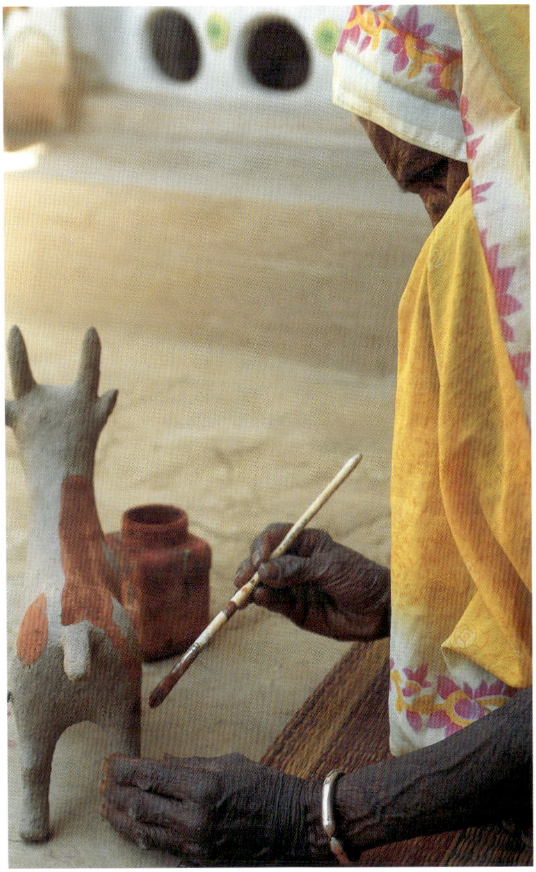

Views of the inside walls of Sonabai's house portray her remarkable artistic embellishments. Sonabai was not trained as an artist; all of her creations were self-taught inspirations.

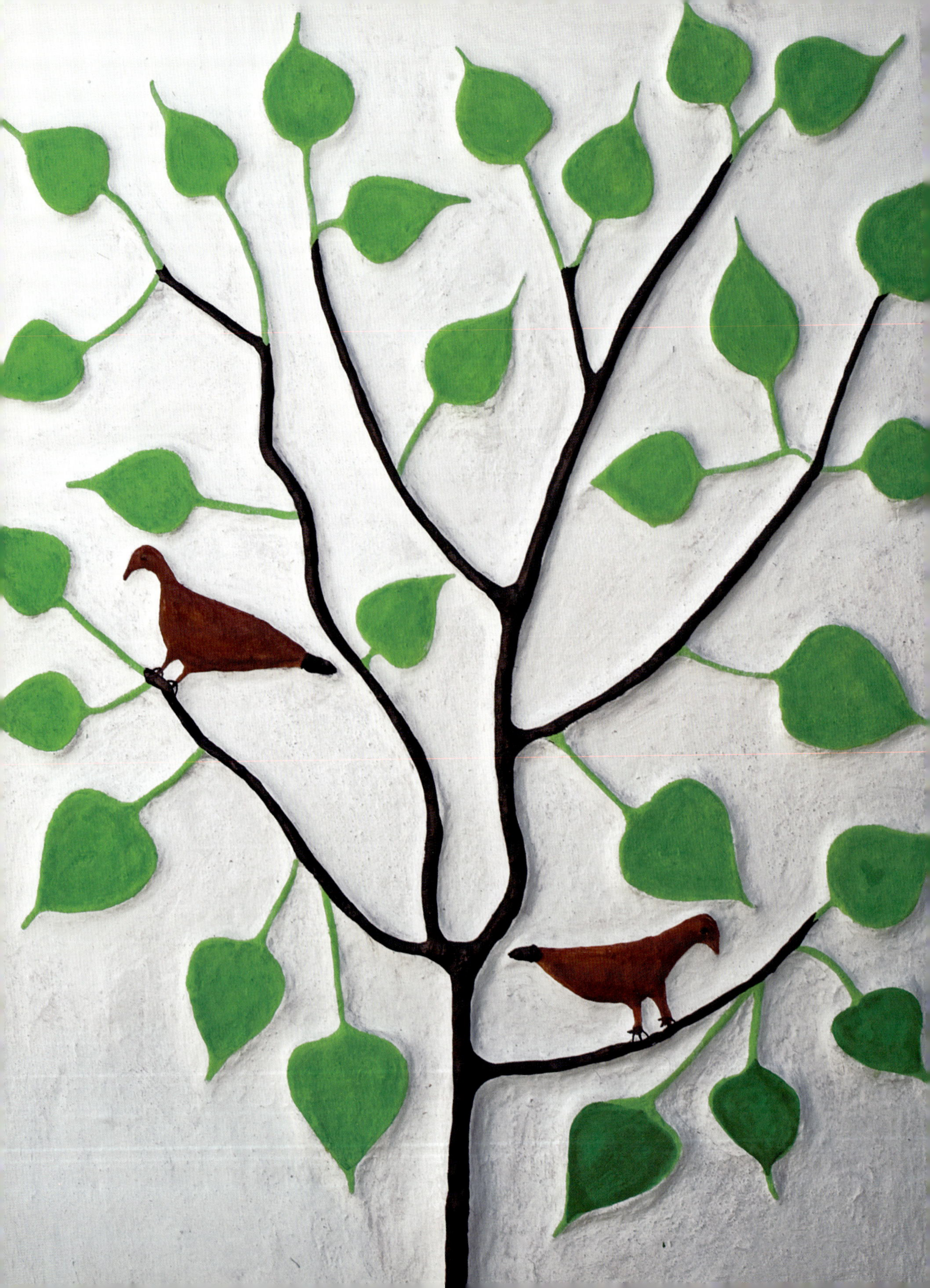

lives in an area one-third the size of continental United States.

It is particularly rare in South Asia for anyone to conduct a profession other than that for which he or she was designated from birth. A farmer is the son and grandson of a farmer with a similar lineage as far back as he can imagine. Teachers come from families of teachers; doctors from those who have been healers for generations; jewelers may be able to trace their lineage back to a succession of jewelers for centuries; weavers to weavers, etcetera. Although the burgeoning Indian middle classes in the late 20th and early 21st century allow an increasing number of career changes, particularly into the newly invented professions that mark our age, this social mobility is still available to only a small fraction of the whole society when compared to other contemporary cultures.

The emergence into the broader world art market of contemporary Indian art is a reflection of this new, highly privileged, educated society. Almost without exception, these artists are the product of art schools associated with urban centers and institutions of higher learning. They may well express the sentiments of modern India, but most are abruptly and intentionally divorced from the values that govern traditional art. In contrast, most Indian artists and artisans pride themselves on being able to exactly duplicate the products of previous ages. Once they have attained this acumen, popular demand requires that their own innovations are only slight adaptations of traditional forms. Artistic originality is exhibited in the choice of concept, color, line, texture and space within these inherited boundaries.

Self-taught art could be defined as creative production that owes no allegiance to an earlier style or tradition and comes solely from within the individual's own psyche: neither learned by being taught by another individual nor through exposure to recorded knowledge. The recent awareness of self-taught art in the West has frequently drawn attention to the troubling biographies of the artists themselves; many are labeled as social misfits, mentally disabled or even criminally insane. Although self-taught art is often excitingly innovative, the subject matter of some is disturbing in the ways it challenges society's most cherished values.

In India, where encrusted traditions overlay one another in a complexity that defies full comprehension, very few examples of self-taught artists have been discovered. Sonabai Rajawar is one of the few. Possessing fine faculties of mind, body and spirit, her only disability, if indeed that word is appropriate, was her enforced isolation during fifteen years of her marriage. Removed from almost everything she had known growing up and with no instruction or guidance, Sonabai generated from within her own memory a vision of life and community with which she began to repopulate her lonely walls. She created an entirely new artistic expression, one completely different from anything ever seen in India before: a world of color, light and whimsy, all her own.

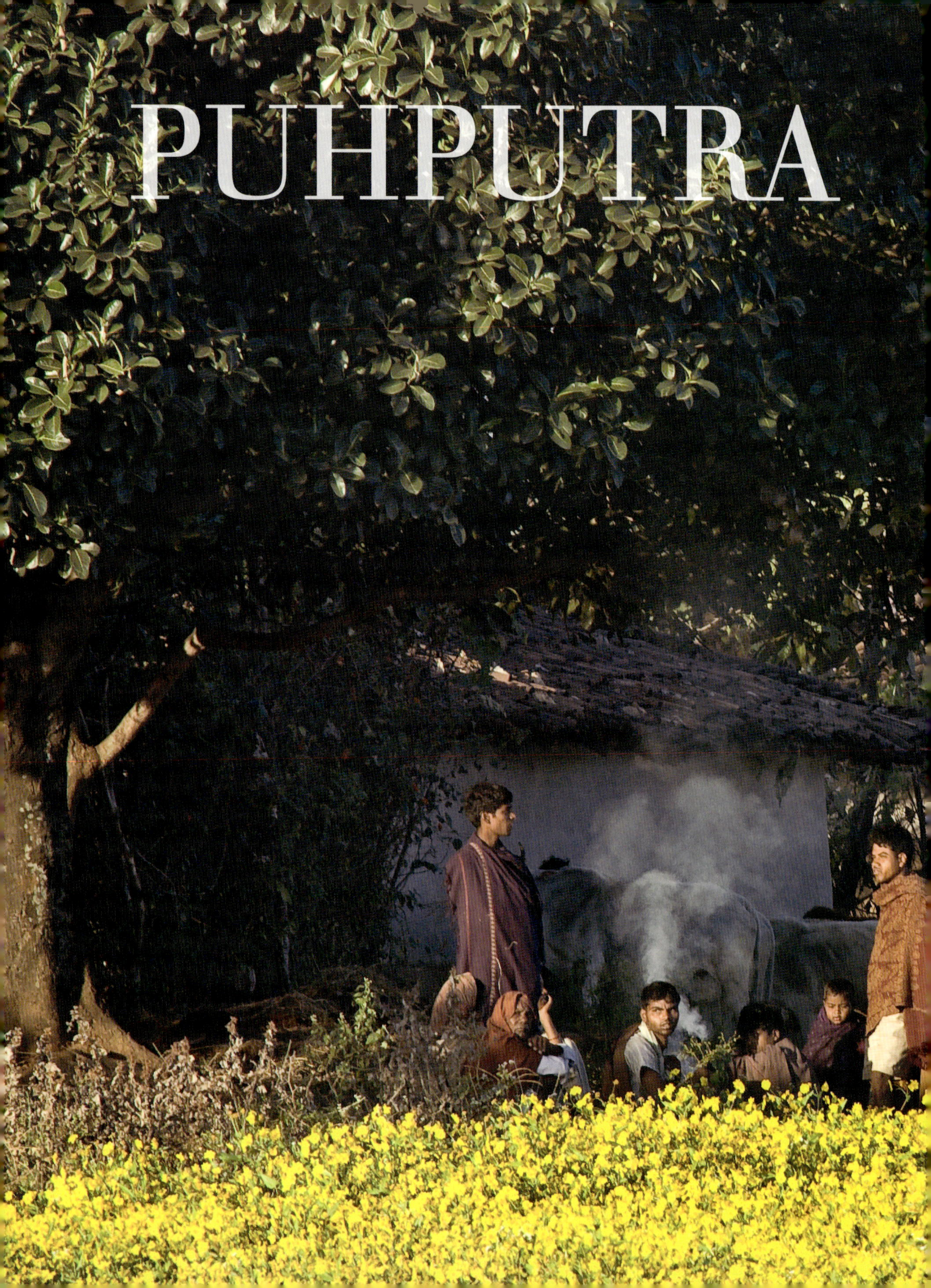
PUHPUTRA

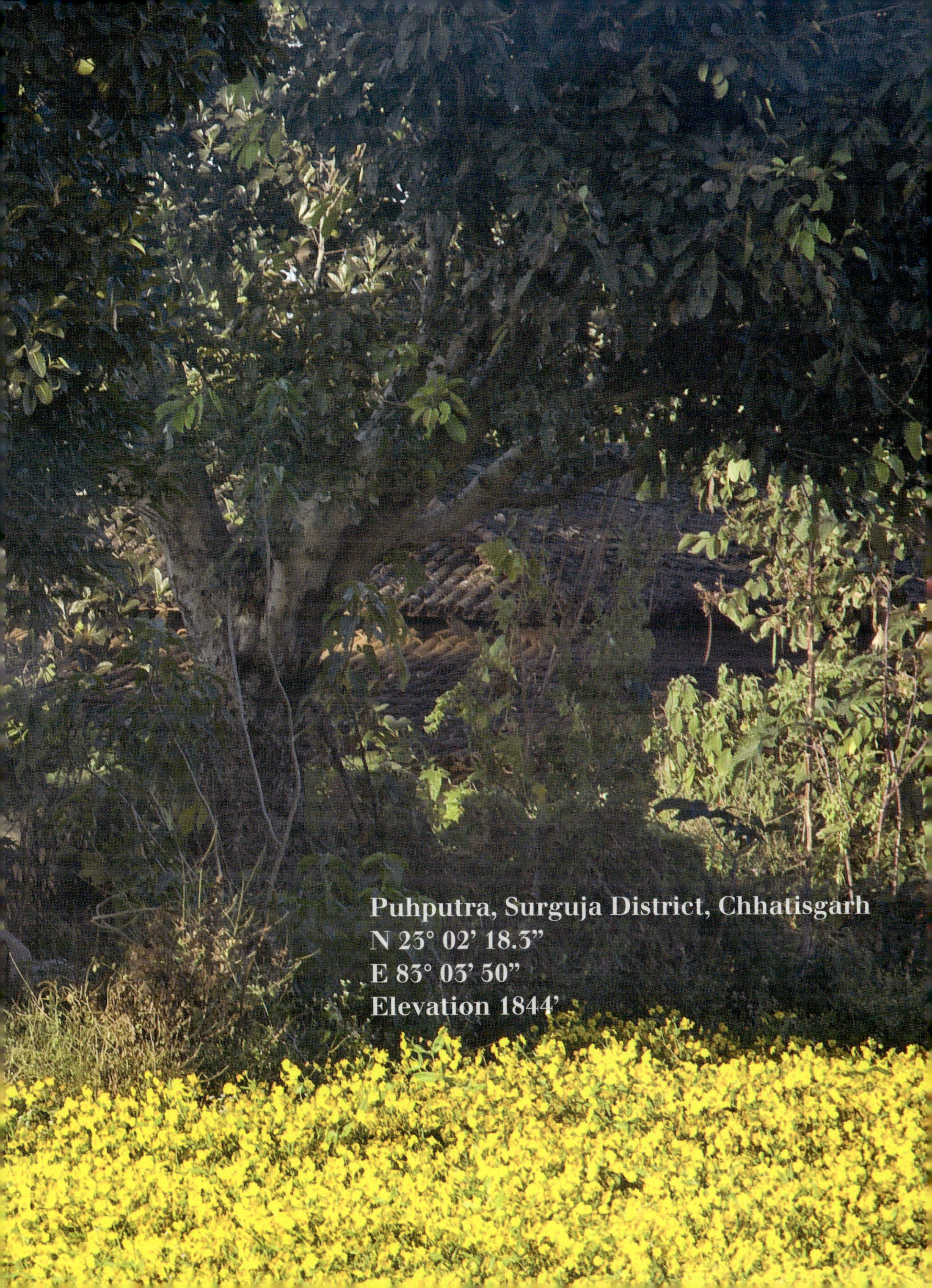

Puhputra, Surguja District, Chhatisgarh
N 23° 02' 18.3"
E 83° 03' 50"
Elevation 1844'

THE MIST PERMEATES THE VILLAGE, blending with the smoke of countless early morning cooking fires to create a gray pall that seems to merge the activities of one person with the next. Puhputra is already busy at 6:30 a.m. Many of its inhabitants have been up since pure dark, getting ready for the day as they do every morning. This is no special day, just one like every other. It is winter, so the chill of the night remains settled deep in the bones until late in the morning. All along the dirt street, villagers are bundled up, their faces peaking out of the saris or shawls wrapped over their heads. Children stamp their feet with the cold. Women, bent from the waist, emerge backwards from the front doors of their mud-walled houses, sweeping out the night's dust and clearing the street in front of their homes to make sure that the village begins its day clean. A group of four men, old and grizzled, is hunched around a fire fueled with cow dung chips, holding out their hands, grunting and spitting. A young father proudly holds up his infant daughter, sweetly singing her little songs as he bounces her up and down. A boy runs from his home into the local shop, impatiently hopping from bare foot to foot as he waits for the vendor to open and sell him some sugar for his family's morning tea. Dogs bark. One snarls and a small fight ensues, ending in the high-pierced yipping that indicates more wounds to the pride than the body. Each house has its cows. Some have already been milked and are happily munching their day's ration of rice straw. In the barn at the front of one home, a nine-year-old girl nudges aside a pink-eared white calf and squats down to squirt a thin stream of milk from the udders of her complacent cow into a red plastic bucket. Goats emerge from many of the houses and, if not watched closely, try to eat everything in sight. Old women yell across the street at them; in response, children run to catch them.

It is busy everywhere, and this is just the beginning of the day here in the heart of Sonabai's village. But her house is far from the bustle of community activity, on the farmlands of her husband, Holi Ram. There the morning remains very quiet. They almost seem like two worlds, one within the other: the serene, sequestered home of Sonabai and her family isolated at the village boundaries, and Puhputra, a typical Indian village filled with the vibrancy of life.

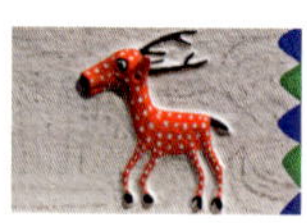

THE VILLAGE OF PUHPUTRA is truly in India's heart, as removed from its major urban centers and industrial hubs as any place can be. Sonabai remembers that when she was a little girl in the 1930s the majority of Surguja District was dense jungle. Tigers and wild elephants still abounded. Monkeys plagued all the houses with their mischievousness. Now there is hardly any jungle left and few wild animals. The need to feed, fuel and house India's burgeoning population has meant that many of its forests have been cut down. Mismanagement and lack of foresight have precluded reforestation. Now most of the area surrounding Puhputra has been tamed. Farmlands stretch in all directions, mostly rice paddies that alternate with other seed and vegetable crops. There is almost no industry in the region. Virtually everyone is dependent on the land.

Ambikapur, Surguja's district headquarters, is the nearest large town. To reach it, villagers must walk three miles on a rough dirt track to the highway and wait (often for an hour or two) for the bus. The highway is always in bad repair and although it could take only forty minutes to reach the town directly, the bus usually plies its way slowly and arrives after a couple of hours. Villagers generally figure that going to Ambikapur will be an all-day affair. Two smaller towns are nearer the village and it might be possible to hitch a ride to them on a passing lorry. The two towns' shops have little to offer, but the selection is still much better than in Puhputra. No one in Puhputra owns a car, but a few of Puhputra's inhabitants now have motorbikes and their new mobility has completely altered their perceptions of time. They are now able to make a decision and complete the action in the time it might have taken to just reach the highway a few years ago.

Just 4200 people currently live in Puhputra, but—as elsewhere in India—the population is growing all the time. Everyone farms, although members of some families are involved in other activities such as running the four tiny shops in town or teaching in the two elementary schools. All the villagers are Hindus; most worship the God Vishnu and his pantheon as their primary

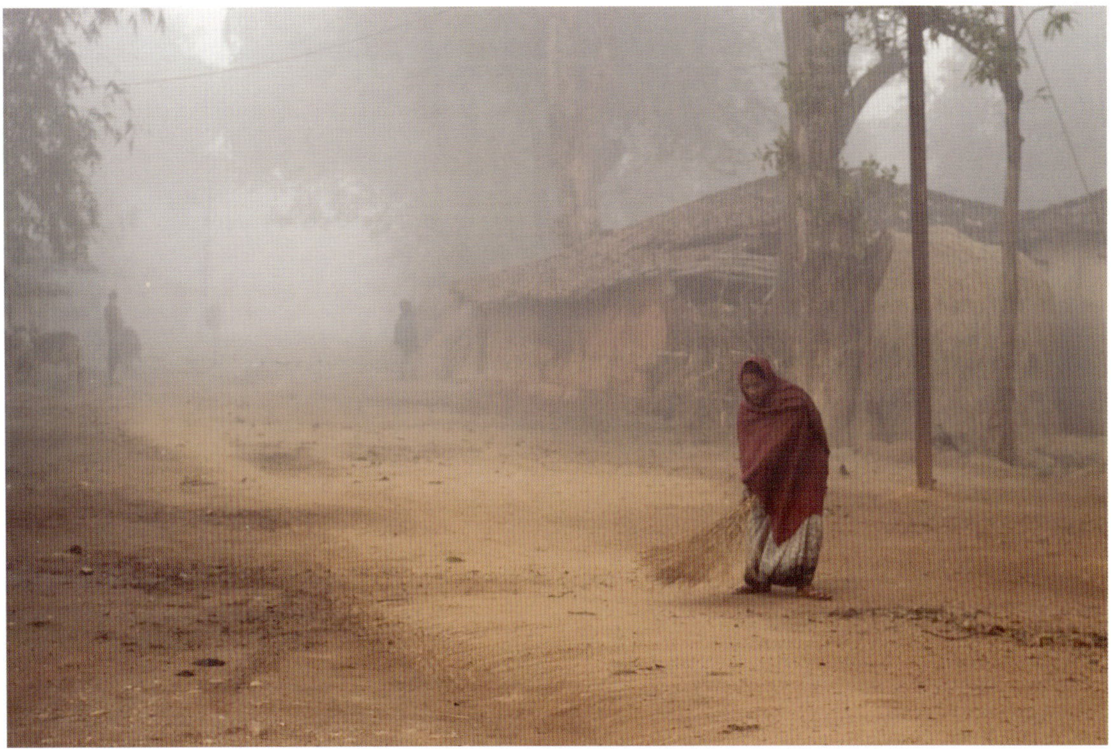

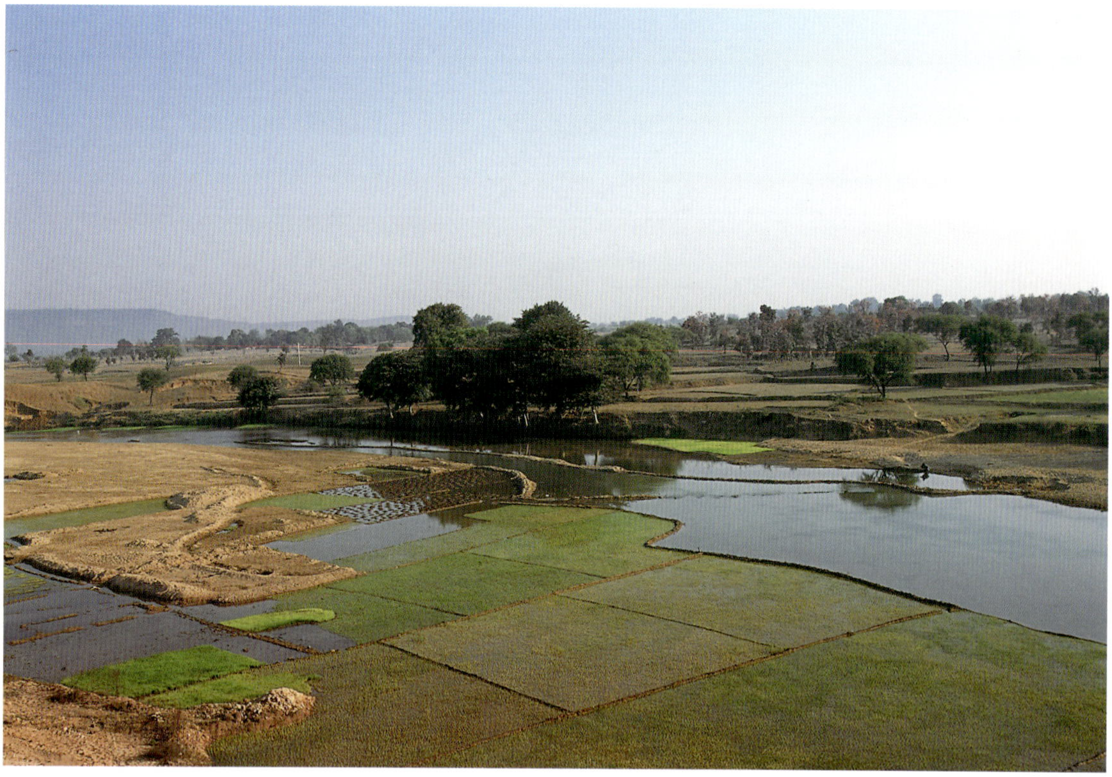

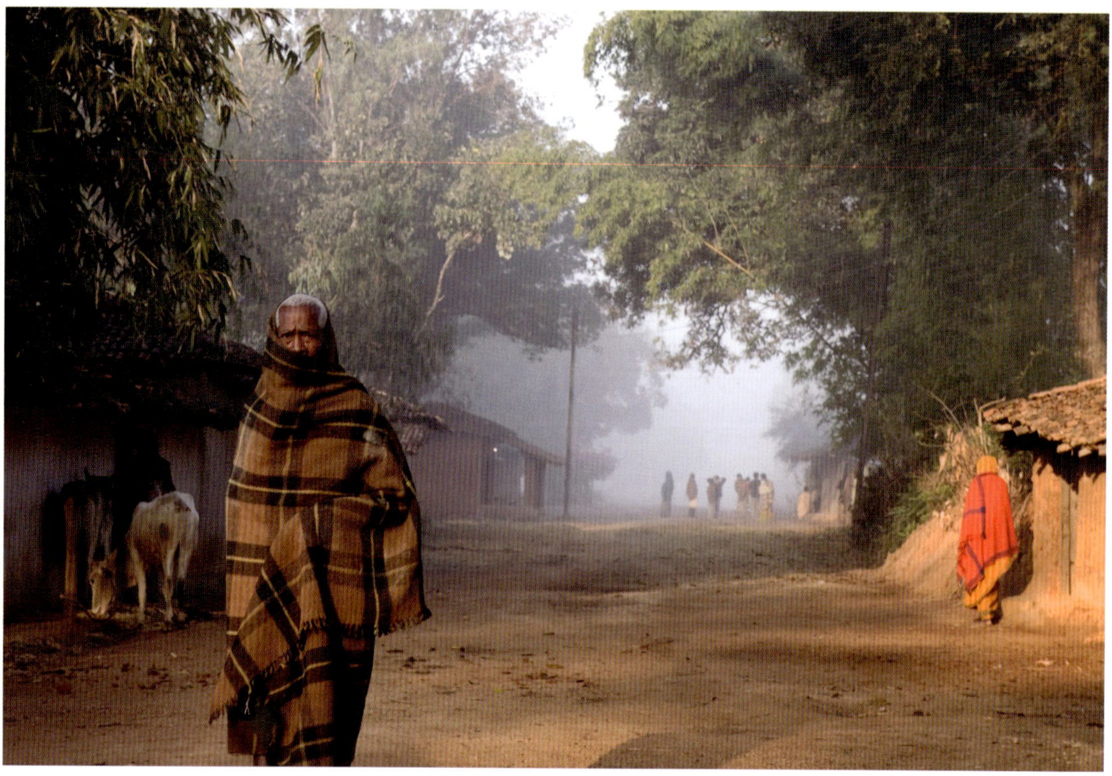

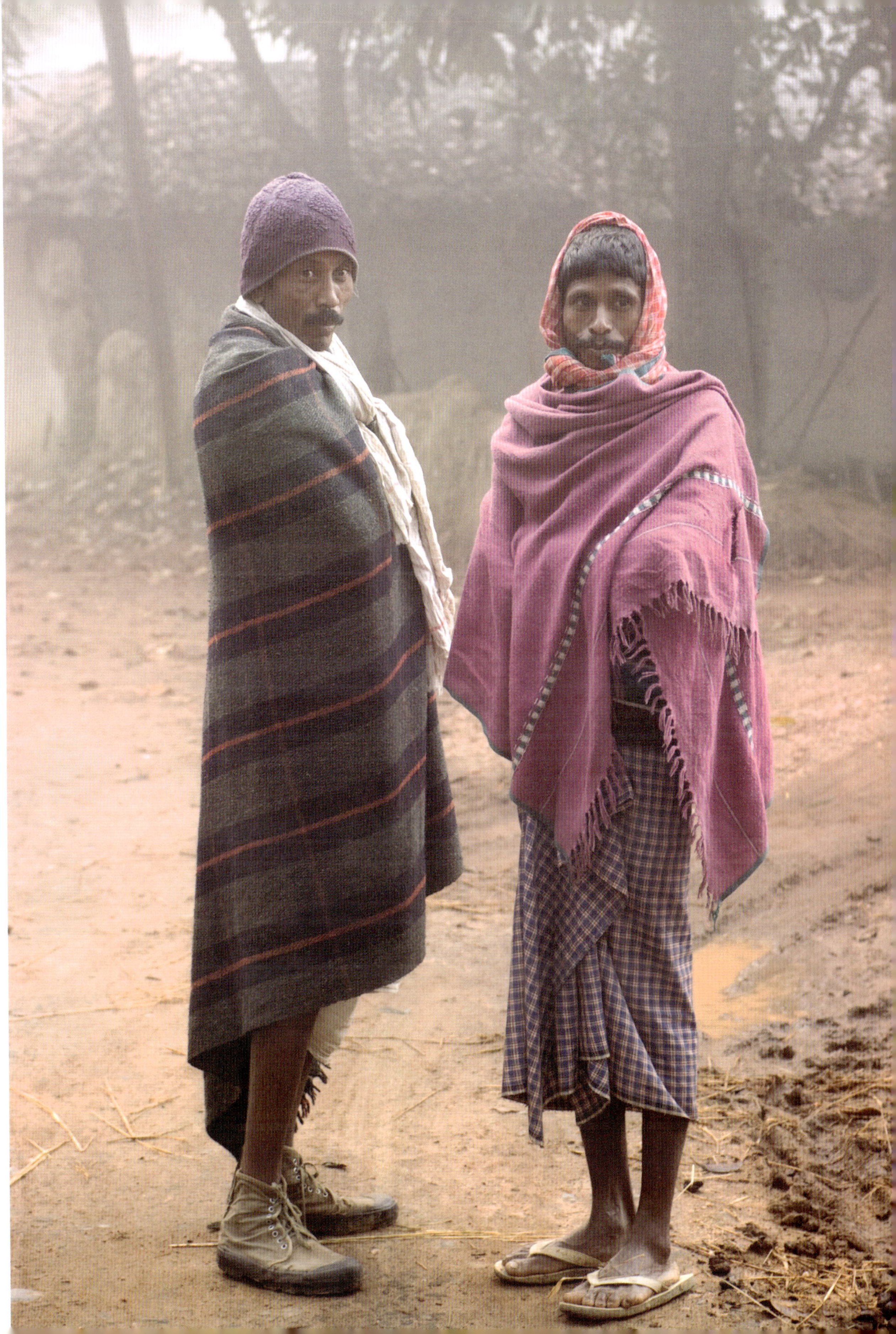

deities, rather than Shiva. Compared with many other communities in India, Puhputra has very little social regimentation. Almost everyone is in the same economic bracket. Local decisions are made by a *panchayat*, an elected council governed by a Sarpanch, who is much like a mayor. Most inhabitants, like Sonabai and her family, are Shudra, members of the broad caste of farmers that is spread throughout the Indian subcontinent. A few Brahmins run the local temples and shrines, help conduct festivals, marriages and other rituals, and provide sons as teachers for the schools, but most of their family members are hard-working farmers like the rest. Some Dalits, members of the social order that before Indian independence was labeled as "Untouchable," live in a tiny hamlet at the opposite edge of Puhputra from Sonabai's house. They divide their time between working their own farmlands and helping as poorly paid laborers on other farms and as cleaners for a few of the larger dwellings in the village. Life is not easy for them, but neither are they destitute.

As the people of Puhputra are endogamous, they usually marry someone from a background and family very similar to their own, but always outside their own physical community. It is forbidden to marry within the village. This custom means that even though their community remains geographically isolated, each person in town has close cousins in many other towns and villages, near and far. They visit them during festivals and for family weddings. Marriages in Puhputra are always arranged, usually by the parents of the bride and groom. It is still common that newlyweds are strangers to one another, or will have met just once briefly before the actual wedding ceremony. Nevertheless, the villagers feel that most of their marriages are successful. When told of foreign individual choice and divorce rates, they express disbelief and indignation.

Puhputra is typical of most of India: it is patrilineal and male-dominated, but as elsewhere the strength of its women should not be discounted. It is true that women's roles are strictly defined from birth. Girls are trained to be demure, thoughtful and attentive to the wishes of others. Boys are given far more freedom. Their games are rougher and simple misconduct likely to be overlooked. Most children in the village attend elementary school and many progress to higher education in nearby Lakhanpur, but it is common for girls to leave school earlier than boys in order to get married. Usually their new in-laws will not allow them to continue their educations after marriage. All youngsters must show deference and respect to their elders, waiting on them without complaint even without being asked. Young women are taught to cover their heads modestly with the ends of their saris in the presence of all non-family males, to hide their faces when they laugh, and to speak quietly. Young men are often self-assured, outspoken and aggressively dominating in the home, the marketplace, and on the street. In all their interactions they convey an overriding sense of entitlement. Yet Puhputra's women are not victims despite their apparent position of servitude to their men. They have full and active lives and consider themselves happy. Women are involved in community activities. There is a full annual calendar of rituals that are only conducted by women. Many village women are musicians and storytellers, and evening events are filled with wholly female entertainment that maintains a heritage of relationships between mothers, daughters, aunts, cousins, neighbors and friends. Alongside India's patriarchy, a vibrant and effective sorority still pervades its village cultures.

Throughout India, one of the ways that women express their creativity is through household decoration. Geographic and social diversity has defined a broad variety of subcultures in India, each of which has its own customs and artistic styles. Increased population and rapid urban development

---

In many ways Puhputra, the village where Sonabai was kept in isolation, is typical of Indian communities. Even though men and women have specific gender-based roles, they also have vibrant social lives.

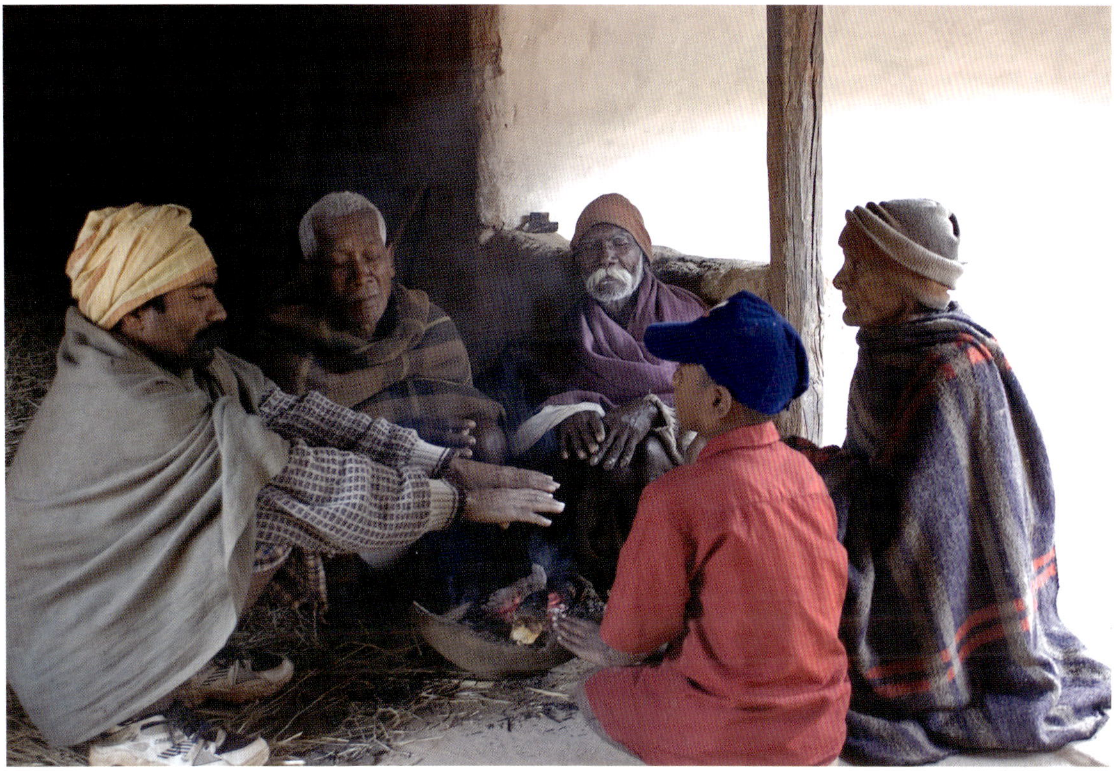

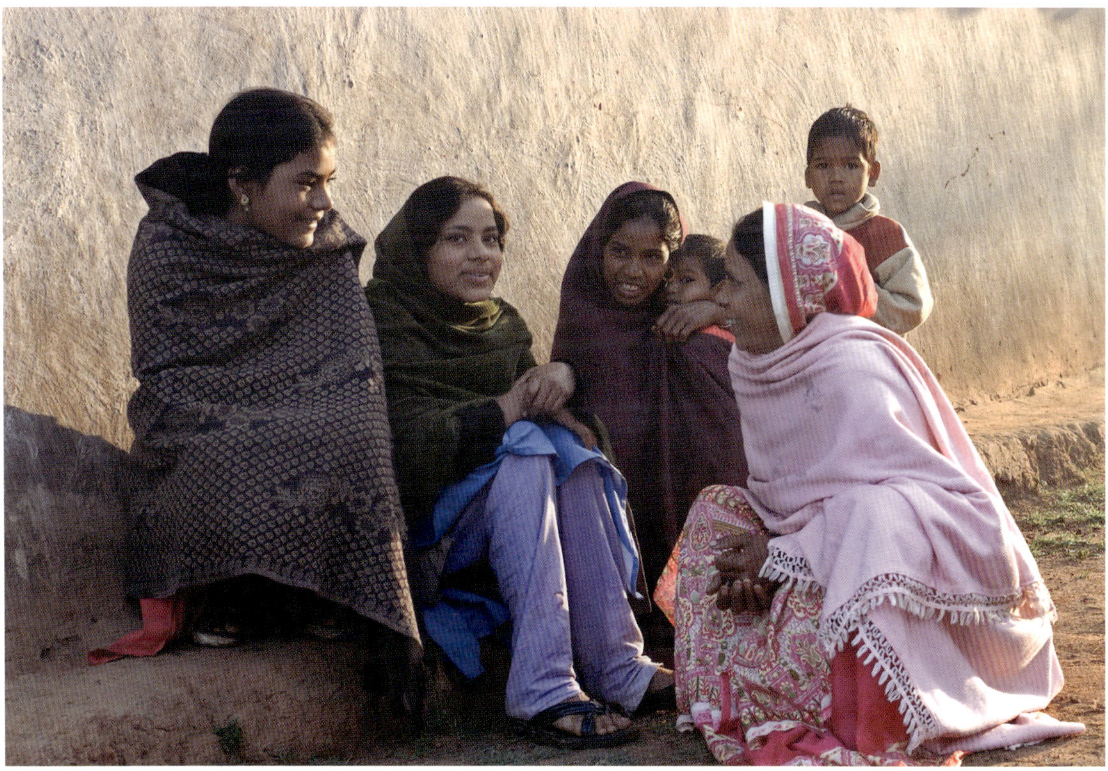

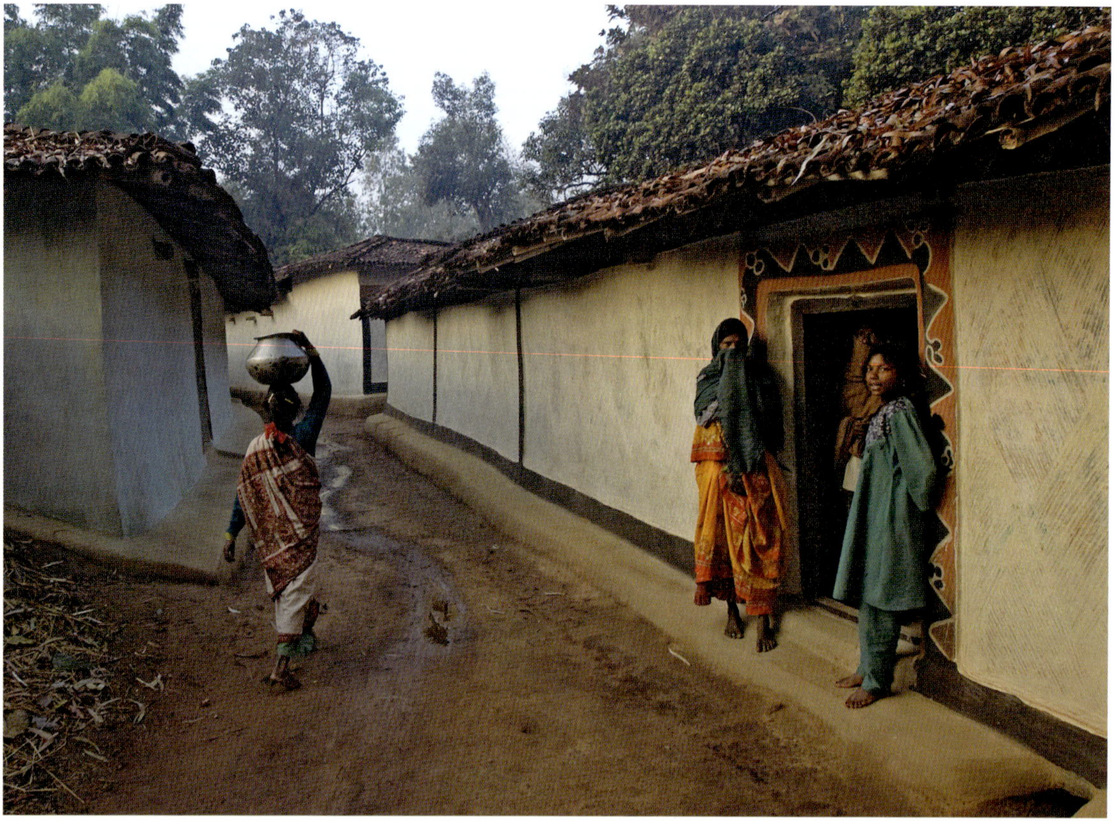

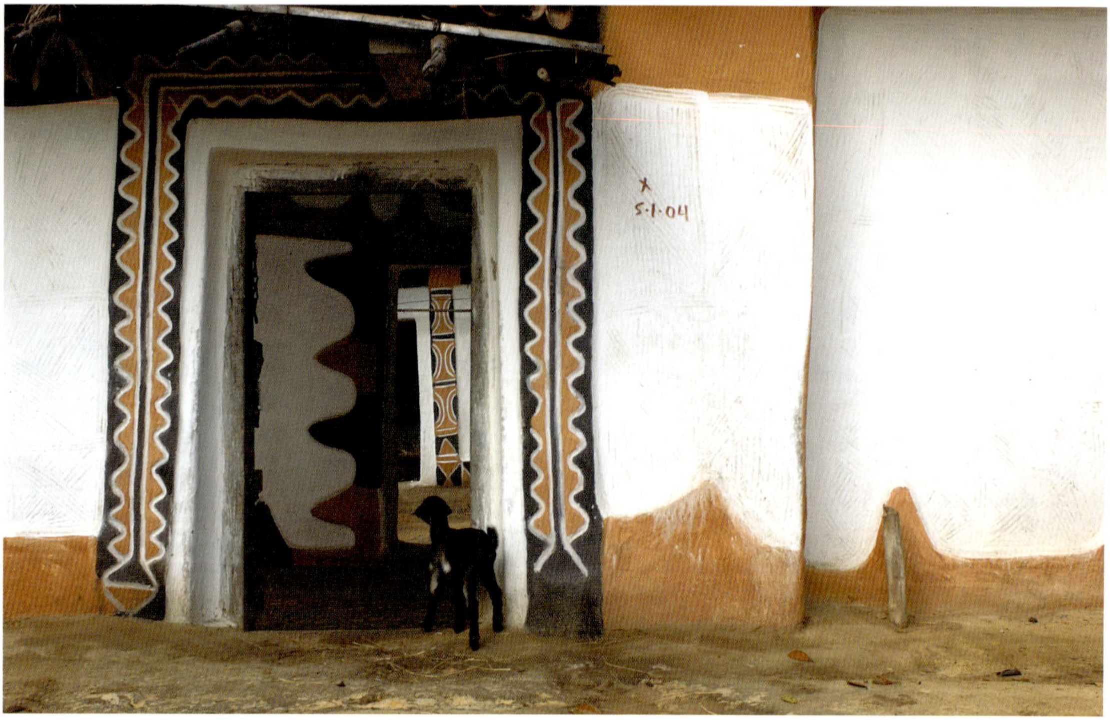
5·1·04

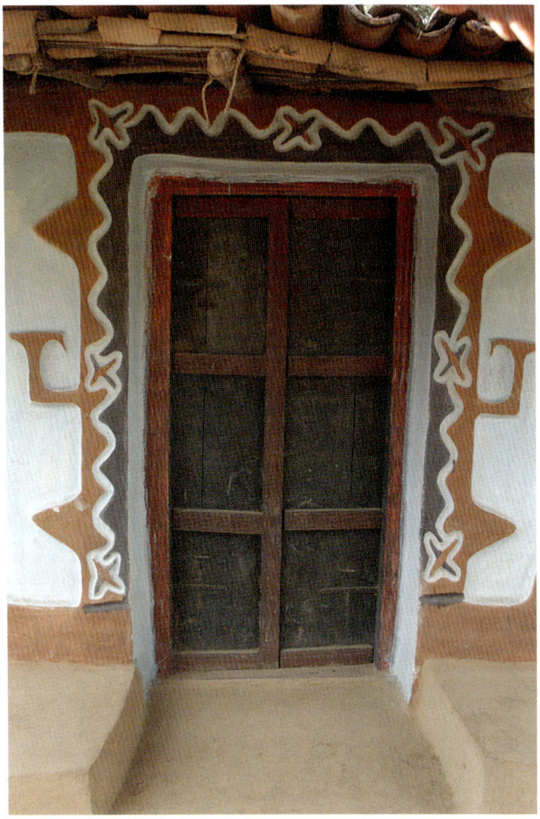

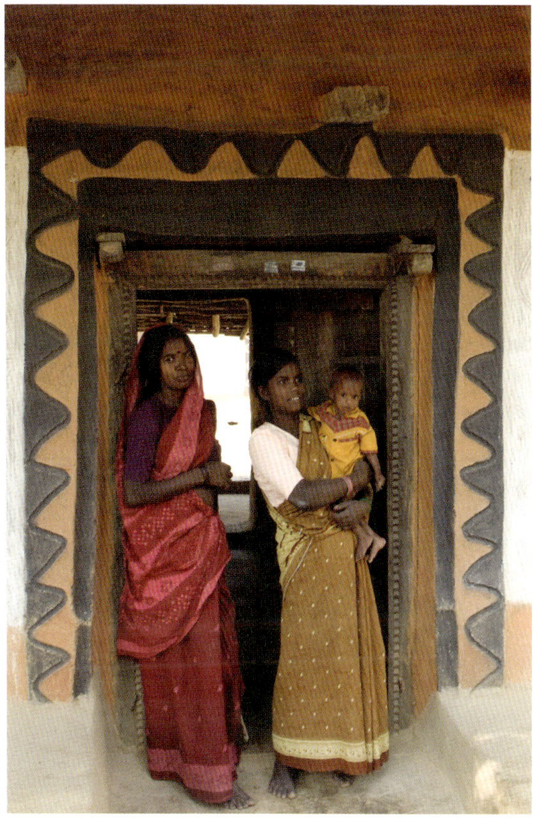

everywhere during the past fifty years have produced new cities and towns that are almost bursting at the seams. Few traditional decorative techniques have made the transition. But 770 million people—nearly two-and-a-half times the population of the United States—still live in rural communities (defined by the 2000 Census of India as having a population that is 75% agrarian). The range of styles of women's wall and floor decoration are far too complex to cover here[1], but the following are a few examples. In preparation for the annual Lakshmi festival in late January or early February, the farming women in verdant northeastern Orissa use rice paste to decorate the walls and floors of their mud houses. Employing a wide variety of motifs (among them lotuses, elephants and peacocks and other birds and flowers) they transform their homes into temples to the Goddess. They paint her symbolic footprints to guide her spirit from outside on the street through the courtyard and into the inner room. In contrast, the poor wives of camel and goat herders in the far western desert of Rajasthan have so little water that they can only resurface their walls once each year during the October–November festival of Divali. Covering their surfaces with fresh camel dung mixed with clay, they paint broad geometric designs that are intended to draw the attention of Lakshmi, the goddess of abundance and prosperity, into their desolate homes. In the southern state of Tamil Nadu, the women in more than a million homes use rice flour to draw intricate sacred diagrams on the ground outside their front doors every morning of the

1 Jyotindra Jain, *Other Masters: Five Contemporary Folk and Tribal Artists of India*, p. 50.

The traditional style of Puhputra's wall decoration is unique to this region, but is entirely different from the art Sonabai invented when in isolation.

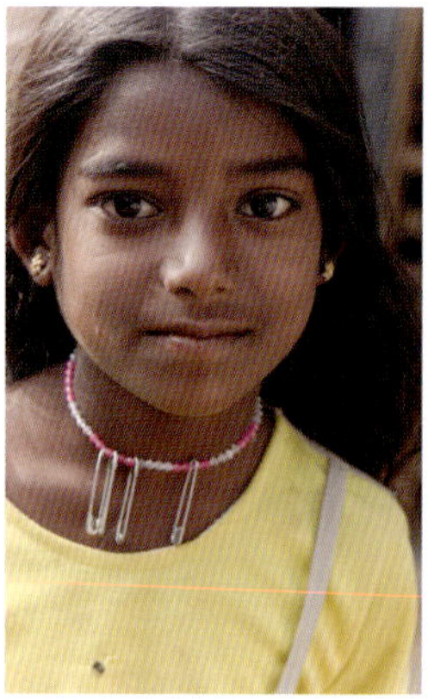
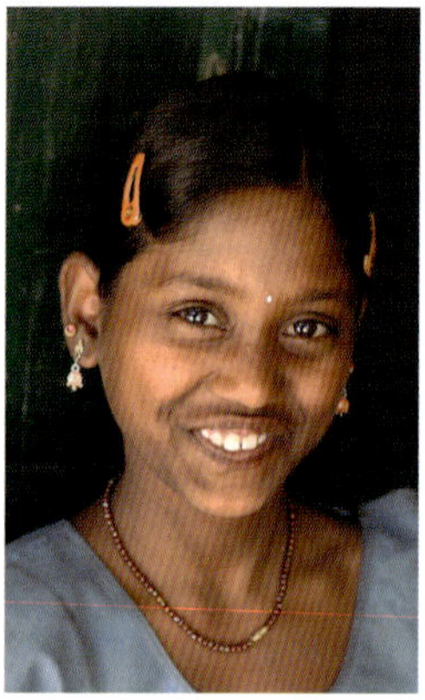
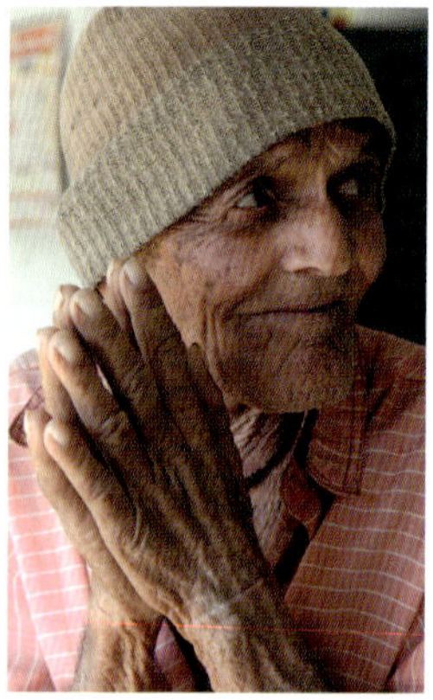
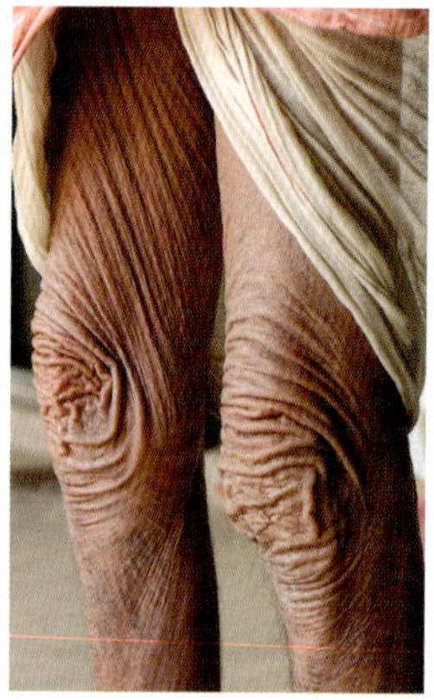
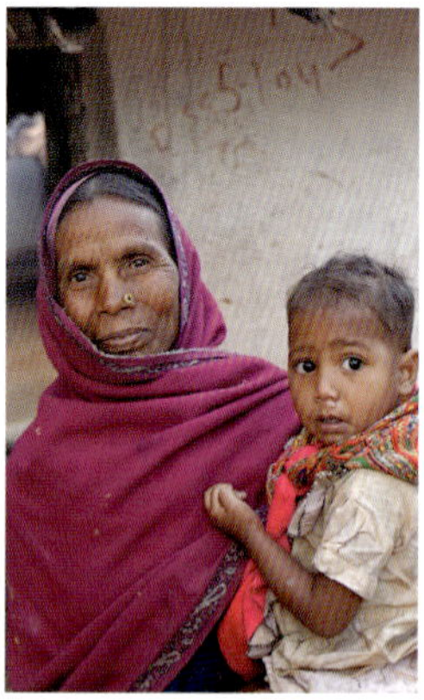
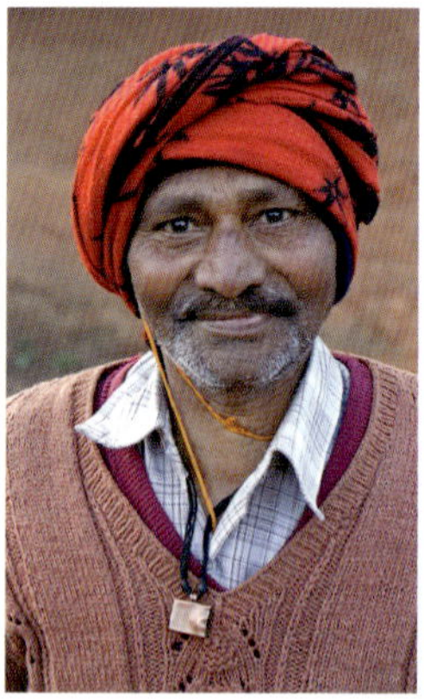
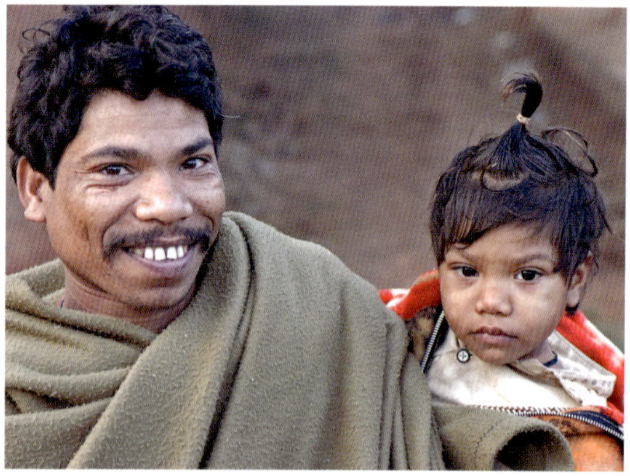

year (except during the wet monsoon season). They pride themselves in never repeating a design. As these works of art last only minutes before they are blown away, walked upon or driven over, it is the moment of making that is considered important. The women claim this art is their own form of yoga: a chance for meditative self-expression removed from their other responsibilities.

Puhputra and its surrounding villages exhibit some of the finest bas-relief architectural ornamentation in India. In rural villages in all the states of north and central India from Bengal to Gujarat and from the border of Nepal through Madhya Pradesh, women sculpt clay bas-reliefs on their mud walls during construction. The styles of sculpture in these regions vary greatly from extremely minimal to highly complex, yet they are often magnificent in form. No survey has ever been published about them. The refinement of form and design found in the farmers' houses of Puhputra is startling in its sophistication. It is without question the basis from which Sonabai's art springs, the font that nourished her; and yet her sculptures bear almost no relationship to it. They are entirely unique.

Until the late 20th century, all the houses in Puhputra were constructed in the same manner as Sonabai's: wood pillars and beams held together by an adobe-like mortar of mud, clay, cow dung, straw and stones, and surfaced with a tiled roof. Like hers, most are a series of courtyards and rooms. It is the ornamentation that is so completely different. Houses are sculpted when they are first built and again when rooms are added or when mud walls crumble. Usually one woman in a family is chosen for her superior artistic skills. She decides the overall design and either does all the sculpting herself or works while coaching other women in the family. The color palette employed in Puhputra's ornamentation is limited to yellow and red ochre and coal black, all against the whitewash of the walls. The designs are usually either geometric or simplified foliate. The first decorative focus is given to the exterior wall and door. Occasionally the doorway is flanked by a small verandah with a simple decoration running along it, but bas-reliefs always surround the front door and mark the style that defines the primary sculptor's trademark. The first courtyard is glimpsed through the open doorway and most often frames another bas-relief beyond, either in a complementary design or one that purposefully contrasts with it. Around a central space are usually a barn, often a rice mill and a storage room for grain and vegetables. There may or may not be a kitchen here. Each doorway and beam is framed with another adaptation of the same decorative device. One is the entrance into a room that opens into another courtyard, often with its own surrounding verandah and radiating bedrooms for the many family members that live there. Horizontals and verticals provide yet more planes for rows of ornamentation and yet these houses are in no way over-decorated. The artistic heritage of these women teaches them an innate sense of negative space. The yellows, reds, blacks and whites, the lozenges, circles, petals and vines, are kept in check, well balanced against the broad planes of solid mud walls and open spaces. It is a mastery of architecture.

In the twenty-five years since Sonabai was discovered by the Indian art world, Puhputra has changed a little. As elsewhere, its population has grown and the village has expanded accordingly. Sonabai's house is no longer completely isolated. Others have trailed out towards it from the center and some have been built even further out. Some village houses have now been built of brick, although none would qualify as contemporary architecture. A few villagers have been inspired by Sonabai's apparent success and ornamented their mud homes with sculptures in her innovative style. One wealthy landowner hired a professional sculptor from Ambikapur to prepare the interior walls of his brick house with stucco bas-reliefs that depict scenes from the Hindu epics. The deities, heroes and heroines are more reminiscent of Bollywood films and popular posters than traditional art.

Sonabai died in 2007, but her legacy remains alive in her family and in the spirit of her village. Even though she was very removed from their daily lives, the villagers respected her deeply. They saw that she had created a world entirely of her own out of nothing. In her loneliness during those fifteen years of isolation, she employed her own vision and invention to bring her community inside. They were everywhere around her. Over the past few decades, solely because of Sonabai Rajawar, the outside world has begun to take notice of this tiny village in the remote heart of India. The people of Puhputra are bewildered and very much in awe of how this came to be.

SONABAI

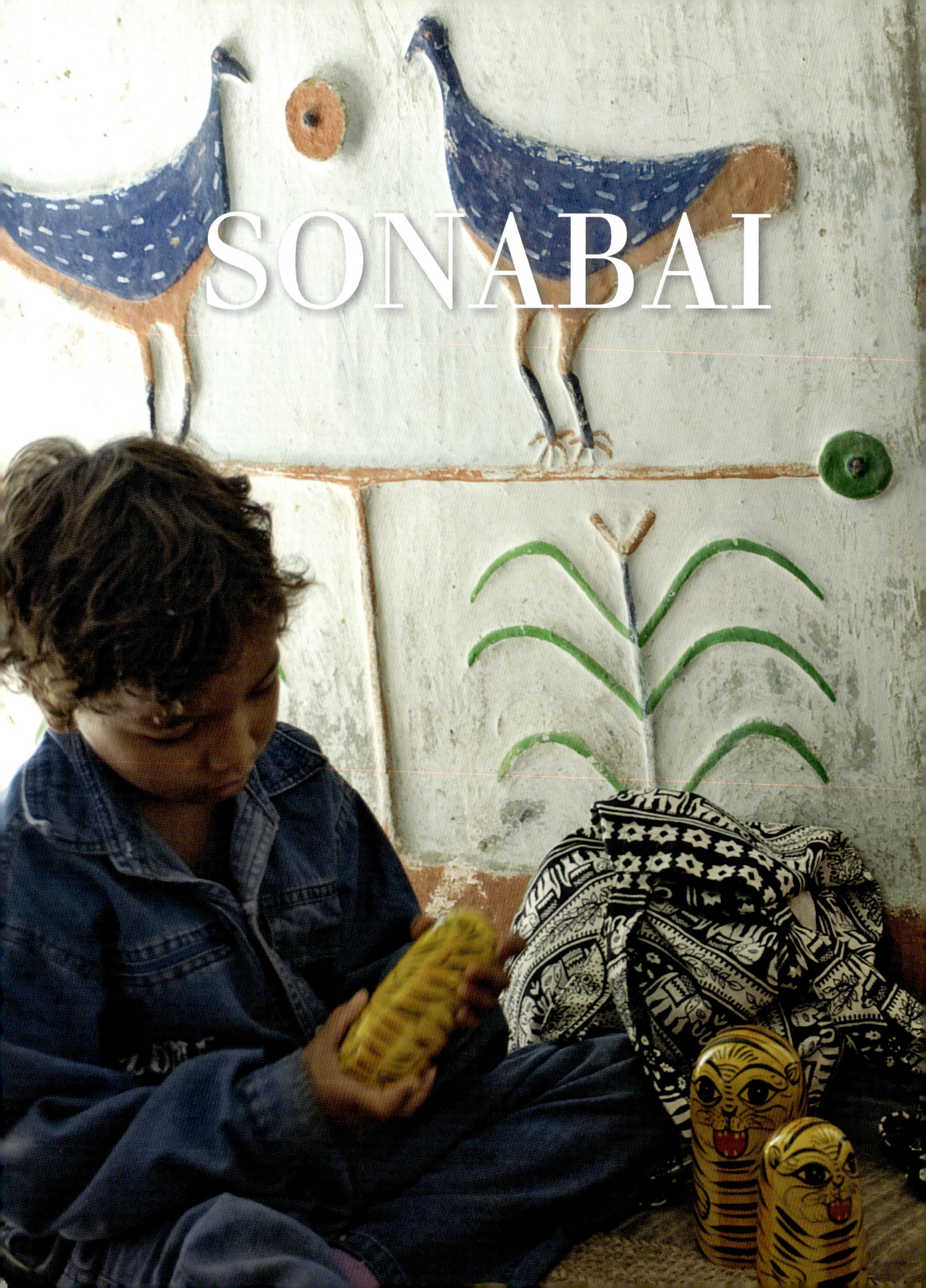

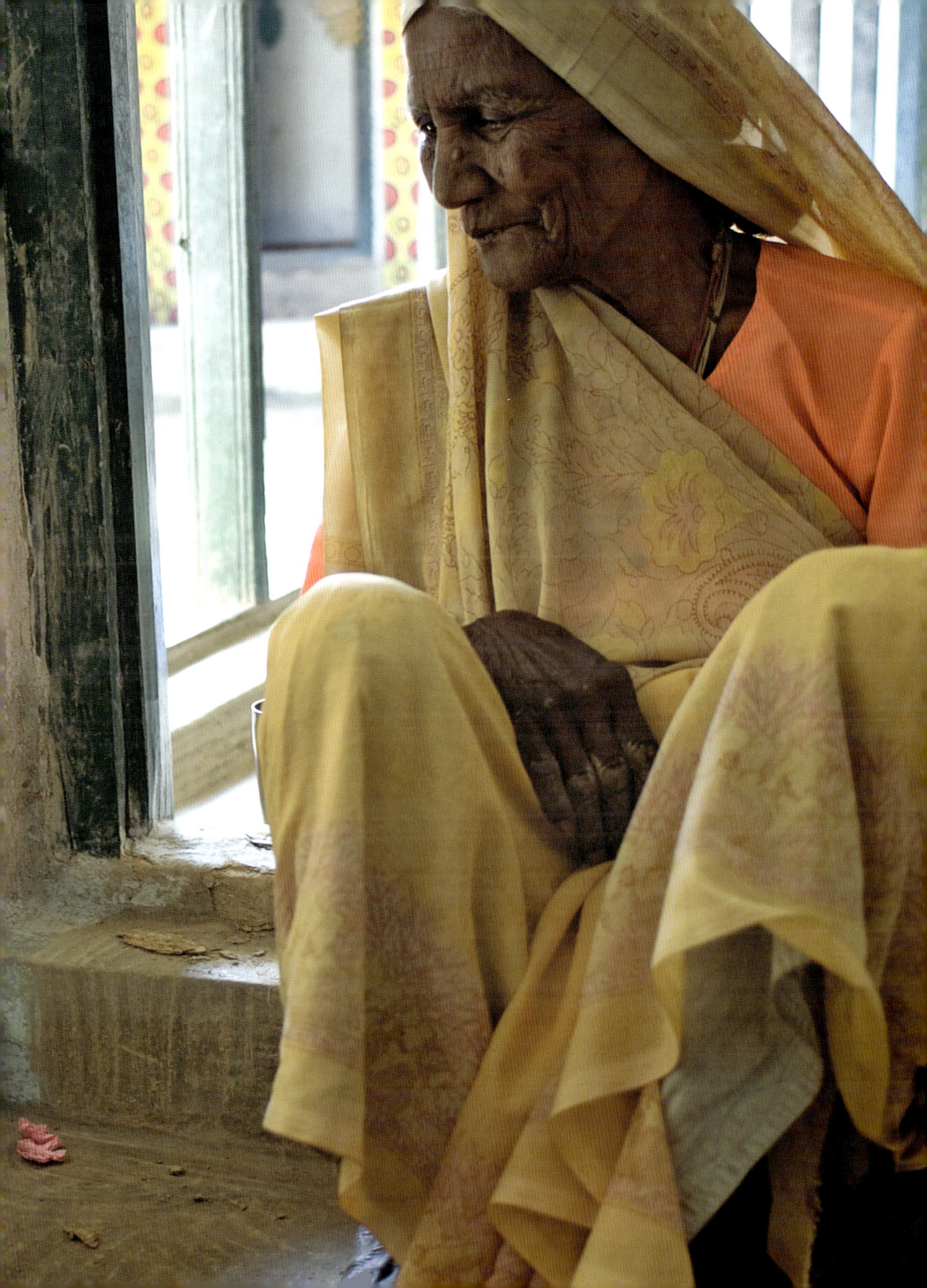

AS SHE SMOOTHES CLAY into the bamboo circles of her *jali* lattice, Sonabai gazes at her old gnarled fingers. They were once small, slender and nimble. Now each movement causes her to wince with pain; she has to stop until the ache subsides. Through the *jali*, sitting in the sun on the other side of the courtyard, Sonabai sees Munita, her grandson's wife, as she nurses Sonabai's great-grandson. There are so many people around Sonabai now! How her life has changed since those early lonely days when she first moved here!

Sonabai clearly remembers her excitement when, more than half a century ago, she first thought of introducing sculptures into *jali*. She began by rolling a long rope of clay and winding it up and through the holes of the lattice. She added a clay ball to its upper end, then pressed the ball flat to become the hooded head of a cobra. The result looked so fine that she immediately mirrored it with a second snake sinuously climbing the opposite side of the *jali*. Standing back to admire the effect, Sonabai realized that the *jali* needed more ornamentation. Employing the same process she had invented to sculpt toys for Babu, she created three parrots. First she wrapped a string tightly around a core of pressed rice straw, squeezing the bundle so that it was roughly pear-shaped, and duplicating the result twice to produce three nearly identical forms. Next she used her thumbs to smooth strips of damp clay into the surface of each, creating the bodies, necks, heads and beaks of three birds. While the clay was still moist, she centered a bird in each of the three largest circles in the lattice facing out into her courtyard. She then let the entire assemblage dry until it was evenly hard.

White lime is the pigment of choice for most household surfaces in Puhputra. Sonabai had used it to paint the entire house when it was first built and she still had enough remaining to repaint the entire *jali*. For this process, she mixed the powder with water until it became a grayish soup and then sponged it on with a cotton rag. As the mud surface dried, it gradually changed into a brilliant white. But Sonabai was determined to make her new *jali* colorful. For weeks, she tried to make pigments in her kitchen, experimenting with different vegetables, herbs, spices and minerals in order to achieve durable, true colors. It was not easy. With a mortar and pestle, she would grind ingredients into a paste and mix in drops of cooking oil until it reached a consistency she liked. Finally she created some pleasing colors: bright green made from leaves, a yellow mixture of spices and mineral ochre, red ochre that she was able to brighten with another spice, and black made from black clay and burnt leaves. For blue, she used the powder that she added to bleach in order to whiten her wash.

At last, Sonabai was ready to paint her *jali*. To make a small brush, she chewed the end of a stick until it was fibrous. Sonabai poured some green pigment into a dish and with methodical strokes covered each parrot with the color. With two smaller stick brushes, she sparingly daubed red for their beaks and black for the eyes. Carefully washing her large brush, she painted her two slithering cobras yellow, defining their hoods and eyes with black and their forked tongues with red. She marveled at the metamorphosis these bright sculptures wrought in her courtyard. They brought it alive! She had to create more.

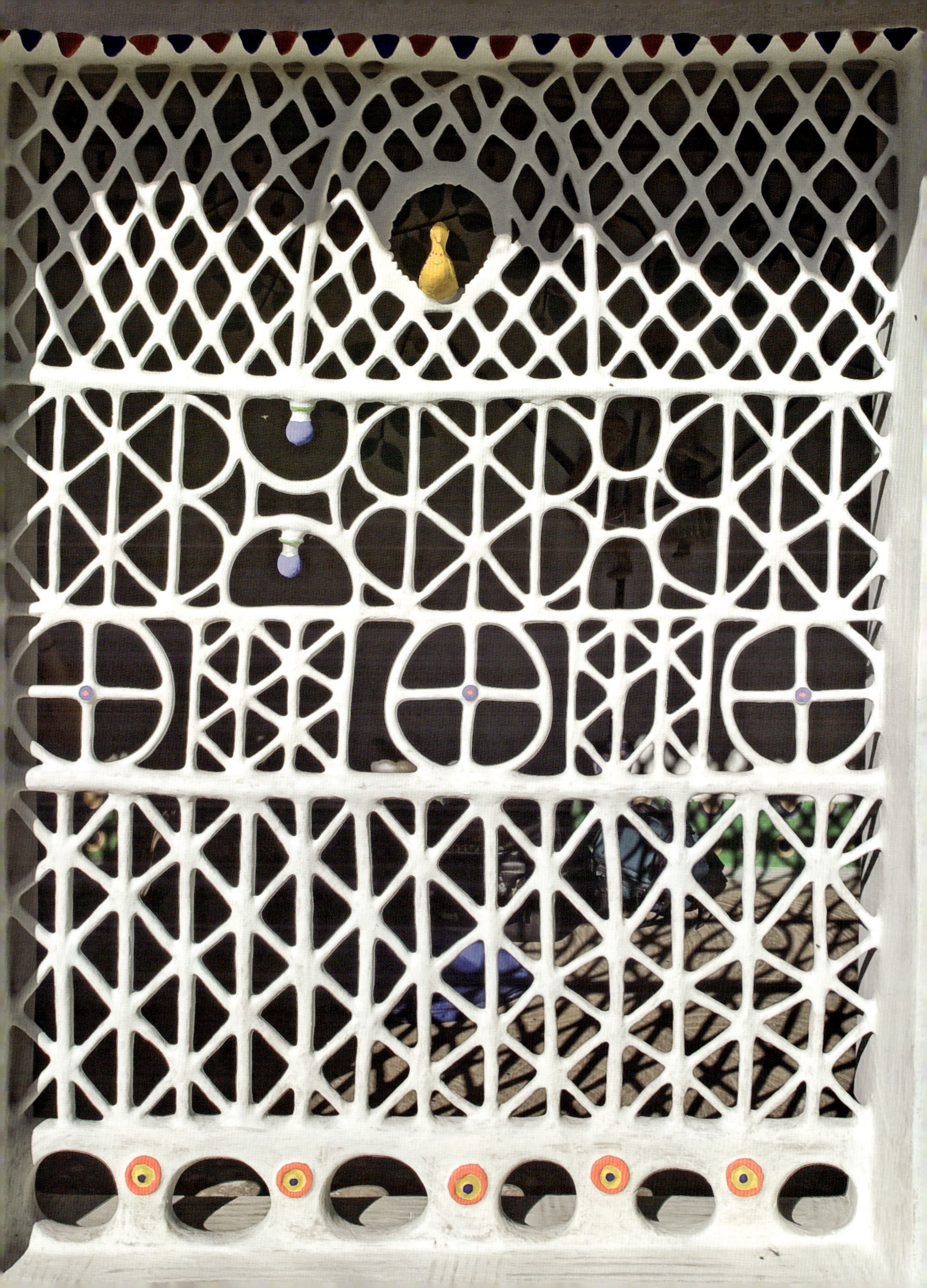

Over the next months Sonabai was very busy. She already had a full workload just caring for Holi Ram and Babu, doing the household chores, cooking for them and helping in the fields. But now there was no stopping her, and Holi Ram didn't try. He never even commented on the changes she made in their home. Sonabai sculpted new *jali* between other columns surrounding the courtyard. Into these she put different sculptures: a villager playing a horn, a woman dancing, more birds, more snakes—it was all so much fun! When the sun was just right and Sonabai stood in the courtyard looking through the latticework, she loved the way shadows played tricks on her eyes, how the foreground and background became intermixed and confused. Holi Ram and Babu created a completely different set of forms and patterns when they walked by inside. It made Sonabai think. What if she mounted sculptures to the walls behind the *jali*? Wouldn't they add even more dimensions?

Sonabai began the entire transformation of her home. She consciously considered every space, every angle, each wall, doorway, beam and pillar. Then, during any spare time she had as little Babu grew from infant to young boy to teenager, she sculpted. The result is a wonderland of color, form, light, texture and whimsy. Fish swim along a baseboard; musicians play under the eaves; monkeys climb trees on the walls in search of fruit; a calf suckles at a cow's udders; women dance energetically in a row; a gazelle leaps; the winsome Krishna frolics with his handmaidens. Everywhere there are stories; all is a delight in perfect balance, thoughtfully composed with an innate understanding of negative space. Not too much. A community of vibrant life expressed within one woman's withdrawn world.

Now nearly eighty, Sonabai has spent almost sixty years surrounded by her creations. Babu has grown into a mature and respected man, a village elder himself. Holi Ram has been dead for decades. That long painful time when Holi Ram would not even let her talk to anyone else is far in the past. Sonabai's life is good. She is content to sit warming herself in the sun for long stretches of the day, watching her grandchildren and great-grandson and occasionally helping Babu and his wife Rajenbai as they carry on the new family profession of sculpting. That is what she is doing now, stretching her fingers again around the forms of a *jali*. This one is going for exhibition in the United States! She begins to think about the sculptures that she will add to it. Perhaps Krishna and his flute? Maybe she will balance him with an image of Radha, his consort… Sonabai has stopped working and is so silent in her deep thought that it is almost as if she is sleeping.

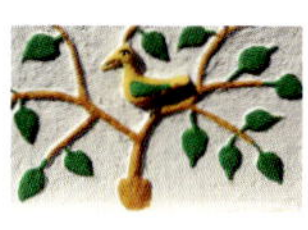

THE STORY OF SONABAI RAJAWAR is unique. She sculpted her own distinct identity against almost impossible odds. Yet her message is universal and very familiar, rooted in the experiences of all of us. In many ways, Sonabai represents everywoman. Although she is self-taught, expressing her creativity in a form unlike that of any other human being, she is herself an archetype of the unrecognized woman who creates beauty in her life. Throughout the history of mankind, it is the males who have demanded attention, who beat their chests and brandish their weapons, whose buildings are acclaimed, whose art is framed and exhibited and whose books are published and read. Exceptions exist, but they are rare. Perhaps the mood is changing globally, but it changes slowly. Where are the women of history? Who were they? How many were kept away, sequestered from the mainstream of activity? How did they blossom? What was their art?

On the outskirts of a village that not long ago was in the midst of a jungle, a village virtually unrecorded and unknown until a few decades ago, lived one woman in almost absolute isolation. Her life could easily have been miserable had she given into its enormous pressures. She did not. Sonabai Rajawar pulled from deep within herself a creative vision that transfigured her entire environment. She counterbalanced a depressive situation with images of bright humor, literally and figuratively bringing light into her dark world. She never sought public acclaim and was uncomfortable with it when it came. Sonabai was most content when she was sculpting, enjoying the love and activity of her growing family.

No record exists of Sonabai Rajawar's birth. She and every member of her natal family were illiterate and no one even knew the year she was born, although it was sometime between 1928 and 1932. "I am not sure how old I am," she commented a couple of years before she died, "maybe seventy-five or eighty. Do you know, Babu?" She turned her rheumy eyes towards her son, whose real name is Daroga Ram. (Babu is a common nickname in Indian families.) Daroga Ram answered that he was unsure. He thought his mother was somewhere around eighty It is probable that Sonabai was in her late seventies at the time of her death of a stroke on August 17, 2007.

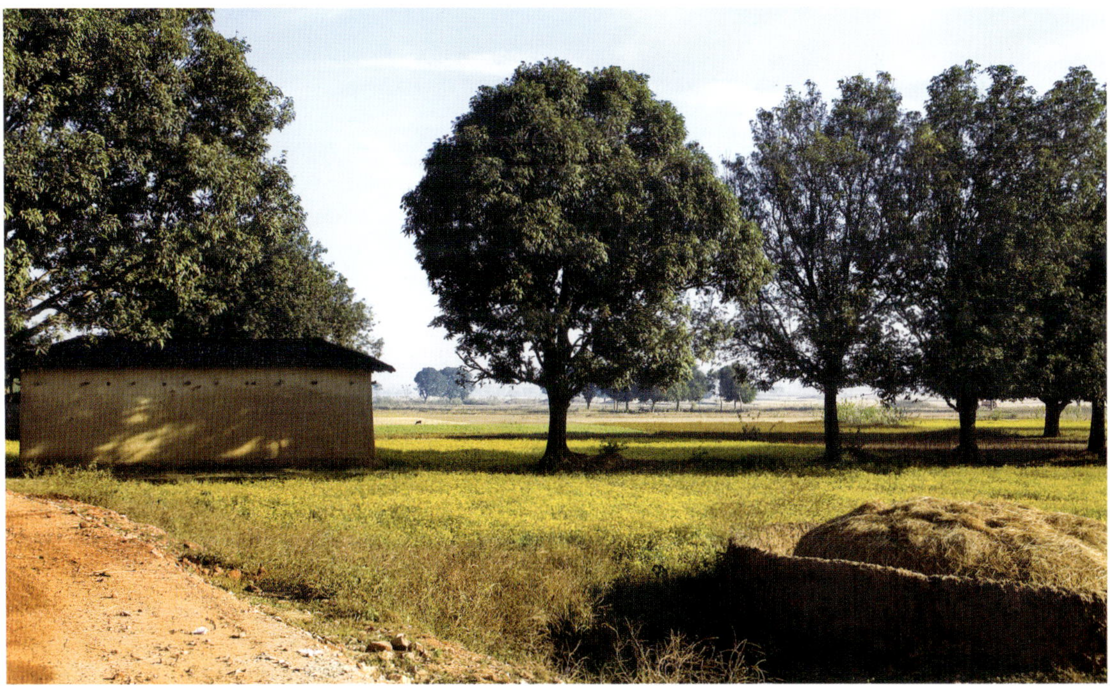

Sonabai was born in the village of Kenapara, near Ganeshpur, not far from Puhputra. "There were eighteen living in my house when I was growing up: my grandparents, my parents, three brothers and three sisters, my uncle, my auntie, and five cousins. We were all together in that one small house. It was crowded, but we were happy." The family house remains right in the center of Kenapara. Compared with others in the village, it is particularly plain, exhibiting only minimal decoration. Many other buildings are elaborately ornamented like those in Puhputra. Sonabai stated that no one in her family was particularly artistic and that art had not been part of her training. "I didn't do any chores around the house. I would talk to people, I would go around the streets in the village, but I never did any sculpting in my home. And once I moved into the first house with my husband, I never did any sculpting or artwork there either." Sonabai's parents were lenient with her, allowing her a great deal of freedom. "I didn't want to go to school... instead I took the buffaloes to graze and then I ran away into the jungle. I never learned to read and write. But now I have received all these awards. Why would I need to learn? What good would it have done me? Rajenbai and Munita (her daughter-in-law and granddaughter-in-law) have both gone to school—but it is me the government calls. They feed me and like my art and love me and invite me around the world."

It was common in that day and age for village girls to marry young. Sonabai's parents believed that Holi Ram would be a good match for her. She was not consulted. As the middle son of a rice farming family, Holi Ram had inherited his own lands when he married his first wife. Both she and their first baby had died in childbirth. Sonabai remarked: "I had never seen my husband before he came on the horse to my house for our marriage. I was so shy. I do not remember much about the wedding... I was fourteen, I think, maybe fifteen... I remember afterwards we all got into a bullock cart, all his family, and left my family behind. We went down the road to my new village. I thought I would never see them again. I cried and cried..." Little did she know how insightful her premonition was. Holi Ram rarely allowed her family to visit and never allowed Sonabai to go to her village again. It was less than two miles away.

Sonabai's isolation from her own family is particularly cruel and unusual in India. Even though brides always marry grooms from other communities, they still keep in close contact with their natal families—returning home for festivals, family marriages, pregnancies, and birth and death ceremonies. When Sonabai was in her late seventies, she was taken back to Kenapara. It was her first visit in decades. She was welcomed by many of the villagers who knew of her national fame. She wept when she met old friends that she had not seen since her childhood. She marveled at how little the streets and houses had changed. In her old home, now owned by a great-nephew and occupied by many cousins of all ages, Sonabai was deeply awed when the women of the family bent before her and washed her feet, bestowing on her what honor they could. Sonabai was the one among them who had been heard and seen. She had made her mark and been recognized by the President of India. Her return to this place of her childhood left Sonabai speechless for days.

Decades before, as a new bride, it was a big shock to Sonabai when she moved with Holi Ram into his parents' home in Puhputra. It was crowded there. As the newest member of the family, Sonabai was given the largest share of work. She had to care for her father-in-law, mother-in-law, brothers-in-law, sister-in-law and new husband, always at their beck and call, fulfilling every whim. It was very difficult! Sonabai commented: "I first learned to cook

During her years of isolation, Sonabai was allowed no contact with her family, friends or anyone apart from her husband and young son. Decades later, when she finally returned to visit her natal home, her relatives washed Sonabai's feet to show their respect for her courage and creativity in the face of adversity.

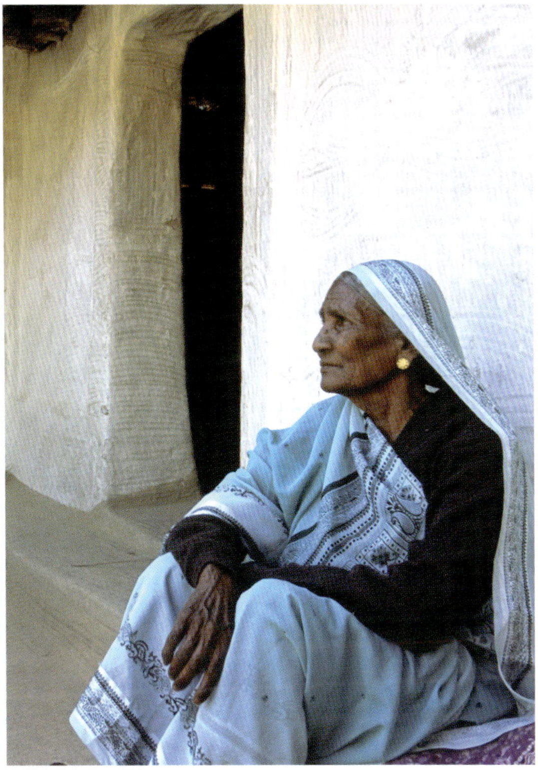

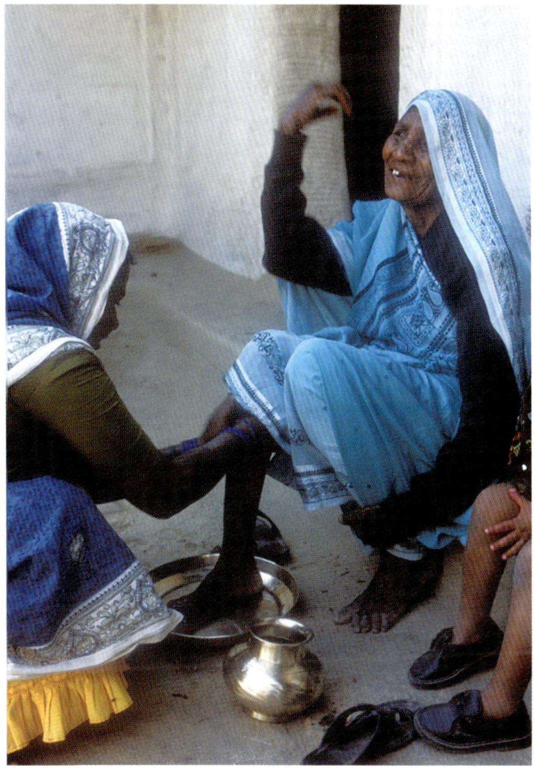

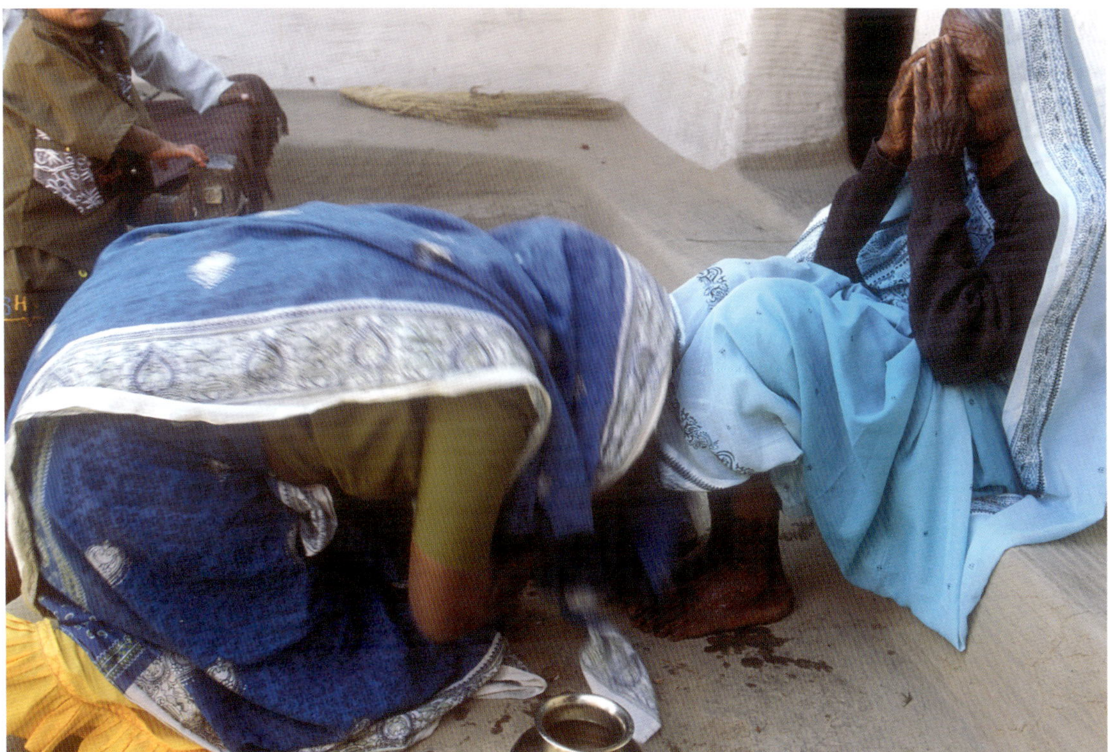

there. I made rice, *dal* and spinach, and I learned other things. They were so demanding! But when the burden of work is dumped on you, you must do it whether you knew it before or not... We lived in that house for ten long years. It was not a good time. (Conditions) did not improve. I did so much of the work."

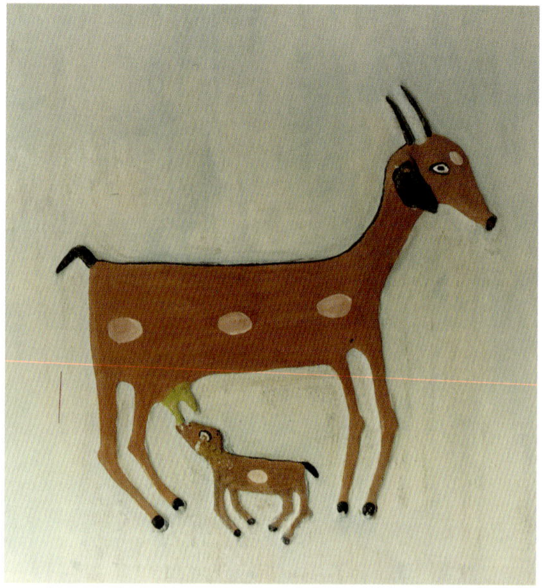

It is not uncommon in India for new brides to be treated harshly at first in their husbands' homes. They are taught the customs of the household and often find their first year or two to be arduous and unhappy. Many complain that they are made to work disproportionately hard when compared with other family members in order to prove their merit. One of the standard traditional gauges of a bride's worth is her ability to produce children, particularly sons. Usually social pressure within her new family eases with the birth of her first son and proportionately with each subsequent son. Women who have no sons are still gradually accepted by the family, but in most cases a stigma hangs over them. Barren women are often rejected as pariahs. For ten years Sonabai did not get pregnant. She was the shame of Holi Ram's family. Her life in that house was almost untenable.

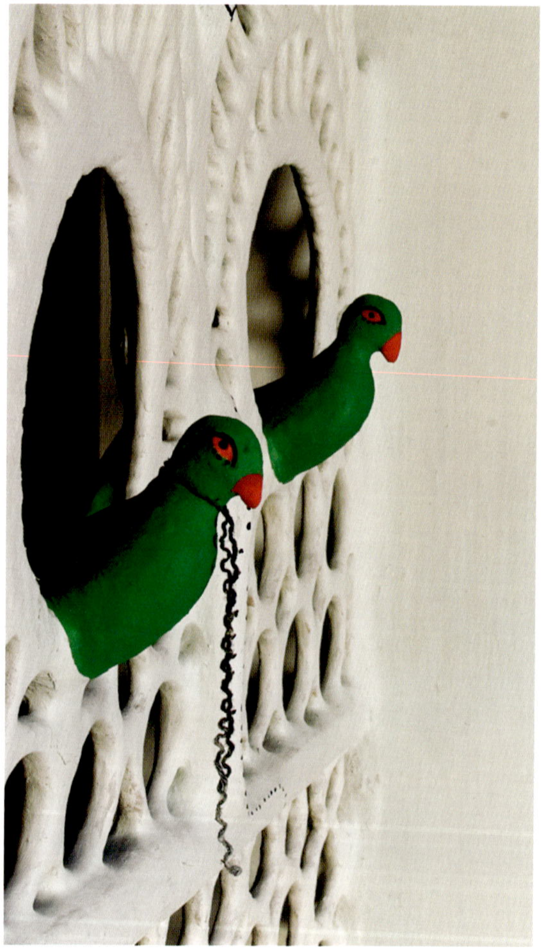

Finally, in 1952, Sonabai conceived a child. This change proved nothing to the family. They did not treat her more kindly or lighten her load. It felt to Sonabai as if they made it even worse. In 1953, Daroga Ram was born. "For the first five or six days after Babu's birth," Sonabai remembered, "he was not well. We saw no one until it was proved that he was healthy and I was no longer called *baanjh* (barren)." Once they saw Daroga Ram, Holi Ram's family immediately adored him. This fact slightly improved Sonabai's position in the house. Nevertheless, she was relieved when Holi Ram made the decision to move out three months later.

At first Sonabai looked forward to living alone. She was naturally shy and reclusive. She enjoyed the peacefulness and the time for reflection. She liked building the house with Holi Ram. He was a good builder. He understood construction and planned it well. It was only a few months after their move that Sonabai began to realize her predicament. Holi Ram was a

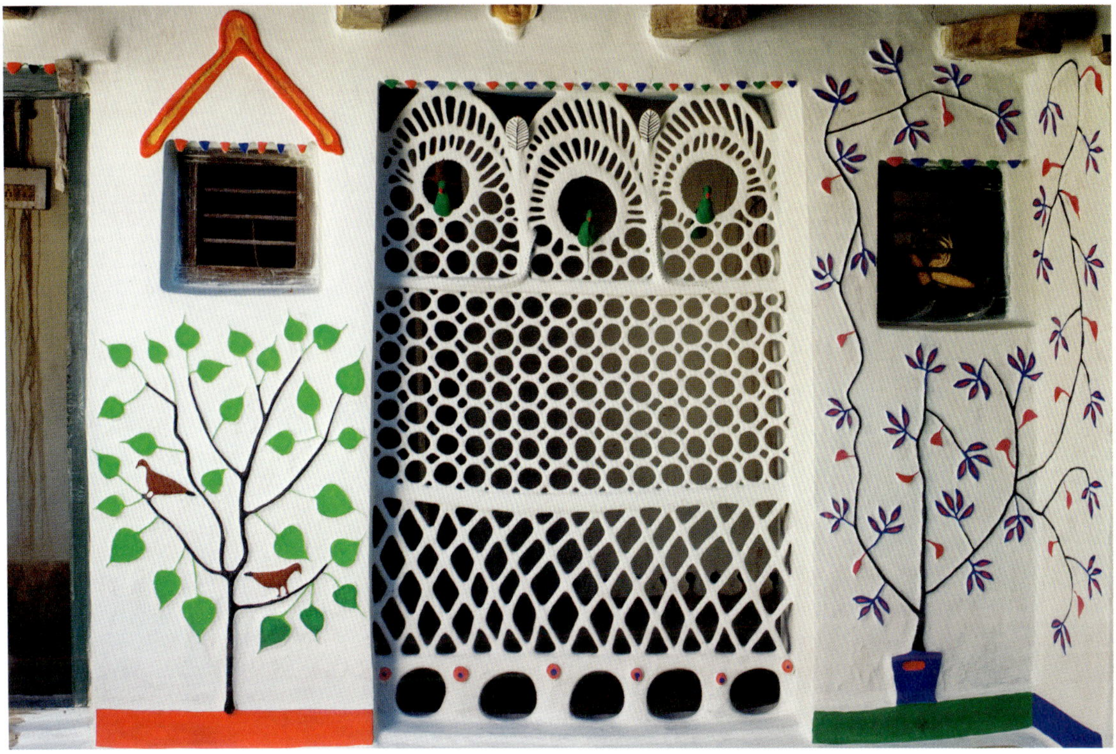

powerful man and told her forcefully that he did not want her to meet with others. "He kept questioning me again and again when I asked to go out. So I never went outside. He always advised me not to leave our home." The force of Holi Ram's demands hit Sonabai hard and she felt very lonely. "I had nothing to do. I had come from this large house, full of people, three brothers and three sisters, and suddenly there was no one, only Babu, and he couldn't talk. Holi Ram was gone during the day. He left me alone. I was so miserable… There was a saint, Baba, who came to meditate under a tree near my house. One early morning when Holi Ram was already gone, I came to Baba. He said: 'Why are you so sad, so lonely and so depressed? Why are you crying?' I told him of my situation and Baba said: 'What more do you need? Just show me your palm.' He took my palm with both his hands and said: 'You will get whatever you want in life. You will get wealth. You will get fame and recognition. Just go home and wait.' It seemed like such a strange thing, but I came home and shortly after that I started to make toys for Babu…"

In order to supplement their meager farm income, Holi Ram began to build houses for other people in Puhputra and the neighboring villages. He proved to be so good that his work was in demand. Sonabai remarked: "He built the houses of different people, even for the Maharajah of Lakhanpur and Junagarh." This new work reduced the little time that Holi Ram already spent in their house. His requirement that she stay at home meant that she was truly isolated. "I was all alone for the first time with just little Babu after all my life living with a big family, first my own brothers and sisters and then my sisters-in-law and their children. Also I needed to keep Babu occupied, so I started to make toys. I would just take a piece of clay in my hands and show him how a monkey or a bird was made out of it. After the cooking and the cleaning of the house, I would have time on my hands. I first made these toys to stop him from crying."

As Daroga Ram began to grow into a cute little boy, Holi Ram's family (the boy's grandparents, uncles and aunts) doted on him. Holi Ram didn't want these relatives in his

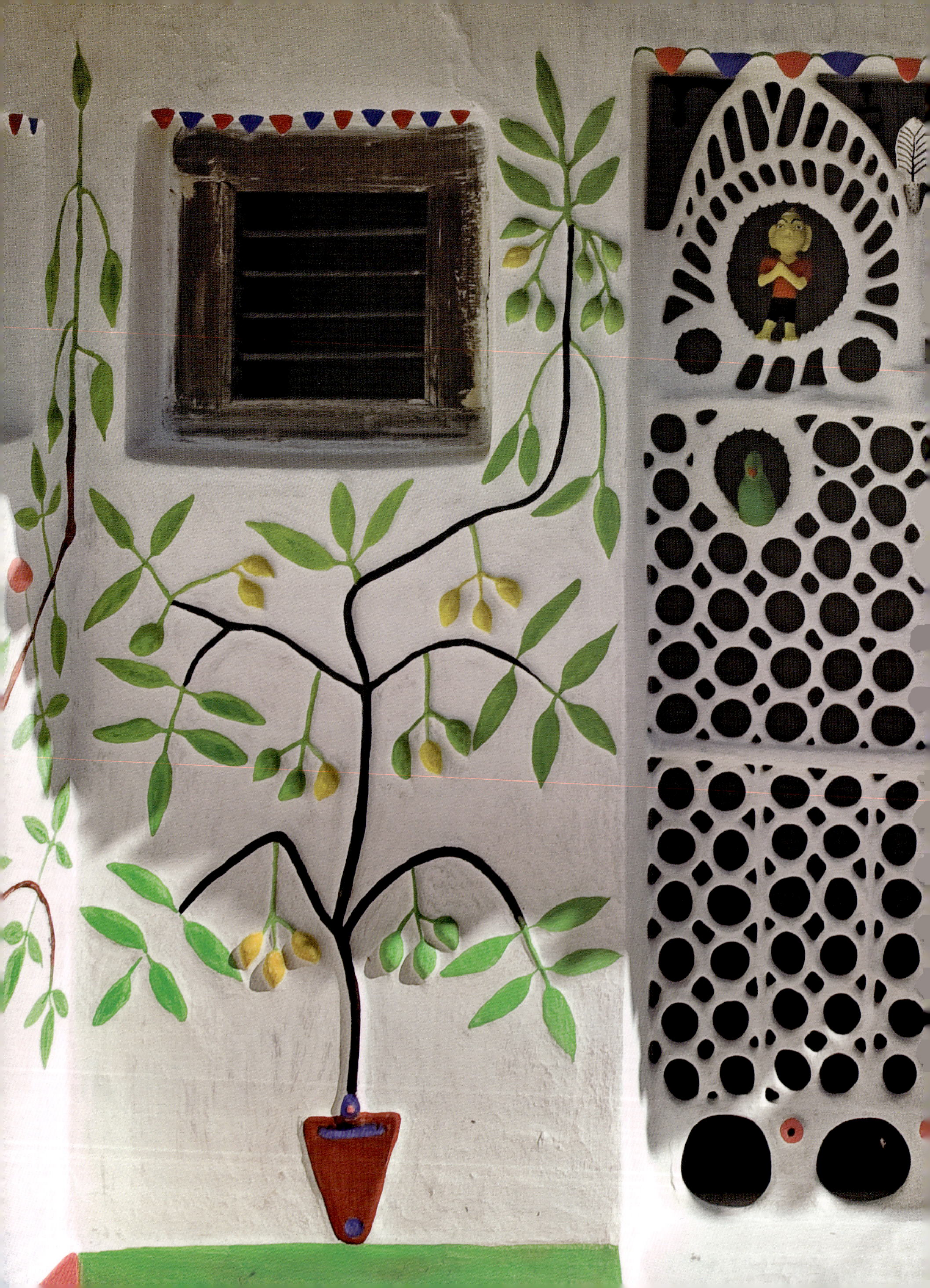

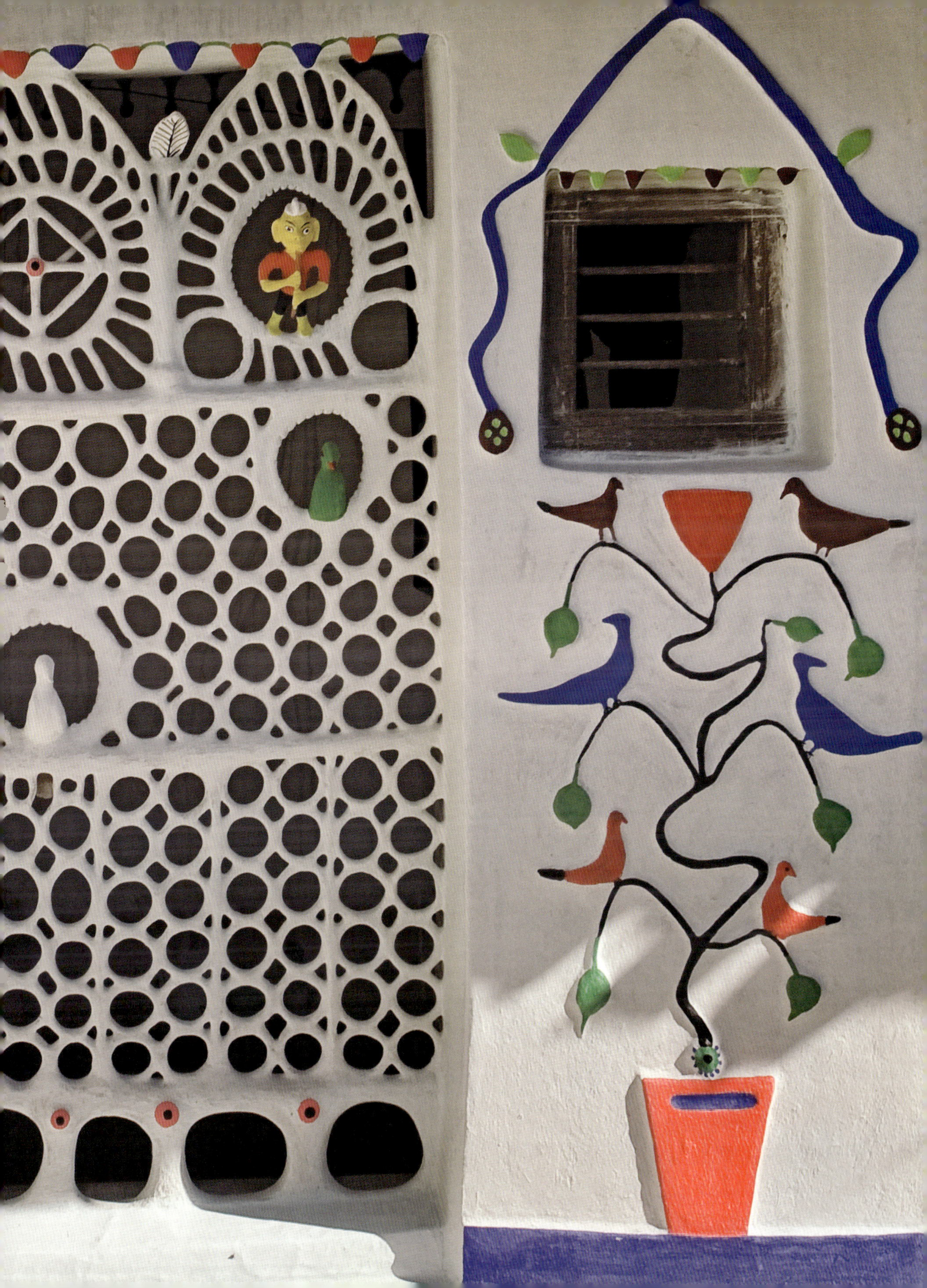

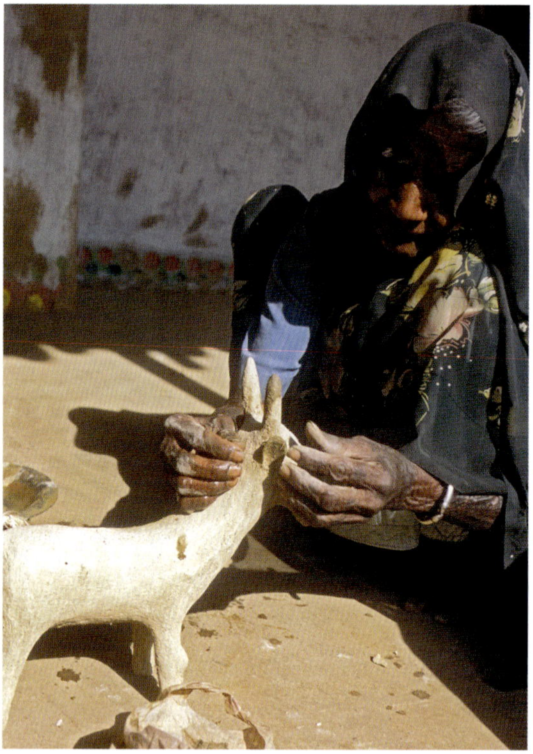

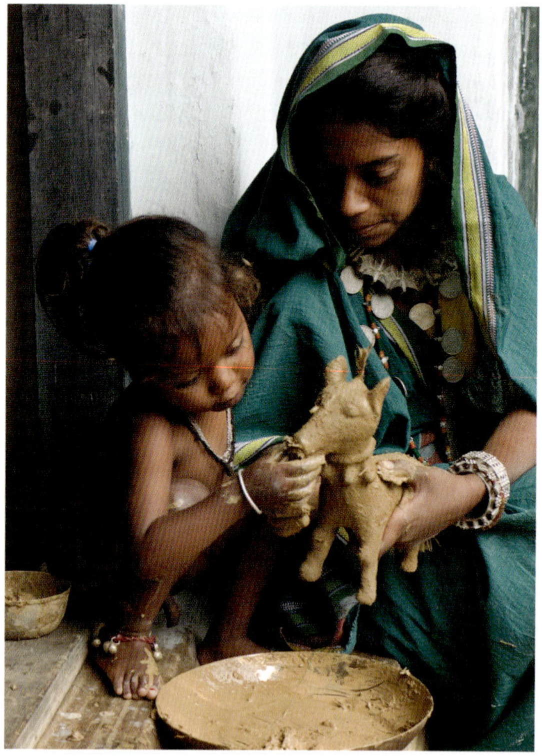

house, so they came often to take the child away with them, leaving Sonabai entirely by herself. As she said: "Everybody in his (Holi Ram's) family liked Babu and took him from my home, playing with him and feeding him. This happened almost every day. I hardly had any time to spend with my son." Sonabai's increased isolation gave her more time to sculpt toys and, as Daroga Ram began to grow, to decorate the house. Sonabai commented on the way in which her entire process of wall decoration began: "When the new house was being built by Holi Ram, there was lots of mud lying about. I would start playing around with it. A design would just come into my head and I would try it on the walls. Immediately I began making these kinds of figures." (She points out trees and leaves.) "They were the first designs I made on the walls—at the top and the bottom. Then the courtyard was finished and to while away the time I started making these *jali* in the open spaces. I had never visited any place where they were and had not seen any photographs of *jali*. I just thought of doing them and made them with bamboo sticks." She reminisced: "It was a large house, my son was small, my husband was away the whole day and I was terribly lonely. I had no one to talk to. To occupy myself and to have company, I began to construct clay figures of human beings, deities, birds and animals all over the house. They became my companions."[2]

Sonabai began by sculpting toys for her infant son. As no record of this time exists, the photo in the upper right is a recreation depicting Munita, her granddaughter-in-law, wearing Sonabai's own dowry jewelry and a sari typical of those bygone years. Sonabai's great-grandson is being taught to sculpt.

It is difficult to ascertain the exact order in which Sonabai's sculpting style developed. As an old woman, she would tell her story a certain way one time and a different way the next. Daroga Ram was careful never to contradict his

2 Jain, *Other Masters*, p. 50.

mother and was almost as hard to pin down. The progression of her art was a random blend of long planning and momentary inspiration. It is likely that Sonabai began immediately after constructing the house, as she stated, with simple foliate decorations on friezes at the tops and bottoms of the walls. These decorative friezes were shallowly sculpted of clay added directly to the existing wall surfaces. Although Sonabai continued to sculpt in this manner throughout her life, she later introduced much more elaborate three-dimensional sculptures into her bas-reliefs that became one of her trademarks. Sonabai often asserted that her first sculptures were toys for Babu. Without question she would have been exposed as a child to the temporary festival images of the Goddess Saraswati sculpted by local potters upon foundations of sticks and straw. Although Sonabai never credited this source, her own toys and sculptures were created using a similar technique and it can be assumed that she was partly inspired by the Saraswati sculptures. Sonabai's sculpted lattices, however, were entirely original. *Jali* are not traditional in the architecture of the region. Prior to Sonabai, none of the villages in at least a sixty-mile radius of Puhputra used *jali* in their houses. Consequently, regardless of the fact that *jali* is employed in royal architecture in much of north India, Sonabai did invent it within her own context. Her technique of tying strips of bamboo into circles, binding these circles into a frame, and then joining the entire assemblage together with clay was unique. Her further creative decision to enhance these repetitive forms with sculptures is masterful. Her creations stretch the boundaries of architectural ornamentation in completely innovative ways.

When Sonabai began to add sculptural friezes to her walls, she again changed the equation. Daroga Ram commented: "When Ma made these animals and birds and put them on the walls, she also made figures doing different things, like Krishna playing the flute, a cow feeding her young, and maidens listening to Krishna." The three-dimensional bas-reliefs that Sonabai invented had to be sculpted when a wall was first built or when a section of it was replaced. The original structure of Sonabai's house was complete when she was first inspired to sculpt them. Consequently, she was required to remove entire sections of existing walls before she was able to begin. This required remarkably bold determination. While the clay wall was being built, but before the final surface structure was added, Sonabai had to plan her sculptures precisely and gather all of the base materials that she would need to create them. One of her friezes, for example, depicts a tree with three monkeys in its boughs picking fruit. On the trunk is a horn player with a drummer and a female dancer below him. Sonabai sculpted the tree and its leaves and fruit in low relief by adding clay directly to the surface of the wall. She rolled long ropes of clay for the trunk and limbs, balls of clay for the fruit, and large pointed plates of varying sizes for the leaves, blending them into the surfaces of the wall while it was still damp.

Sonabai next built the substructures for all six three-dimensional sculptures in exactly the same way she began the toys for Daroga Ram. For each of the monkeys, she wrapped a rice straw core with twine and used sticks for the tail, four legs and neck. She added a ball to the neck-stick for the head and clay strips to the

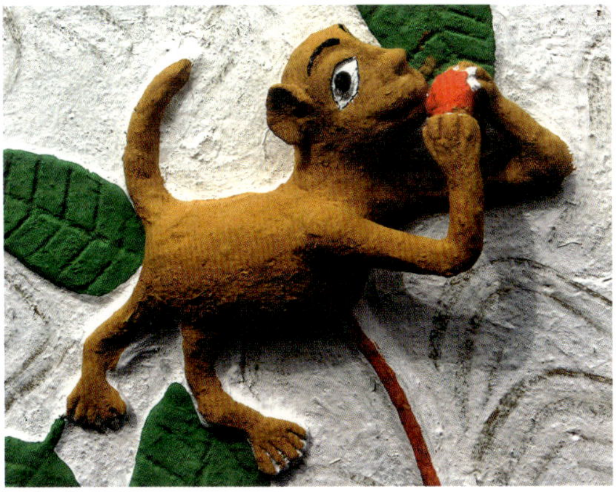

Sonabai's bas-relief sculpture of monkeys picking fruit from a tree is a good example of her enigmatic vision.

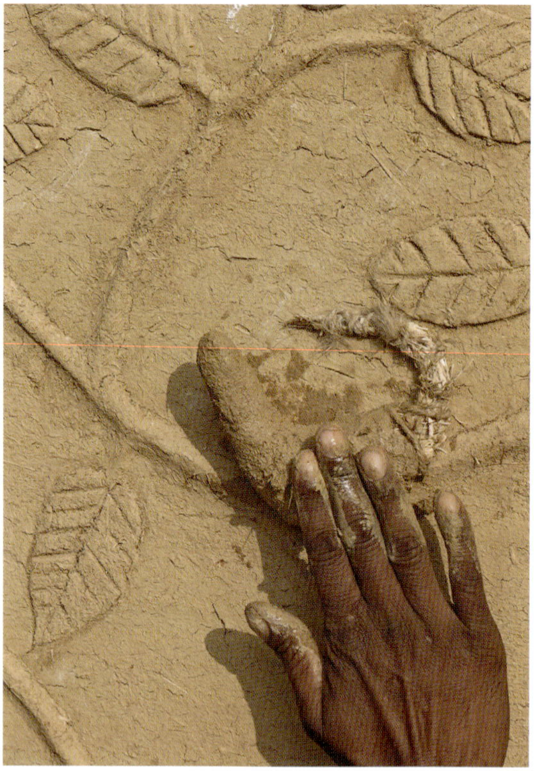

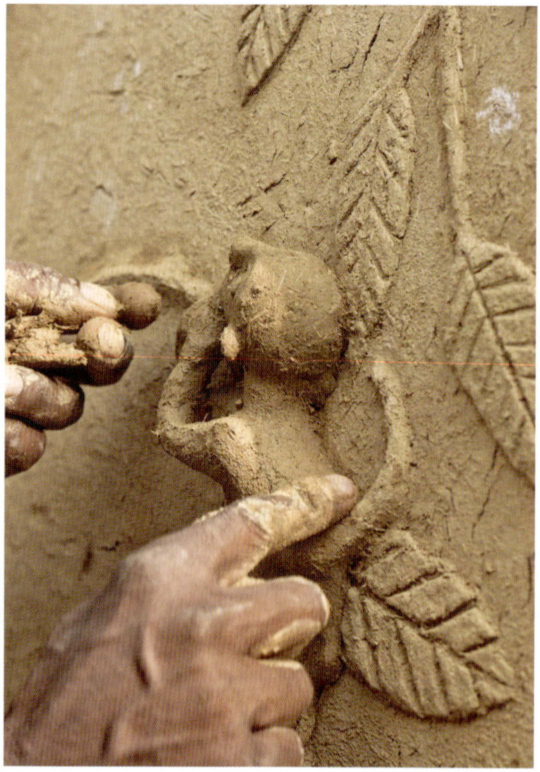

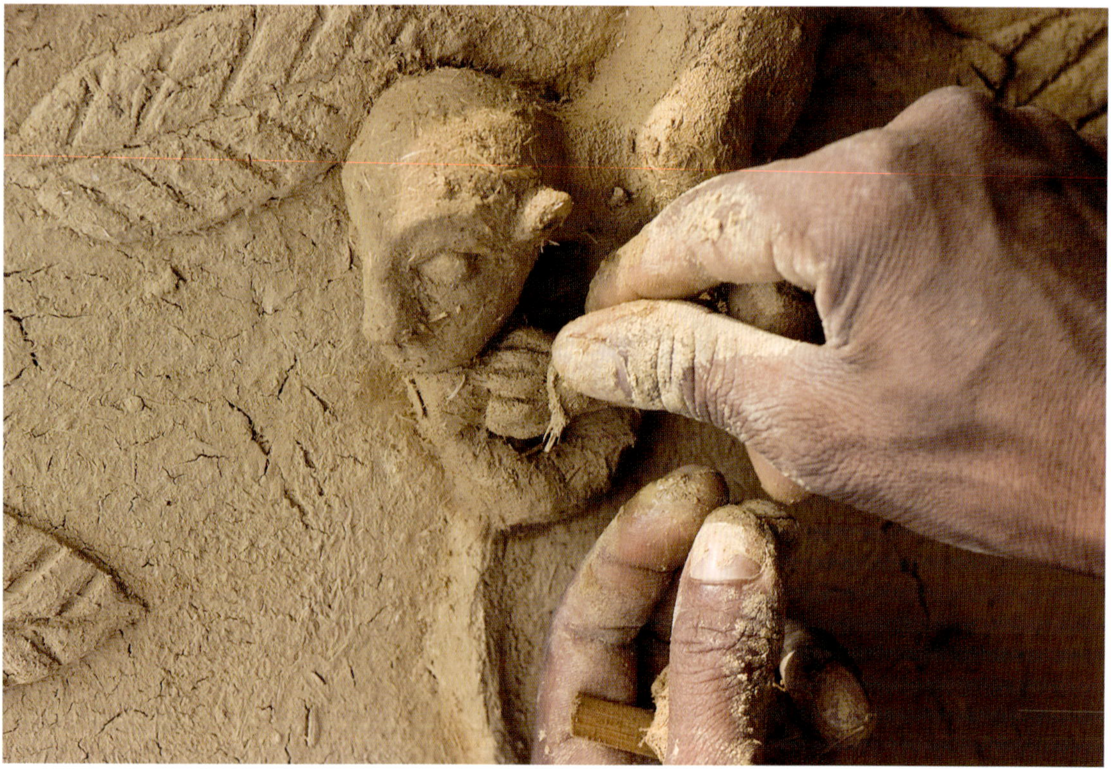

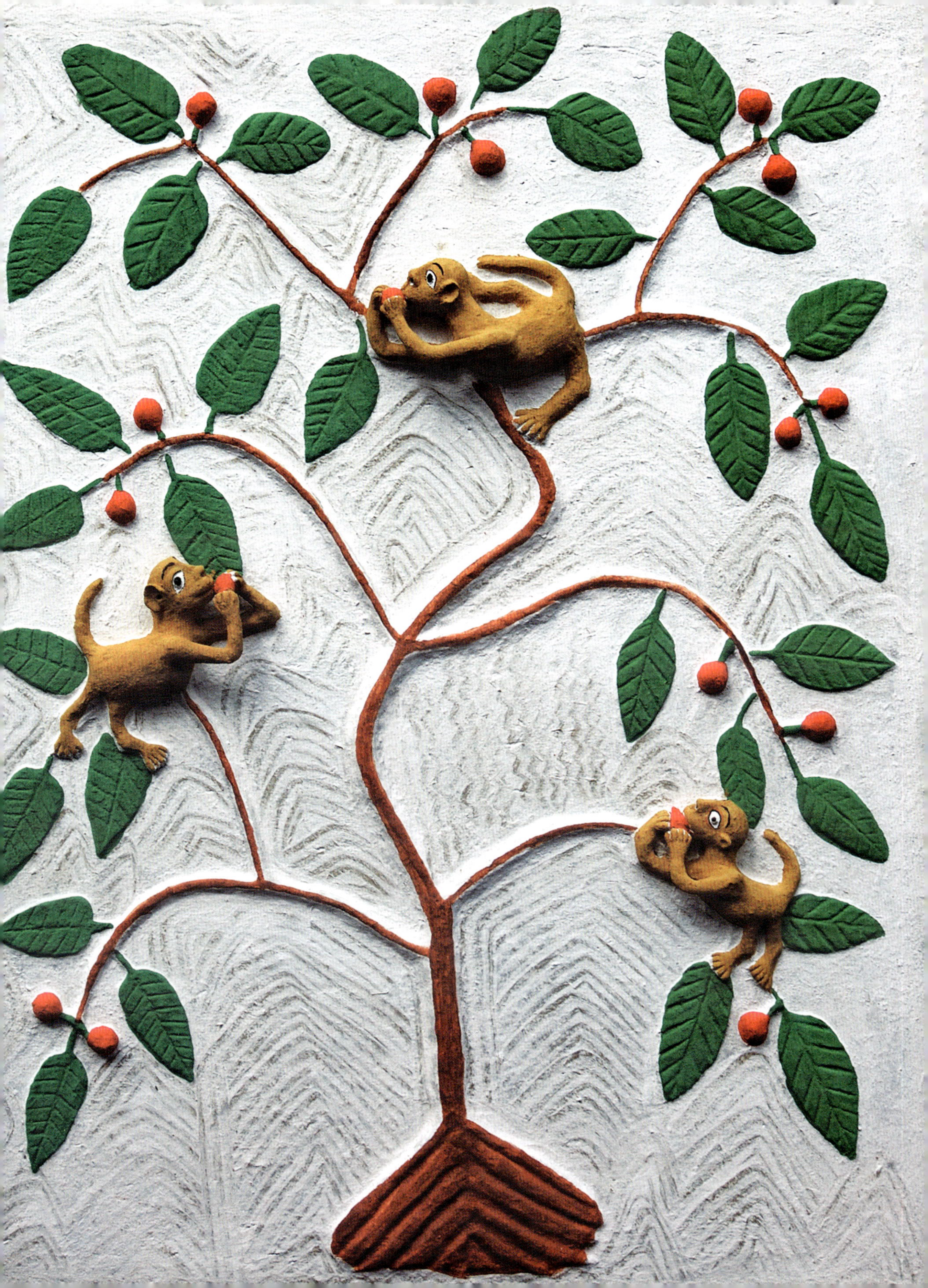

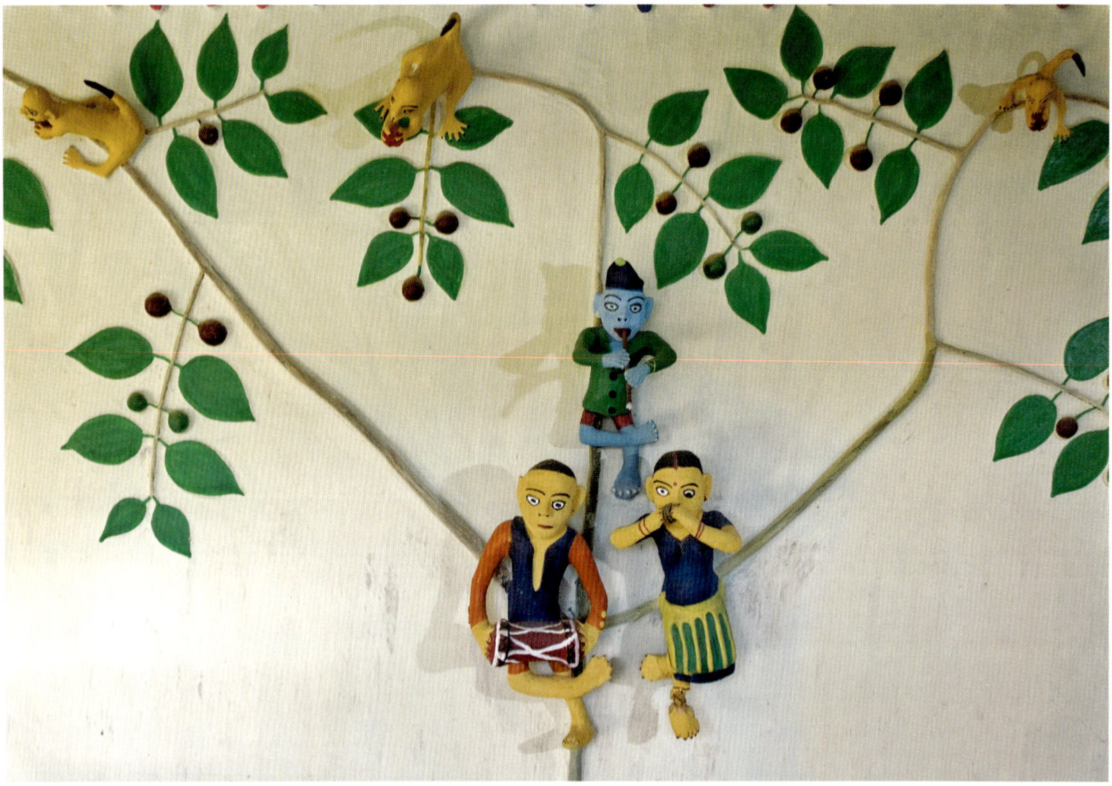

core, molding it into the body, legs, feet, hands, curved tail and face of the monkey. She then placed a tiny clay ball as fruit in the monkey's outstretched hands. Finally, she stuck a heavy stick into the monkey's rear and affixed its other end through one of the branches of the tree and deep into the mud of the wall.

The three human figures were sculpted in a similar fashion. Sonabai created the horn player by using a central stick for the torso and left leg and tying a second stick across it near the top. She then tied two crooked sticks to this cross stick for the arms and a long stick at the end of the arms for the horn. She added a third crooked stick about half way down the torso for a bent leg. Bunching straw around these sticks and binding them tightly with twine, Sonabai created a general substructure for the musician. Finally she covered this entire base with clay, using her fingers and fingernails to pinch and incise the details. The result is a horn player standing on his left leg with his right leg bent onto his thigh. In his hand he holds a long horn similar to those still played in Puhputra today. Sonabai ensured that this sculpture would remain where she placed it by embedding a strong stick deep into the wall and impaling the back of the musician with its other end. She sculpted the drummer and dancer using the same technique. Then, when the entire frieze had completely dried, she painted the tree, leaves, fruits, monkeys, two musicians and dancer with an array of pigments that she had mixed herself. The result was an enchanting depiction of village life that greatly enlivened Sonabai's interior walls. Viewed at a distance through the organic veils of her *jali*, the overall effect was stunning.

Holi Ram continued to farm and to build structures that took him away from home.

Musicians and a dancer stand at the base of a fruit tree with monkeys. Although Sonabai's initial artistic expression was unprecedented in India, she has taught her craft to her son and his family, who carry on this new tradition.

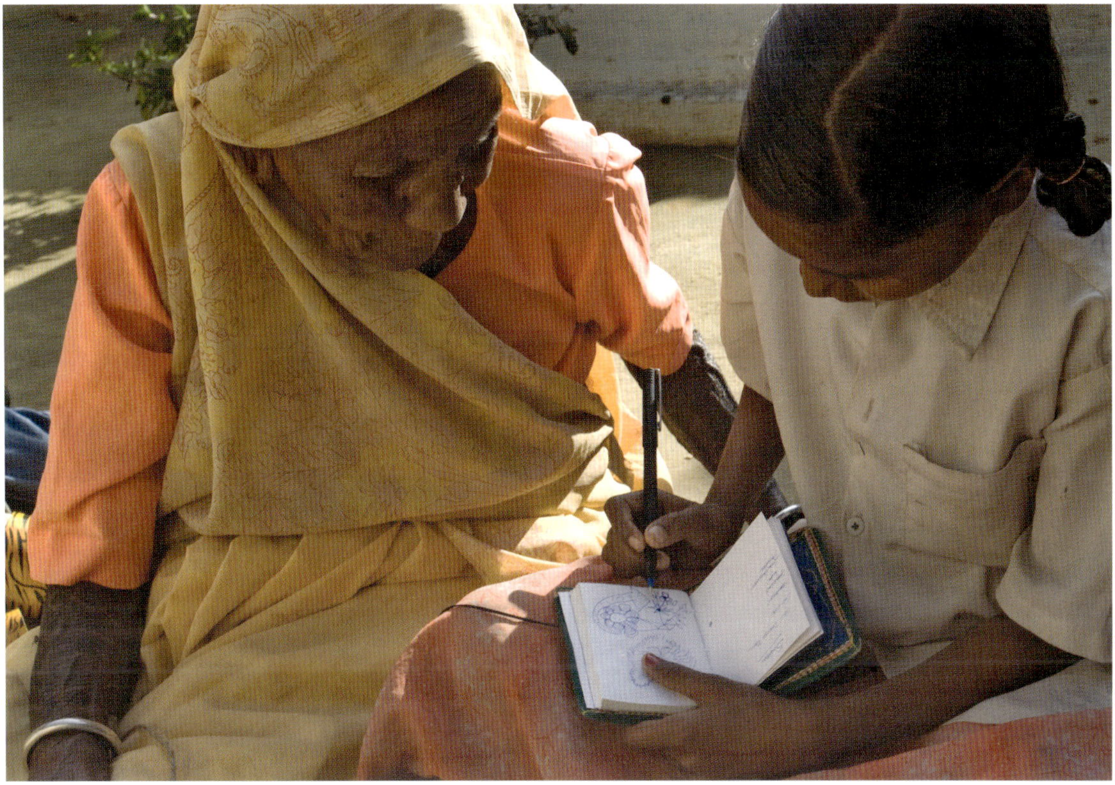

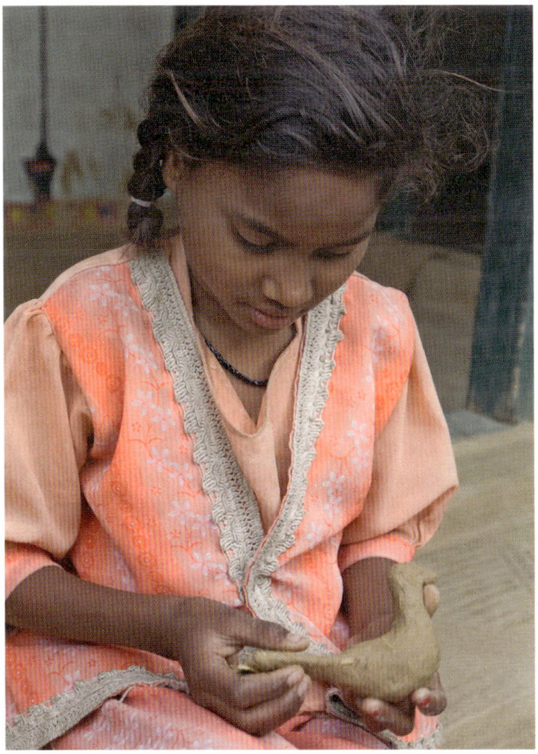

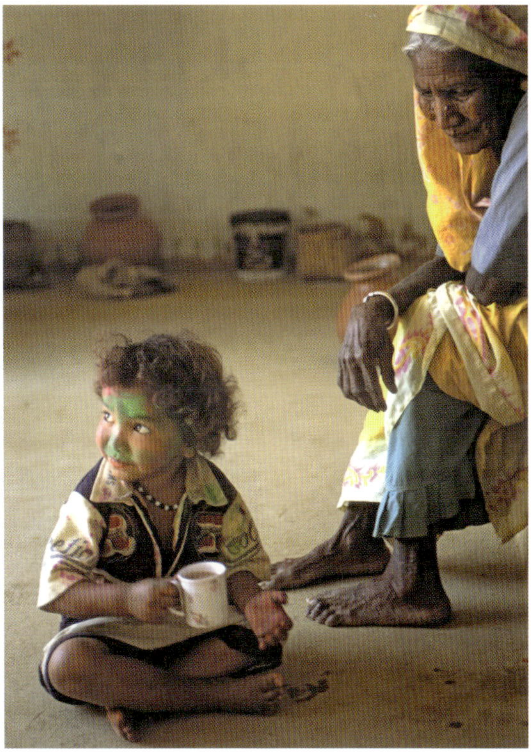

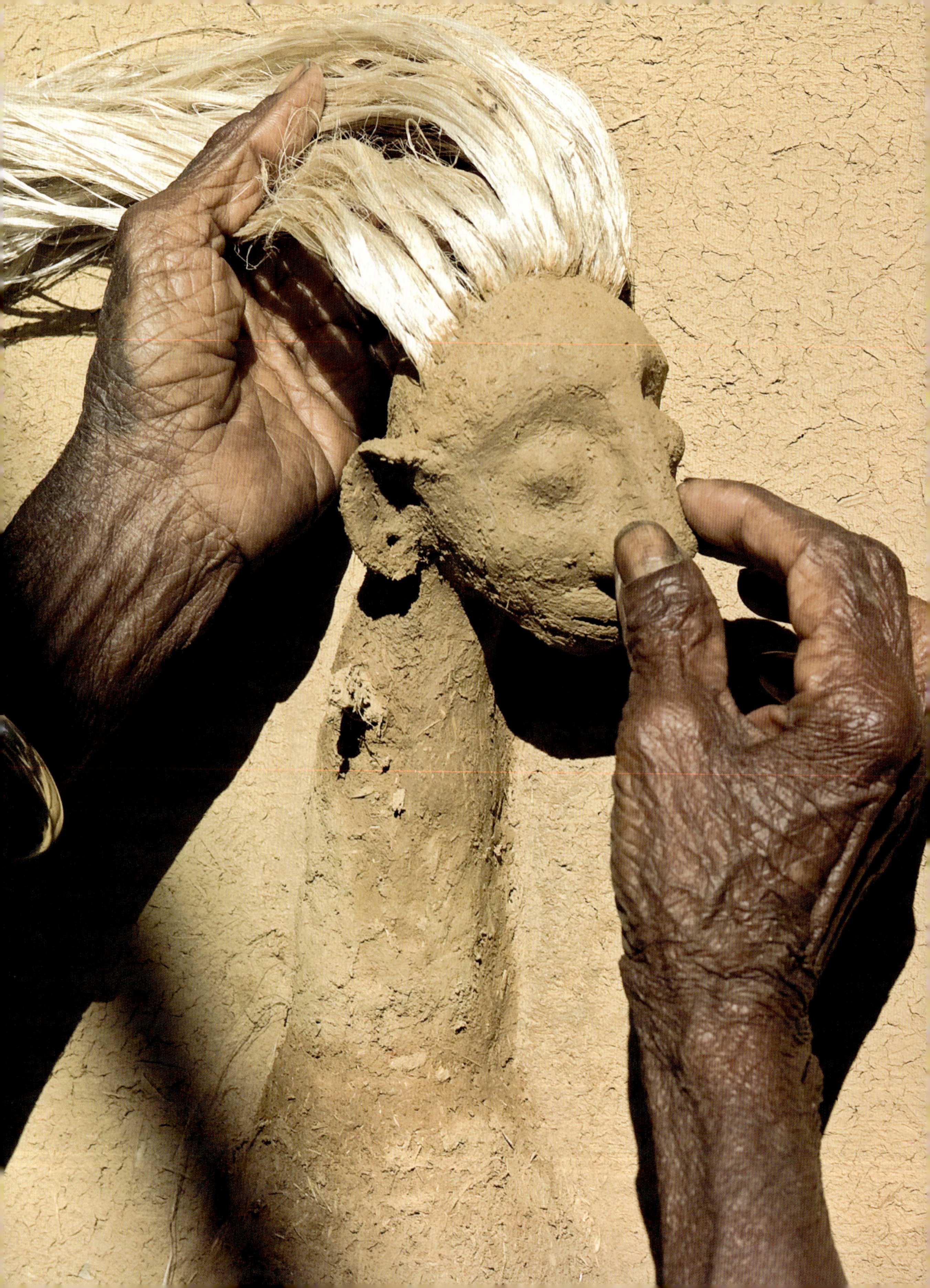

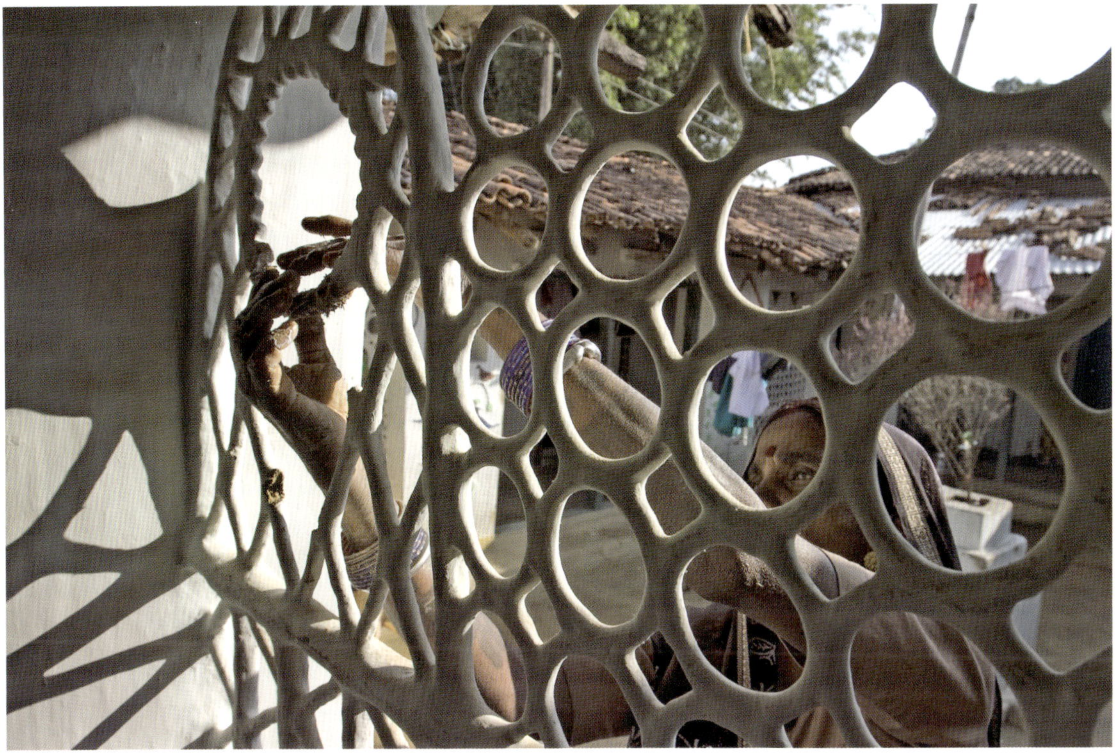

Daroga Ram began to grow up and go to the village school. He studied there until the tenth standard (the equivalent of the tenth grade in the United States) when he left at his father's request to help him in construction and farming. During these lonely years, Sonabai continued to transform the interior spaces of her home until it was unlike anything ever seen in India. Her art was always upbeat: the colors she chose bright and fresh, her patterns imaginative and her figures lively and humorous. Sonabai employed her remarkable creativity and inventiveness to distance herself from the intense provocations in her life.

Fifteen years went by in solitude. Fifteen years of confinement to one house, remote from the rest of humanity. Fifteen years during which Sonabai blossomed as a masterful artist. Sonabai spoke little of those years. When asked, she usually changed the subject. For some undisclosed reason, Holi Ram altered his restrictive attitude towards Sonabai in about 1968. After one and a half decades of enforced isolation, the door to Sonabai's house was opened. Villagers were invited in and Sonabai was allowed to mingle with the community. The effect of this change is immeasurable. Daroga Ram, who was fifteen when it occurred, is also unwilling to comment about the reasons for his father's change of mind. Sonabai's neighbors and other villagers are determined not to voice their opinions on this matter. It remains a mystery. Yet many villagers have remarked on their first impressions upon entering Sonabai's home. A sampling of their comments is: "I had never seen anything like it." "It was like going on a bus trip to a different state. Everything was so different! How could this be right here in our own village?" "I just stared at everything. I could not understand it at first. Where did these ideas come from? Is this what she had been doing all those years?"

Sonabai had come to Puhputra from another village and lived for the first ten years in a hostile home. She had not been able to make any friends during that time and the subsequent fifteen years by herself had cemented her isolation. She had always been a

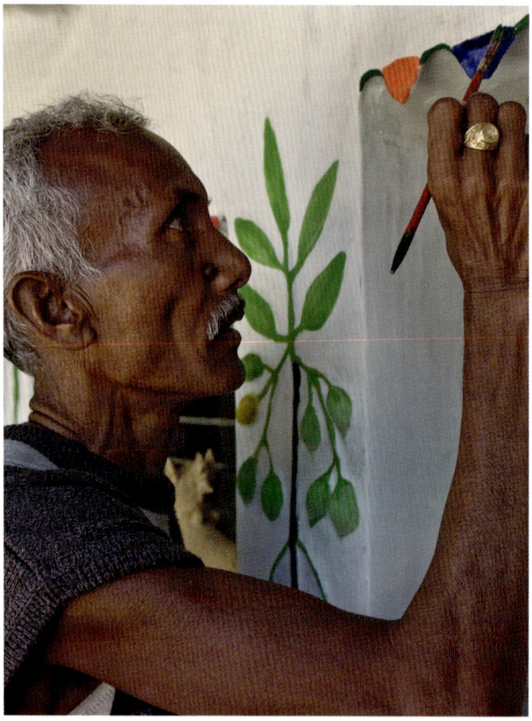

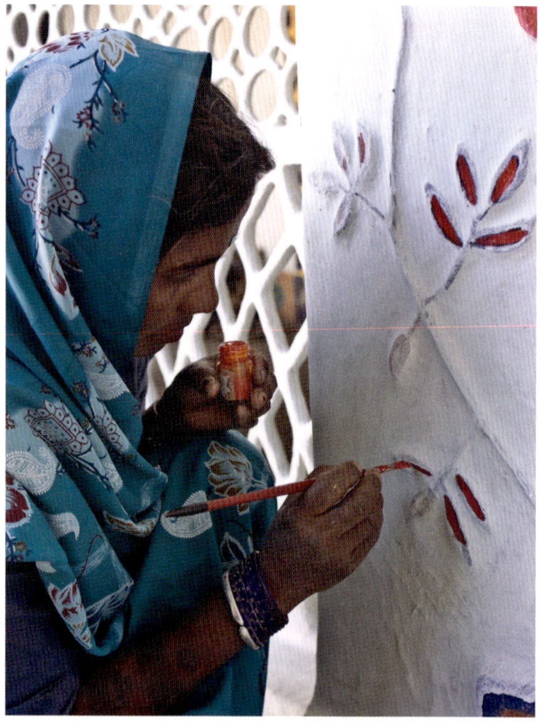

naturally shy, withdrawn person. The habits of solitude had strengthened those characteristics; now that she had the opportunity to actually join the community, she did not know how to go about it and was not really sure that she wanted to. As an old woman, Sonabai stated: "To this day I have still not visited most of this village or most of the houses. In the early years, I was not allowed to. Then I became focused upon my art. Finally I lost any interest in doing so."

In many ways, the next sixteen years continued for Sonabai in the daily routines she had already established. But Holi Ram and Daroga Ram would now invite neighbors to visit and the house was livelier than before. According to Sonabai: "People going by would stop to see my place. Other people who visited the village would hear about it and come to see my house too. They praised it." And yet it took Sonabai a long time to realize that her sculptures were of any particular value. Holi Ram continued to ignore them. One important change in the status quo during this time was Daroga Ram's marriage to Rajenbai in 1972. He was nineteen, Rajenbai a shy twelve. Their marriage was arranged entirely by Holi Ram and her parents. Rajenbai came from Deenkara, a village of farmers not far from Puhputra. She had never met Daroga Ram before their wedding day. It must have been odd moving into this unusual house, but Rajenbai is very reticent and does not comment. Within two years of their marriage, Rajenbai gave birth to a stillborn son. Two years later, the young couple had a daughter who lived. Holi Ram was typically displeased about this granddaughter, but Sonabai was thrilled. She loved to make her toys and play with her. After another eighteen months, her grandson, Vinod Kumar, was born. Now Rajenbai was vindicated in Holi Ram's eyes and could begin to truly settle into the home. During this period Sonabai's relationship with Rajenbai began to blossom into a strong and abiding sisterhood that started to heal the pain of Sonabai's long loneliness.

Sonabai's entire world changed in 1983. Daroga Ram explains: "In 1983, Mushtak Khan (one of a team of field workers from the Bharat Bhavan, a well-respected museum in the city of Bhopal) and a group of three women were doing

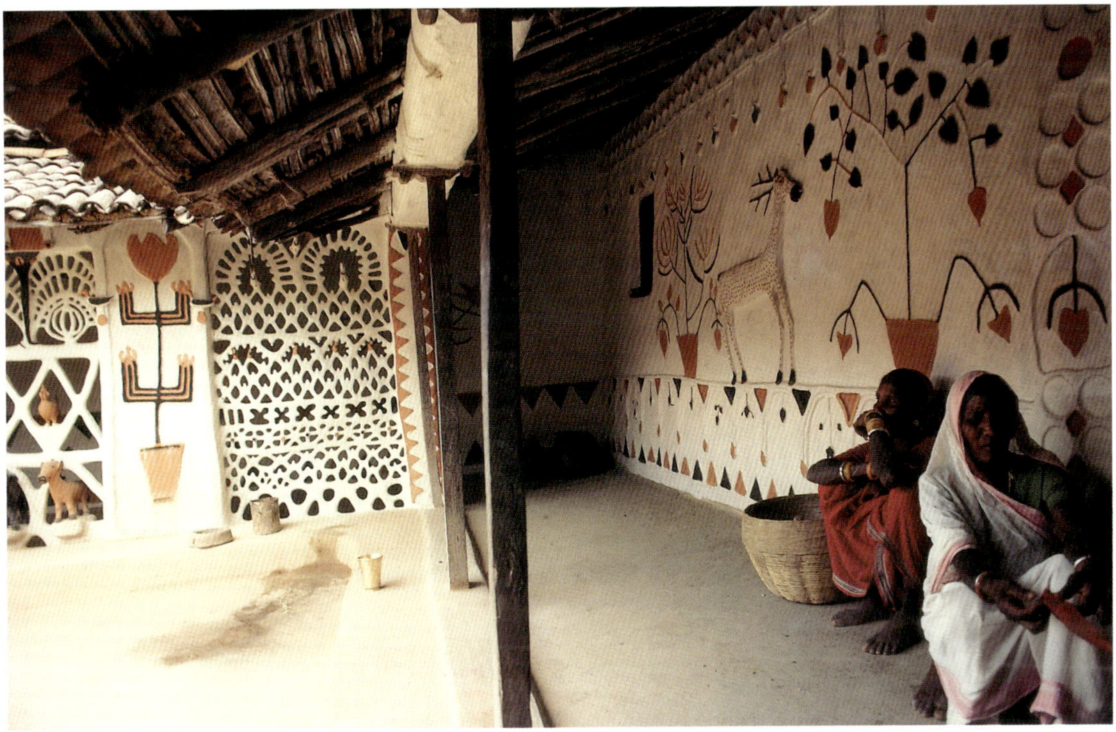

a craft and folk art survey of all the villages of our district. During this survey they had met a potter, Saheba Ram, who made pots on a wheel and was an artist himself. Saheba Ram told them about Ma and brought them to us himself. They were very surprised to see so much work all in one house, work of a type that they had not seen in any other house in Surguja District. They came regularly for the next two or three days, looked at all the work and asked us to give them one of the *jali* right from the wall on the verandah! They said: 'You must give it to us.' I was afraid the wall would break because it was made of mud, but they insisted that they would carry it carefully and they would save the art. They cut the wall with saw blades and kept all the pieces that fell off to paste on later. I was given 800 rupees (US$23) by them to restore the damages done to the wall." Commenting on the pain it caused her to give up this precious work of art, Sonabai said: "When they said they wanted to take one of the perforated screens from my house to Bhopal so that the whole country could admire my work, my throat choked. They were nice people, they had stayed in my house—had given me so much honor. I could not refuse, but when the screen was removed, I could not hold back my tears."[3] These museum scouts also commissioned Sonabai to sculpt examples of her toys and other small pieces that they took with them to Bhopal. Renowned photographer Jyoti Bhatt accompanied that Bharat Bhavan team and made the first photographic record of Sonabai's house. Puhputra is so remote and inaccessible that Bhatt's images were the only record in existence before the photographs for this volume were taken.

When the first people outside Puhputra visited Sonabai's house in 1983, they were astounded by what they saw. In this first photograph taken at that time by Jyoti Bhatt, it is evident that Sonabai's color palette was simpler, yet her inventive creativity and artistic vision are clearly evident. Sonabai, in her early fifties, sits in the lower right corner with a young Rajenbai behind her.

3 Jain, *Other Masters*, p. 56.

Bhopal is the capital of Madhya Pradesh and, at that time, Puhputra was a part of Surguja District in the state's northeastern region of Chhatisgarh. (In 2000, Chhatisgarh separated from this former largest state in India to become its own state, naming the city of Raipur as its new capital, and is about an eight-hour drive from Puhputra.) In Bhopal, the Roopankar Gallery at the Bharat Bhavan was created in 1981 as an innovative museum that attempted to display all the arts of Madhya Pradesh's people—folk and classical, contemporary and tribal—side by side without hierarchical judgment. Its exhibitions were well acclaimed by the Indian art world. In 1985, the Bharat Bhavan gave Sonabai Rajawar a small exhibition, displaying the thoughtfully restored *jali* that had been sawn from her verandah and the other sculptures she had created. Her art caused a major stir. Critics were astounded. Delhi took notice.

Daroga Ram continues: "It was only after this time that my wife (Rajenbai) and I began to work with Ma, but that was more out of necessity. She needed our help. In 1983, the people in our village felt that we had been given money and prestige by our art. Slowly, slowly, other people began to make the same crafts in Ma's style. One of these people was a woman named Sundaribai. She had not made any sculptures before that, but she started now… These people from Bhopal returned in 1984… They again asked us to make pieces for them and at that time they saw some of Sundaribai's work and took some of those with them to Bhopal too… These people asked us to come with them (to Bhopal), but we refused to go. In 1985, we got a letter saying that Ma had received the President's Award (the Rashtrapati Purushkar, the highest award an artist can receive in India) so we traveled to Delhi to receive it! I had to accompany my mother; she would not go alone. Even after getting the letter we were afraid to go, but the local Maharajah of Lakhanpur and his family all came to our home to persuade Ma. They convinced us that we must go and that we would have no problems in Delhi. Even then, Ma was very frightened. I had to talk to her for a long time before she would agree. But we took the train. It took two days and nights and finally we reached Delhi. It is such a huge city! I had never seen anything like it. But they were very good to us. We stayed at the Lodhi Hotel with the other artists being honored and all of us were shown the important sights of the city and important works of art, including the Crafts Museum in Pragati Maidan."

In just two years Sonabai had gone from almost total obscurity to national recognition. The President's Award included a bronze medal and a check for a sum larger than anything her family had ever seen. Sonabai was unable to process the change. It was too much for her. As a naturally shy woman, Sonabai was extremely uncomfortable with the press and public scrutiny, although she was shrewd enough to realize that the limelight brought with it an income that would change her family's future. So she reluctantly acquiesced. Daroga Ram was clearly delighted with the attention, adapting to new situations with grace and aplomb. The natural honesty and humility he had inherited from his mother saved him from being corrupted. Both mother and son were relieved to be able to return to Puhputra, but their relief was short-lived.

"After we came back," Daroga Ram says, "we received a letter in 1986 saying that Ma had been given the Tulsi Saman (a state award for traditional and folk arts) from the Bharat Bhavan in Bhopal. We went there to receive this award and stayed the month of February. There we met Dr. Jyotindra Jain who had come down from the Crafts Museum in Delhi to visit the Bharat Bhavan. He is the one who told us about our invitation to go to America just two months later!" Dr. Jain, one of India's finest art scholars, was to be a seminal force throughout the rest of Sonabai's life. He had proposed Sonabai and Daroga Ram as visiting artists to Mingei International Museum in San Diego, California. As part of the 1985-86 Pan-American Festival of India, the two artists were to demonstrate their sculpting techniques in an exhibition of Indian terracotta entitled "Form and Many Forms of Mother Clay" and curated by Haku Shah. Daroga Ram continues: "We flew there by Air India with two potters from Gujarat and Anil

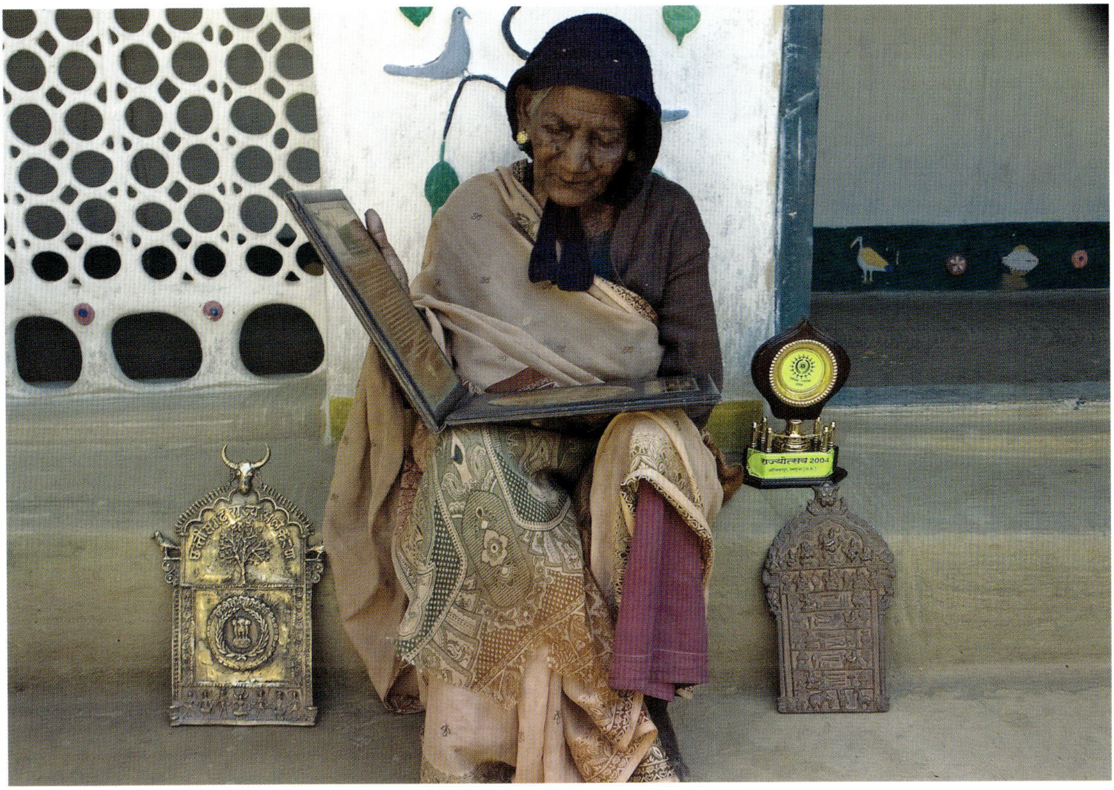

Agarwal (an interpreter escort). The museum arranged for us all to stay two months in a house in La Jolla. It was all so different! We were given daily money (a stipend) and would go shopping at the supermarket for food. You could find everything there, but it was very confusing. Mostly we just bought rice and dal and simple vegetables... Yes, the gas stove and the fridge were very interesting. I remember just standing and turning the stove on and off and on again... They took us to Marineland and the zoo and Disneyland and Tijuana and the beach...The director, Martha, was very nice and we had dinner at her house... During the day we sat in the museum and made *jali* and figures. We had brought some clay, but they gave us more. And they had bamboo and sticks, but it was difficult to get the new clay to work just right... We were only able to make one *jali* and a few other pieces for them... We had brought no colors with us, so they provided us with paint. It was then that Ma began to paint with bright colors."

It is impossible to comprehend the full impact of the dramatic changes in Sonabai's life over such a short period of time. After decades, first of derisive abuse, then of enforced isolation, Sonabai began to slowly reintegrate with her community. Her family of three had doubled in size and although she still felt displaced, she was beginning to feel more accepted. Then, within three years, she was propelled from relative anonymity in a village, not recorded on any map, into the national and then into the international limelight. It was astounding! Whereas another person with a different background might have been deeply changed by all the attention, Sonabai remained unaffected. When asked about California, she remembered almost nothing. Her only clear memory was her fear of flying: "We were floating in the air for two whole days and I was so afraid I would

Late in her life, Sonabai sits surrounded by her many medals awared to her to acknowledge her artistic achievements.

drown in the ocean!" While in San Diego, she deferred to Daroga Ram to take care of her and kept her attention on her sculpture. Other Indian folk artists who were brought to America for the same Festival of India created artworks of their impressions of city skyscrapers, subway systems, and freeways, but not Sonabai. The only noticeable change in her art was her consequent use of brighter, commercial paints.

Sonabai commented: "We came back from overseas after the monsoon. We had missed it. We wanted to go home, but Dr. Jain invited us to Pragati Maidan (the National Handicrafts and Handlooms Museum) to work. They gave us *geru mati* and *pilli mati* (traditional mineral pigments) and those types of colors to use, but they came off in our hands, so we asked for paint. The colors were too strong, so I diluted them and made them softer." Sonabai meant that although the natural pigments that the museum provided were unsatisfactory, the commercial paints available in Delhi were garish and that she softened the hues to make them suitable to her sculptures. Under Dr. Jyotindra Jain's masterful direction, the National Handicrafts Museum in New Delhi (commonly referred to as the Crafts Museum) had become one of the most popular places for the educated elite, diplomats and foreign residents to visit. Exhibitions were always on the leading edge. A constantly changing roster of India's finest folk artists and artisans from all over the subcontinent exhibited their techniques and sold their art directly to purchasers without paying commissions. In the late 1980s and 1990s, Sonabai, always accompanied by Daroga Ram, became a very popular attraction there. They would be given bus and train tickets from remote Puhputra to the capital city. They would be housed for three months at a time in a hostel, given meals and a daily stipend, and at the end were able to keep the entire income from all the sculptures that they were able to sell. It was common during this period for museums and craft fairs in other parts of India to arrange with the Crafts Museum administrators for Sonabai and Daroga Ram to attend events at their institutions or festivals without even consulting the artists. They just went where and when they were told. Occasionally a wealthy patron would pay for them to build an installation (a *jali* or wall frieze) in his home, living in the servants' quarters for weeks at a stretch. Their lives were not their own. They returned to Puhputra whenever they could, trying to insist that they be there to help on the farm during the planting and harvesting seasons.

Back in Puhputra, life was changing as well. The income from the awards and the subsequent money that they saved from their per diems in San Diego and from payments in Delhi and elsewhere meant that they were no longer poor. "I was able to put money aside for my daughters' dowries," Sonabai confided, "and to purchase the saris and jewelry that we needed to give them. This made sure we could arrange good marriages for them and that took so much pressure off." They were also able to buy more farmlands and to expand the size of their house. In 1987, Rajenbai gave birth to a long-coveted son, Vinod Kumar. Although Sonabai had been happy with granddaughters, a grandson was extremely important to Holi Ram. The larger family now had a second courtyard that was built in front of the first to contain a barn, large open verandah and a storage and grain-grinding room. They also added to the number of bedrooms radiating off the original courtyard. All of this building meant, of course, that Sonabai, now joined by Daroga Ram and Rajenbai, could sculpt many new surfaces. They had entirely new spaces to design and they tackled this task with typical originality and mastery.

For the first time, Holi Ram was suddenly very interested in the sculptures. Sonabai stated: "Before my recognition, my husband neither encouraged nor discouraged my work. After the award, he was very excited and encouraged me very much in all my work for the next six years. He also instructed Babu to spend the time to watch and learn how to help me and to do this work himself. Then he died in 1989. After he died, I was very demoralized and depressed (widowhood is often a time of social rejection in India) but my family was completely supportive of me. Seeing how good my son and

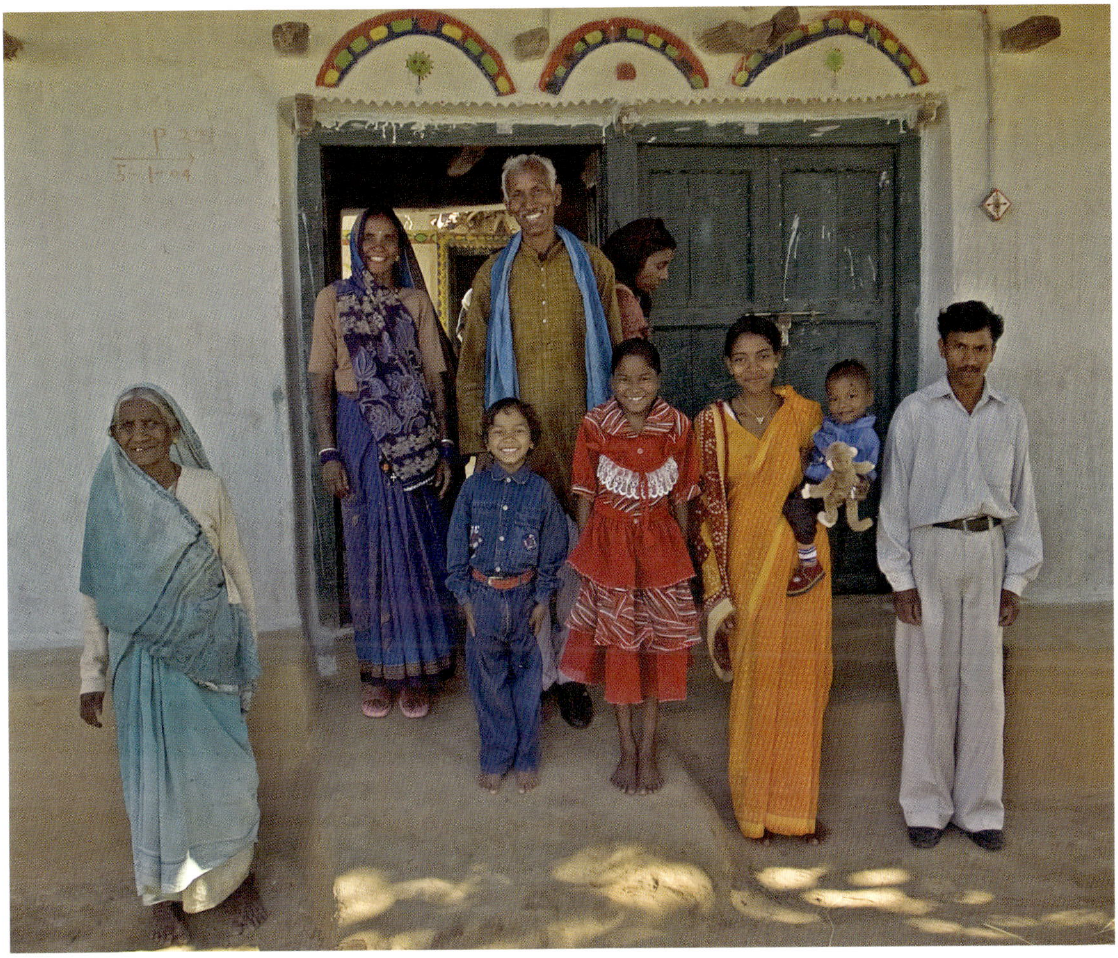

his children were, I began to find myself again and to revive." In another conversation, Sonabai reflected on her loss in this way: "When I first was given the award and traveled to Bhopal, my husband was alive. But then when fame really came, he was already dead and I had no one to share it with."

A few of Puhputra's villagers had begun to tentatively emulate some of Sonabai's sculptures in their own homes. "Slowly, slowly the village began to change," Sonabai remarked, "as they realized that people in other states, even other countries, were interested in my work."

After years of bleak solitude, Sonabai was deeply cherished by her son's extended family in the last decades of her life.

A fundamental boost was given to the spread of Sonabai's style of sculpting in 1991, when the Government of India gave Sonabai a grant to teach ten artists from her region. She had not requested this grant and was perplexed about how to go about teaching, but the artists appeared and she had little choice. Two days a week for an entire year (planting, monsoon and harvest season excepted) she conducted workshops in the new barn courtyard of her house. Several of her students came from Puhputra and the rest from nearby villages. She showed them how to construct *jali*, how to build the substructures for sculptures and how to sculpt in her technique. Several of these artists were subsequently contacted by fairs and festivals and traveled outside of Surguja District to exhibit their craft. The success of the first workshop caused the Government of Madhya Pradesh to give Sonabai a grant in 1996 for a second workshop to train twenty artists over a six-month period. Some of the original artists also took this second course and remain sculptors in this style to this day. It is interesting to note that of all the artists that Sonabai trained—aside from those in her immediate family—only four active sculptors remain today. Practical reasons govern that choice. No local demand exists for the art. Even Sonabai asserted: "Nobody here buys my work. A few people from Ambikapur occasionally buy something, but that is rare. Most of my sales are made through the Crafts Museum." The sculptures are so fragile that they are almost impossible to export without severe breakage, so the artists must travel outside of the region to produce their sculptures either on commission or in hopes of sale to potential buyers. Consequently, the market does not support many artists. Local house owners prefer to sculpt their own walls in styles that have been passed down from mother to daughter for generations. A few have adapted Sonabai's innovations into their own work, but none would consider hiring artists outside of their own families.

Sonabai's life changed again in 1998 when Dr. Jyotindra Jain featured her as one of five artists in an exhibition that challenged the smug complacency of contemporary art criticism. In *Other Masters: Five Contemporary Folk and Tribal Artists of India*, Jain intentionally provoked India's social hierarchy by featuring artists who have been historically perceived by the educated intelligentsia as representing inferior sub-cultures; he proved they should be viewed on a par with the finest contemporary artists. He commissioned three village painters, one potter and Sonabai to prepare masterpieces and displayed the results with a refinement of exhibition skills never before applied to these arts, particularly in India. To Sonabai he gave an entirely separate large room, and she completely transformed it into an installation that astounded the critics. The complete space might be perceived as one organic sculpture: Sonabai painted its walls a soft white interlaced with finger patterns of lines and squiggles and interspersed with sculpted bas-reliefs. Monkeys climbed and picked fruit from a tree on one wall while on another wall Krishna played his flute in a second tree for a bevy of adoring maidens above a small herd of cows. A large sculpted grain storage box stood in the center of the room. Sculpted *jali* created a light and shadow effect in front of a recessed niche. Shelves held three-dimensional figures. The floor too was made of softly brushed organic clay. Every view was a delightful feast for the eye and yet, in a manner typical of Sonabai, all was well balanced by open spaces. Dr. Jain published an excellent book with the same title as the exhibition, the first true publication about Sonabai's work. She was deservedly acclaimed for her achievement. In India, Sonabai was finally accepted as a contemporary artist. Her sculpted installation remains a permanent part of the National Handlooms and Handicrafts Museum.

As a direct consequence of this exhibition, the Queensland Art Gallery in Brisbane, Australia, invited Sonabai and Daroga Ram to demonstrate their art in a four-month exhibition entitled "Beyond the Future," beginning in September 1999. By this time, Sonabai was at least in her late sixties and was suffering from bad arthritis. She was confined to a wheelchair for part of the trip. Daroga Ram later expressed delight at being able to visit rain forests and hold koalas and see kangaroos. Sonabai retained no memory of the trip. In November, 2002, the president of India honored Sonabai again by giving her the Shilp Guru, an award for highest excellence as a master craftsman. By this time, it had become increasingly difficult for this venerable woman to travel. All she really wanted to do was stay at home with her large family.

Rajenbai and Daroga Ram gave Sonabai three more grandchildren during her last fourteen years: two girls (1993 and 1996) and another boy in 2000. Sonabai's two eldest granddaughters were married to prosperous young farmers in the late nineties. In 2000, when Sonabai's grandson, Vinod Kumar, was

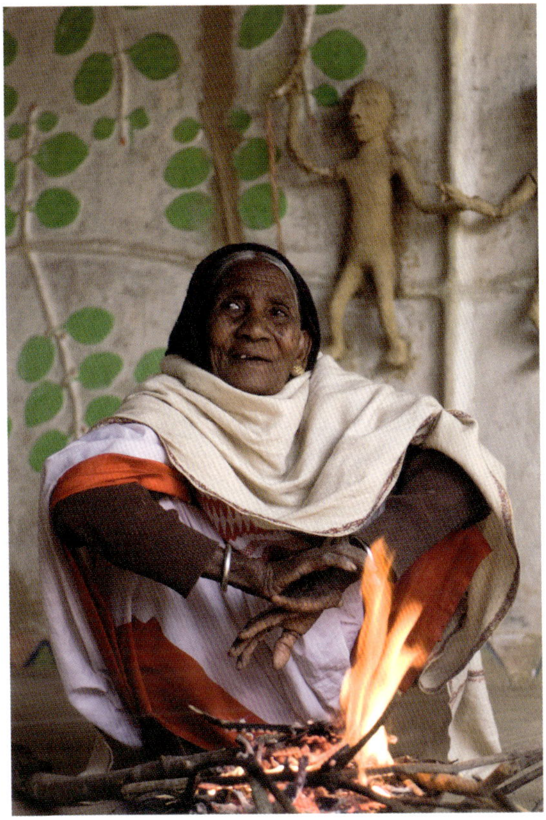

Sonabai died in August, 2007.

just seventeen, he married Munita, a fifteen-year-old educated girl from a distant village. By the time she was eighteen, Munita had already given Sonabai two great-grandsons, one in each of the past two years. In this period, Daroga Ram was recognized by Puhputra for his distinct leadership qualities and was elected for a term as Sarpanch (the equivalent to a town mayor). A new elementary school named for Sonabai was founded amidst the growing number of houses in her neighborhood. Two of Sonabai's grandchildren presently attend this school.

As an old woman, Sonabai had cataracts in her eyes, bad arthritis in her hands, and complained of being forgetful, but she doted on her offspring. She loved to spend her days watching their activities. Daroga Ram tried to refuse all travel on her behalf, but he did not always succeed. At least twice or three times a year, she was required to leave her family to hobble aboard a train and travel the long distances to Kolkata, Mumbai, Chennai or Delhi to participate in an exhibition or to receive another award. None of it mattered to her. Back at home, she generally left the sculpting to her son and his assistant, Buddhi Ram, although she could not help getting involved in the design and some of the hands-on fashioning of figures. On most mornings, she squatted back on her heels and warmed her hands over a fire of cow dung patties, ruminating on her life. In the afternoons she would sit in the sun, watching Daroga Ram sculpt or the children play. Perhaps her granddaughter, Sunita, would make a clay bird and she would get involved in the process. She might watch little Pradeep as he zoomed around the courtyard with the energy of a bee. She ate little, she drank tea. Occasionally, another village elder would visit, but the two generally had little to say to one another. Sonabai was just content to rest surrounded by the entire world of color, form and whimsy she had created from her own imagination. Hers was truly another way of seeing.

Puhputra is different since Sonabai's death. The villagers recognize that this single woman changed their lives. One of their very own, in some ways a person that they had regarded as the least of them, had made a profound artistic statement. From the humblest of beginnings, Sonabai was honored by the highest in the land. She changed the fortunes of her own family and in some ways the fortunes of the entire community. She never sought acclaim, nor was she comfortable with it once she had it. She truly lived for her art and for her family as it grew. In the crucible of her own years of torment and isolation, Sonabai discovered a unique transformative vision. Her inner joy was in self-expression fostered in solitude and manifested in sculpture. Luckily, unlike that of so many other anonymous women in history, Sonabai's vision was not lost. Her door was opened. The world was allowed inside and Sonabai's art has had a profound impact on all who have seen it.

LEGACY

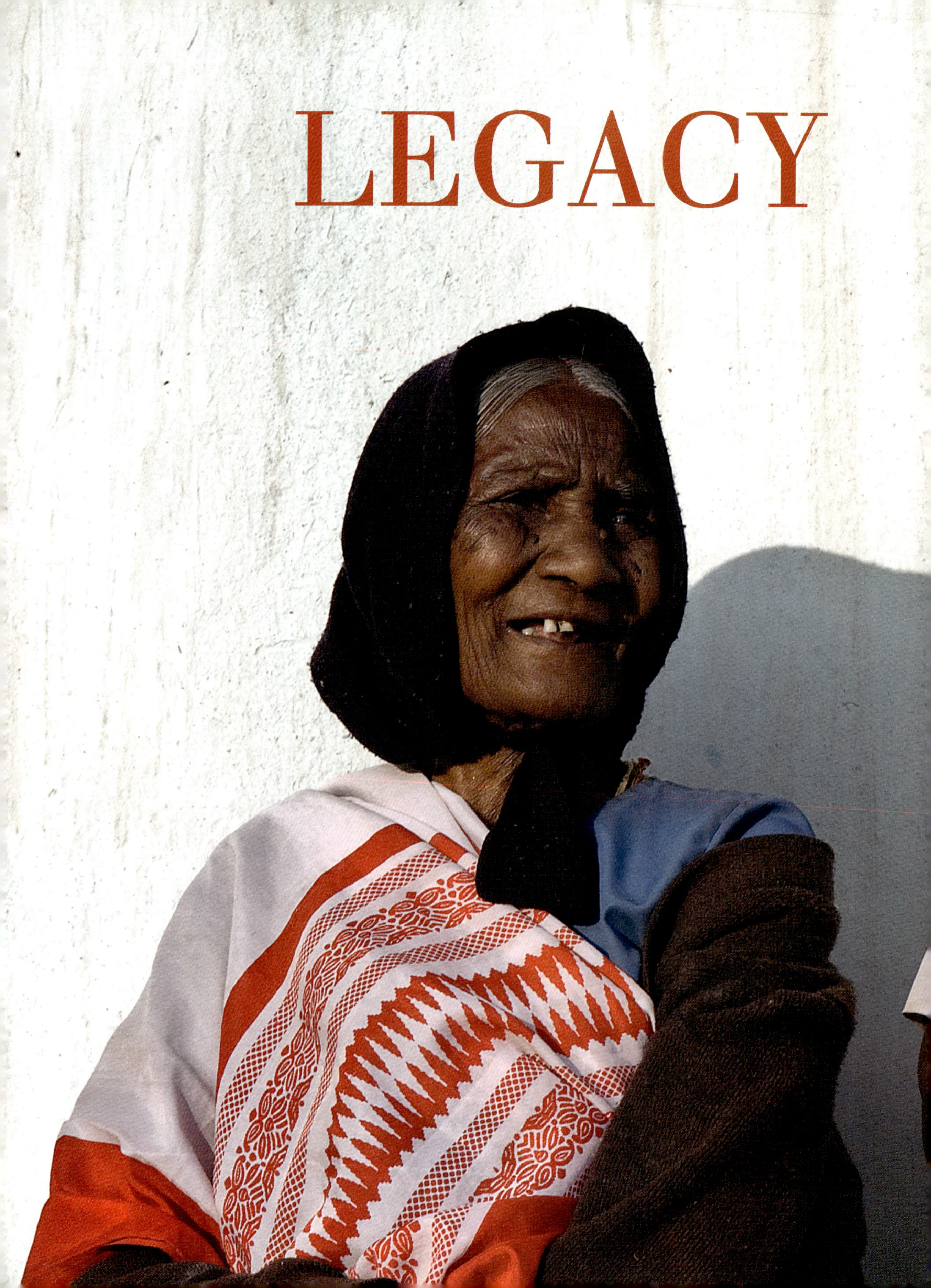

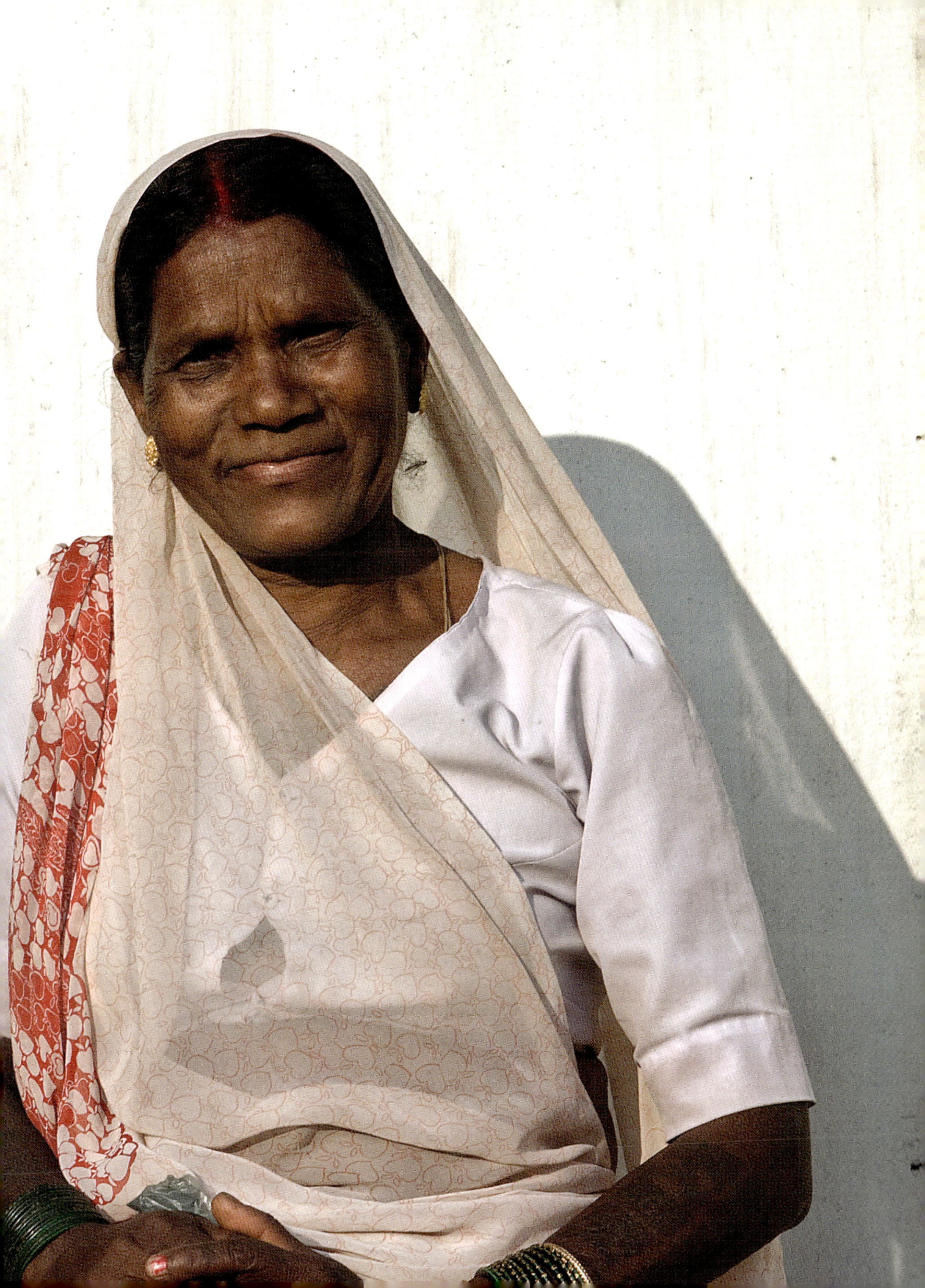

ENTERING PUHPUTRA SEEMS DIFFERENT now without Sonabai there. It is still just as remote and difficult to reach: a sleepy, dusty village in the midst of a large plateau of rice paddies that not too long ago were all dense forests. Life continues as it always has. People rise in the predawn dark to get ready for arduous days in their fields, planting or weeding or harvesting rice. Little children, barefoot and ragged, play in the dirt streets. Older ones, proud in their matching uniforms, sit in school chanting in unison their alphabets and sums. Girls, when they aren't busy helping their parents, talk shyly in small groups while boys show off by playing cricket at a distance. Elderly men and women singly sit hunched in front of their houses keeping watch on the village, missing nothing.

Nevertheless, their community has lost a pivotal force. A great woman has died, an artist whose vision and commitment to her art changed life for each one of them. Although it seems the same, Puhputra is transformed. Sonabai has left a legacy. Her home, once far outside the village boundaries, is now within its northern precincts. As Sonabai's art was by nature ephemeral and transformative, her family has decided against preserving the house purely as a static monument to her memory. They are artists themselves, all trained and nurtured by her, and they are continuing to enhance Sonabai's original vision with their own creativity as she would have wanted.

Other artists in a few houses in Puhputra and some villages beyond were either directly trained by Sonabai or so influenced by her art that their own professions have been altered because of it. They are driven by urges to sculpt, to express themselves in new and innovative ways. They do not view themselves as replicating Sonabai's art, but use it as a foundation upon which to build an entirely new future. Most have been successful and are recognized both within and outside their communities as independent artists, occasionally requested to travel to distant cities and states to display their art. Like Sonabai, they are changing the economies of their own families and, indirectly, that of the entire region as a broader national awareness is increasingly generated of an identifiable "Sonabai" or "Surguja" style of sculpture. The real question remains: As its fragile, ephemeral nature makes this art almost impossible to export, is it sustainable in the future? Can these artists find ways to blend and adapt these artistic visions with practical twenty-first century needs?

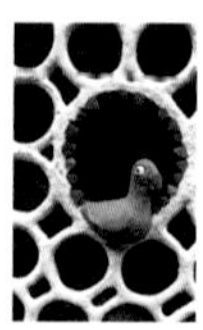

DAROGA RAM AND RAJENBAI RAJAWAR

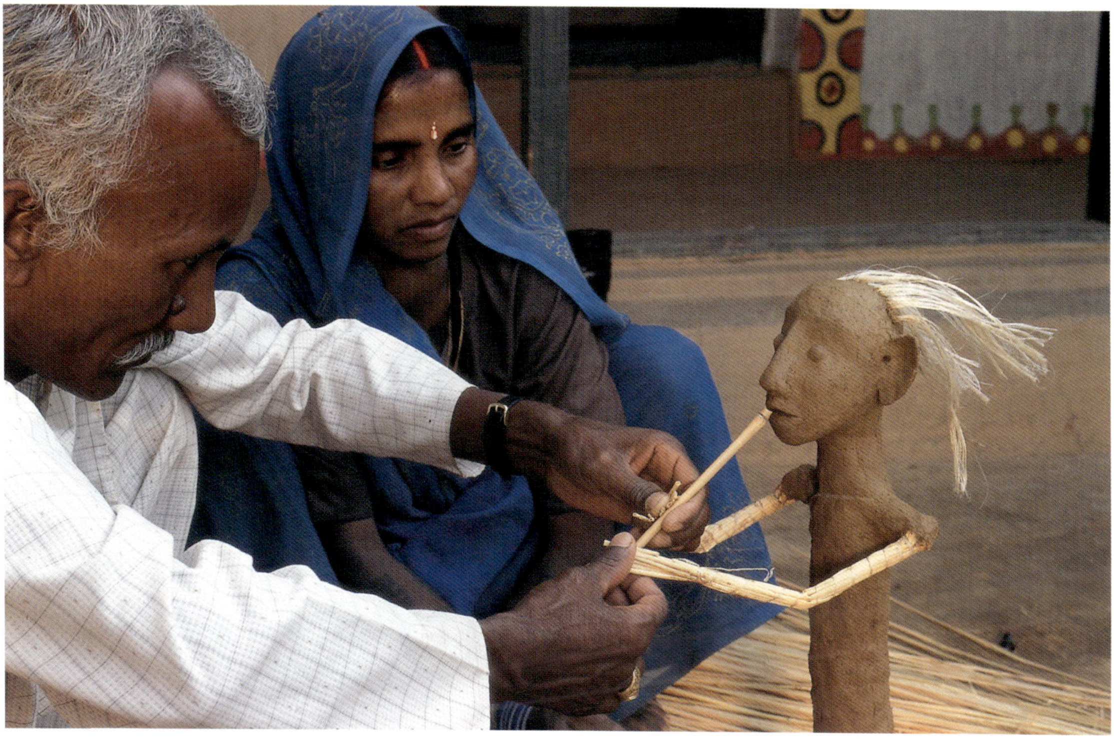

DAROGA RAM is a kind and patient man, a good father and grandfather, loving to his family and affectionate to his wife, Rajenbai. In many ways, his profile strongly contradicts that of his father, Holi Ram. Like his mother, Sonabai, Daroga Ram is quiet and reflective with an easy, charming sense of humor. Unlike both, he has effectively bonded with his community, impressing almost everyone with his forthright honesty and clear intelligence. Using his sense of fair play and justice, he naturally mediates during squabbles between neighbors. Consequently, Daroga Ram's qualities of leadership caused his fellow villagers to elect him as their Sarpanch, the local equivalent of mayor.

Above all, Daroga Ram is a masterful artist. From infancy he watched his mother sculpt. He was there when she first made him toys, invented her *jali* and began to add sculptures to them, and later to sculpt her walls. He observed the slow transformation of his home from everyday house into a fantasy dream world. Although for his first twenty years his father took no interest at all in Sonabai's art, once the world began to take note, Holi Ram encouraged Daroga Ram to learn from her. It was not hard. Daroga Ram had always been attentive, watching Sonabai closely as she sculpted. When he was finally allowed to help, the process came naturally. Sonabai would not travel without Daroga Ram. He accompanied her everywhere, to every museum or craft fair. Daroga Ram was with Sonabai when she met Indian dignitaries, diplomats, scholars and art critics as well as the president and prime minister. He traveled with her to California, to Australia and the length and breadth of India. He acted as her liaison, her intermediary, speaking for Sonabai when she was too shy and helping her to overcome the hardships. In each place, Daroga Ram sculpted alongside his mother, improving his art, learning and maturing. In true Indian fashion, he was her *chela*, her disciple, and always let Sonabai take all the glory. But in

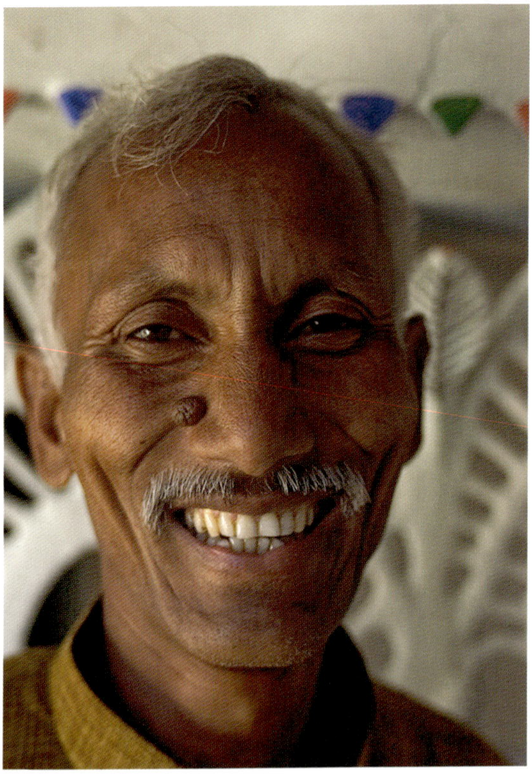

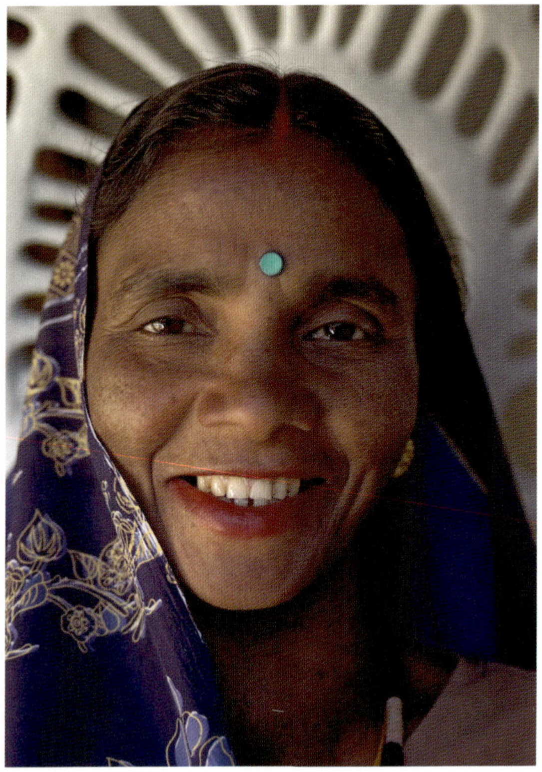

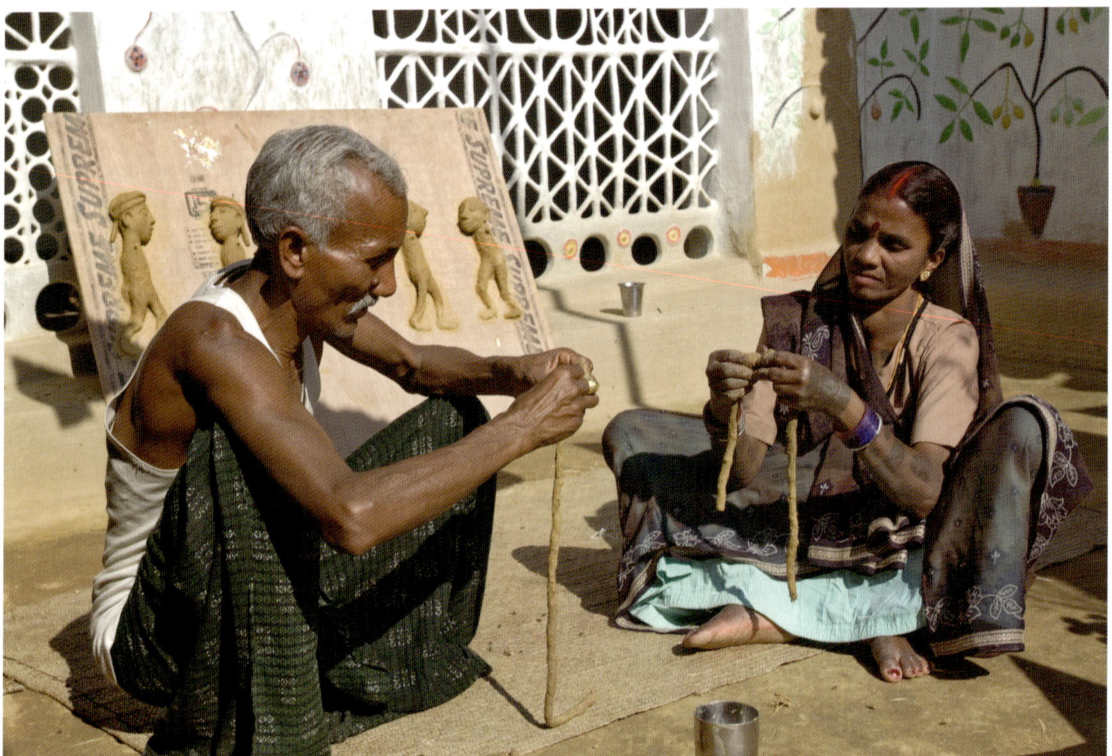
SUPREME
SUPREME

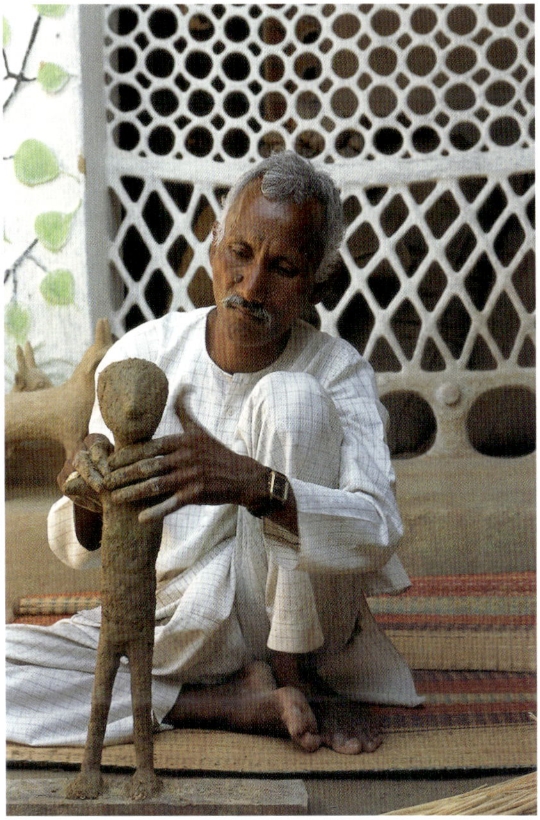

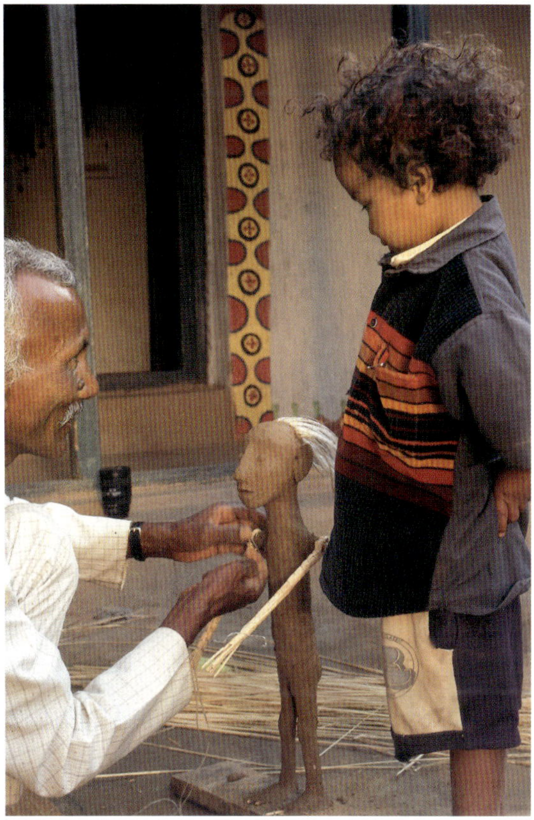

fact, Daroga Ram was emerging with his own mastery of art.

When Rajenbai married into Sonabai's family, she had no particular training as an artist. Women in her birth home sculpted in clay when new walls were built, as they did in virtually every home in the region, but their style was minimal and repetitive and the color palette was simple. Rajenbai did not know what to think when she first entered her new home on her wedding day in 1973. She remarks that it was like a different country! Her father-in-law was foreboding, her mother-in-law shy and withdrawn, and her new husband sweet but diffident. It took Rajenbai several years to feel truly at ease in this house. Daroga Ram was kind to her from the beginning and they soon became friends. Rajenbai was in awe of Sonabai, finding her stiff and awkward, yet marveling at the imagination that was made manifest through her remarkable fingertips. Rajenbai's first years were spent adapting to household customs and to the two daughters she had, one after another. These grandchildren delighted Sonabai and melted her reserve away, beginning a bond between the two women that lasted thirty-three years until Sonabai's death. Holi Ram remained harsh and critical of Rajenbai until she finally gave birth to her first son in 1986. This change in status coincided with Sonabai's international recognition, and Rajenbai was never sure which situation mellowed Holi Ram more. In any case, her life improved. Since that time Daroga Ram and she have had three more children; their eldest three are married, and they now have several grandchildren.

As an artist, Rajenbai was truly under Sonabai's shadow. She helped both Daroga Ram and Sonabai in the sculpting process, but she did not travel with them and was rarely allowed to create pieces on her own. She prepared the clay and the wall surfaces. At home, she made the bamboo structures for *jali* and covered them with clay, but it was always her mother-in-law

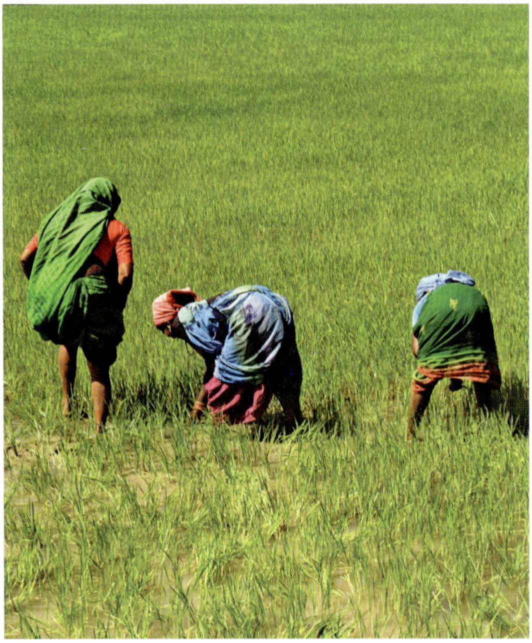

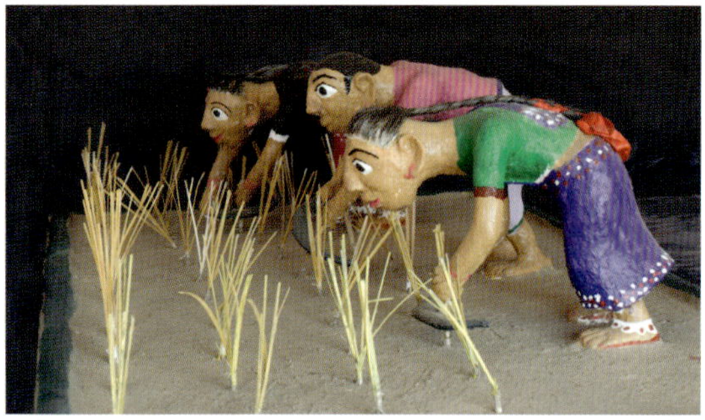

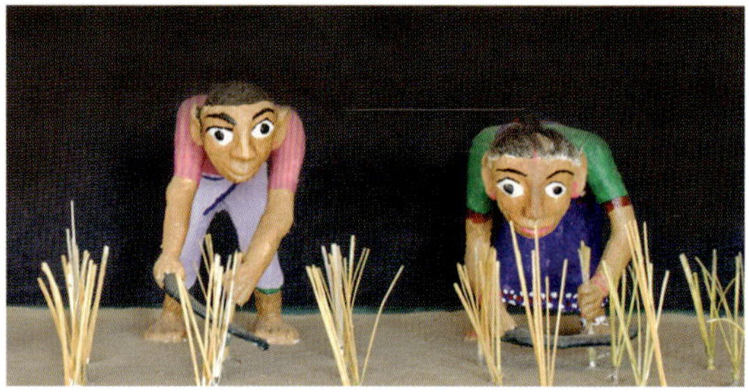

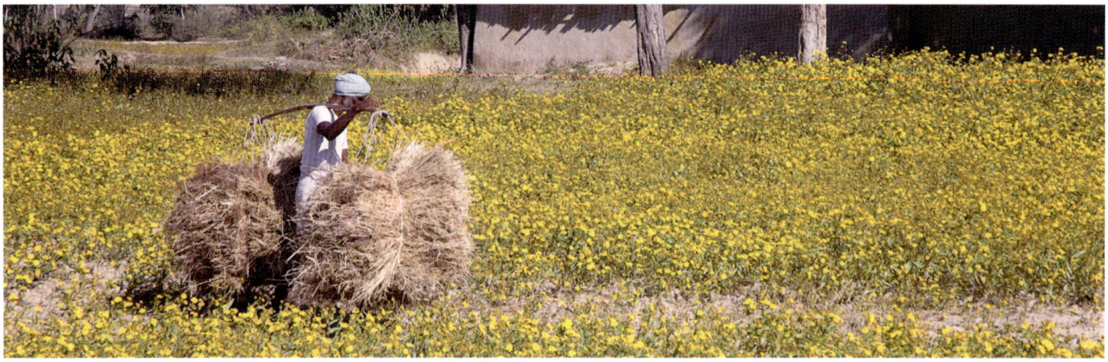

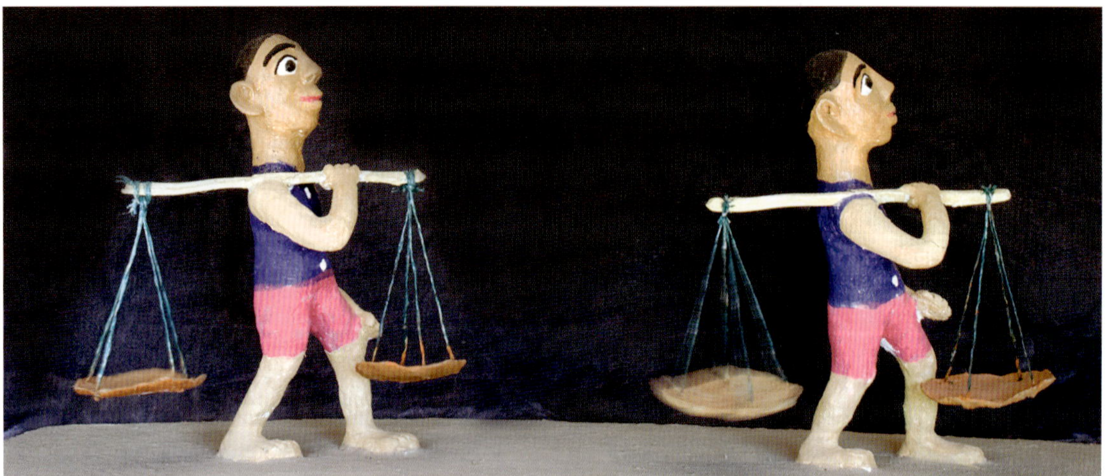

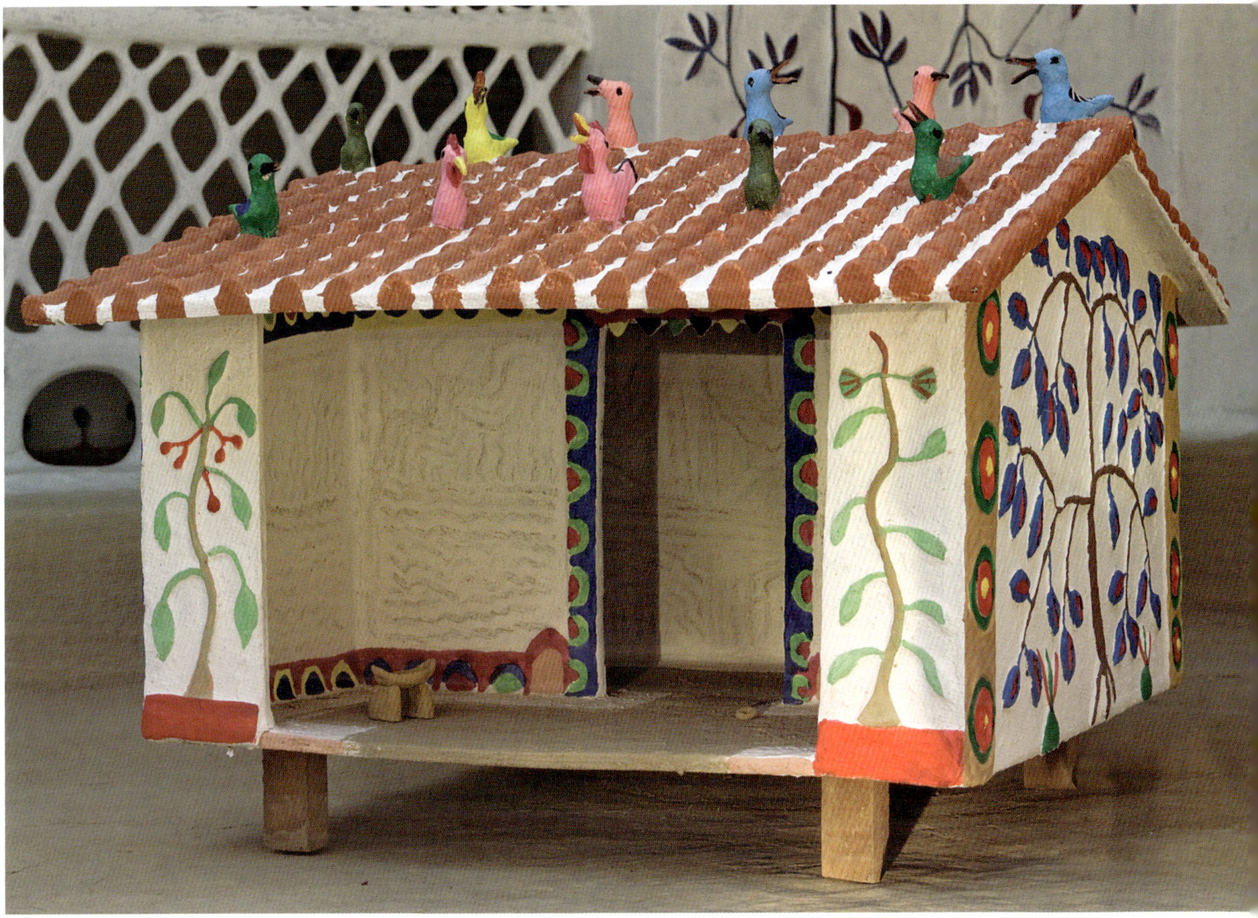

or husband who actually made the sculptures to adorn them or the walls. Rajenbai is adept at using her fingers to trace the complex patterns in whitewash that are often used as counterfoils to Sonabai and Daroga Ram's bas-reliefs. During all of those earlier years Rajenbai internalized her own creativity, deferring to her mother-in-law's and husband's art. It is only since Sonabai's death that Rajenbai has shown her own prowess as a sculptor. Now in her mid-fifties, she is just beginning to travel and emerge as an artist in her own right.

As a sculptor today, Daroga Ram is determined to preserve the style of art and techniques of production that his mother invented. Consequently his work reflects a relative conservatism when compared to some younger artists in the field. Nevertheless, Daroga Ram still expresses a bold and assertive vision that portrays a mastery of the medium that is unexcelled by anyone else. Like his beloved wife, Rajenbai, Daroga Ram is exploring new avenues of creativity now that his mother is gone, trying to find new ways to preserve the art and make it more marketable. Recently, in conjunction with several of the other artists, including Rajenbai, Daroga Ram has been spearheading an attempt to learn the technique of papier mache in hopes of adapting it to his mother's sculpting style. The project is so new that the results have yet to be seen.

SUNDARIBAI RAJAWAR

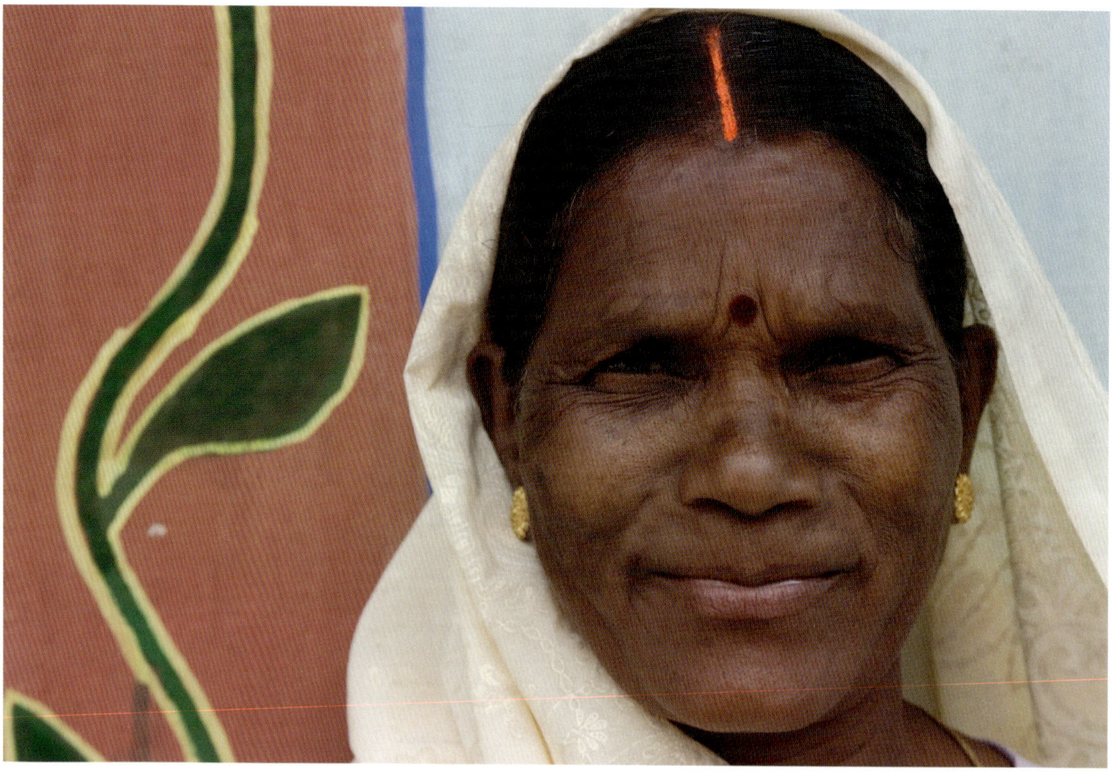

SUNDARIBAI, like Sonabai, has achieved national and international acclaim as an artist. This goal has been a driving force in her life. Sundaribai was born in Puhputra in about 1945, around the same time that Sonabai first moved there as a young bride. She also does not know her exact age, nor her age when she was married, although she believes that she was eleven or twelve years old when her husband, Kenduram, took her to live in his village of Sirkotanga, just a mile from Puhputra. Sundaribai's claims about the development of her art vary according to her interviews. In some she states that she has been creating jali and sculptures since she was a small child, that she evolved her style completely independently from Sonabai and that she has never even been in Sonabai's house. The author of this book first met Sundaribai prior to those published statements, and inside Sonabai's house, a place with which she was clearly very familiar. Sonabai and Daroga Ram stated that she had been a guest in their home off and on for many decades. When Sundaribai and Sonabai were interviewed together, Sundaribai's story was different from her earlier published ones. She affirmed that she had first visited Sonabai when she was a young woman, after the community had been allowed to enter Sonabai's home. (This fact would make it sometime after 1968, when she was in her mid-twenties.) That is when she was first inspired to begin sculpting by herself.

Without question, Sundaribai is a fine artist who has shown tremendous personal initiative. Her creative response to Sonabai's unusual vision caused her to begin her own explorations of the medium without instruction, and she excelled at her craft. Sundaribai was very inventive and enterprising. She was strongly affected by the visit of the Bharat Bhavan scouts to Phuputra in 1983 and by their purchase of Sonabai's sculptures for their museum. When they returned the next year, Sundaribai was ready to show them a variety

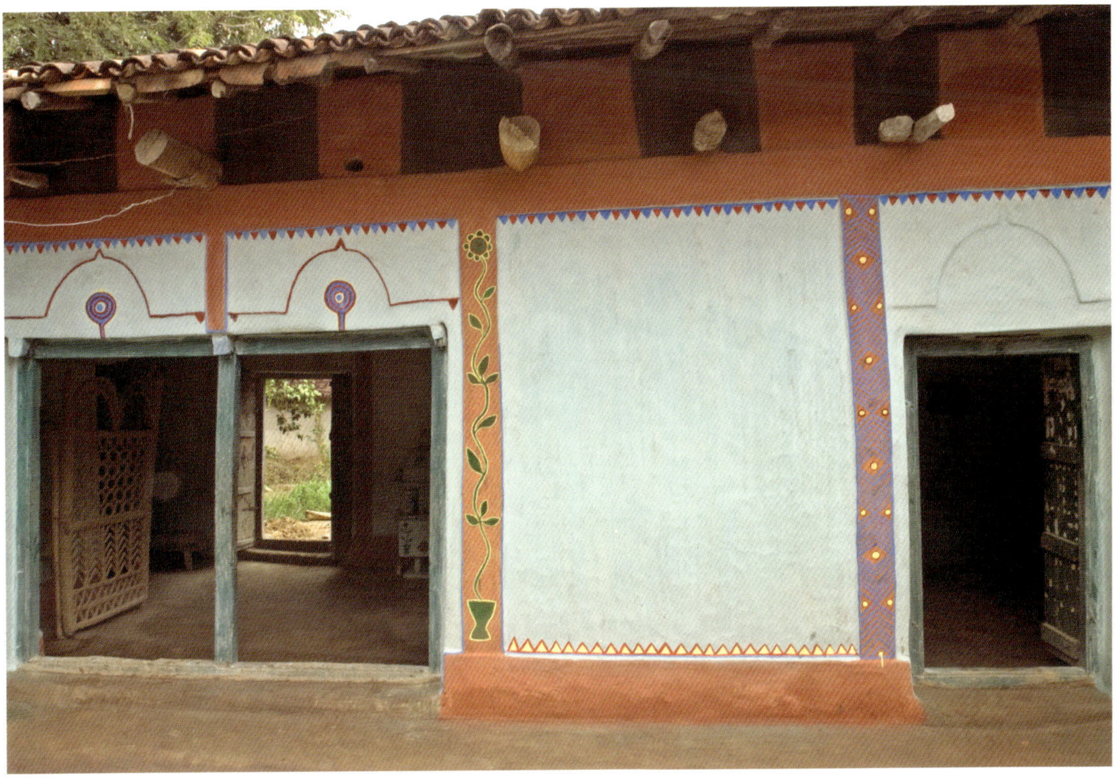

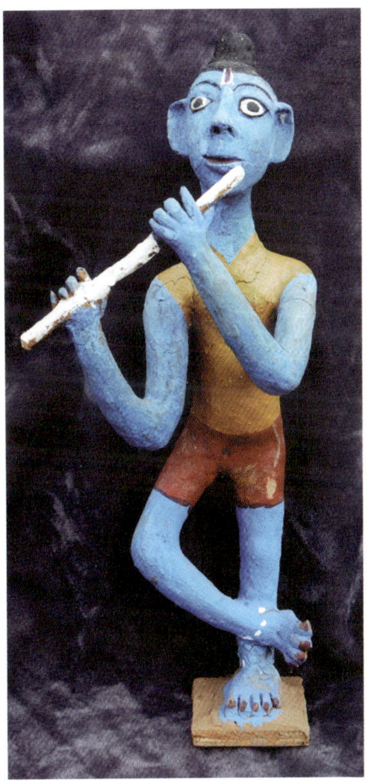

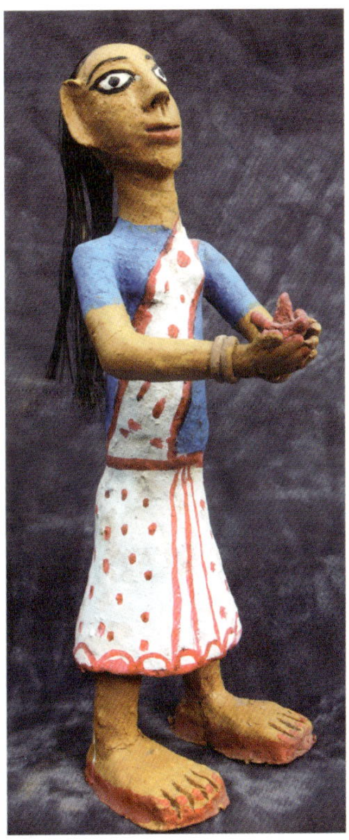

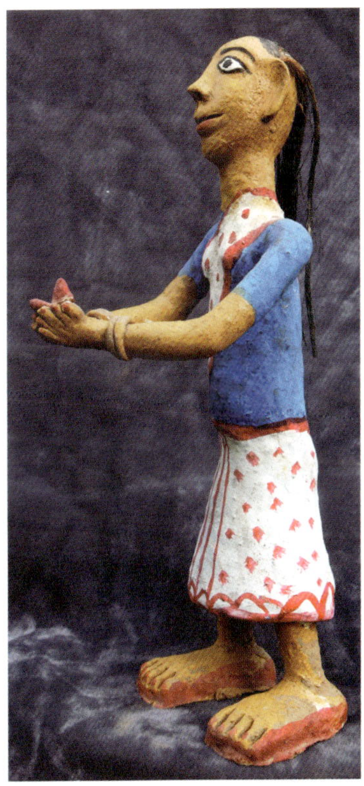

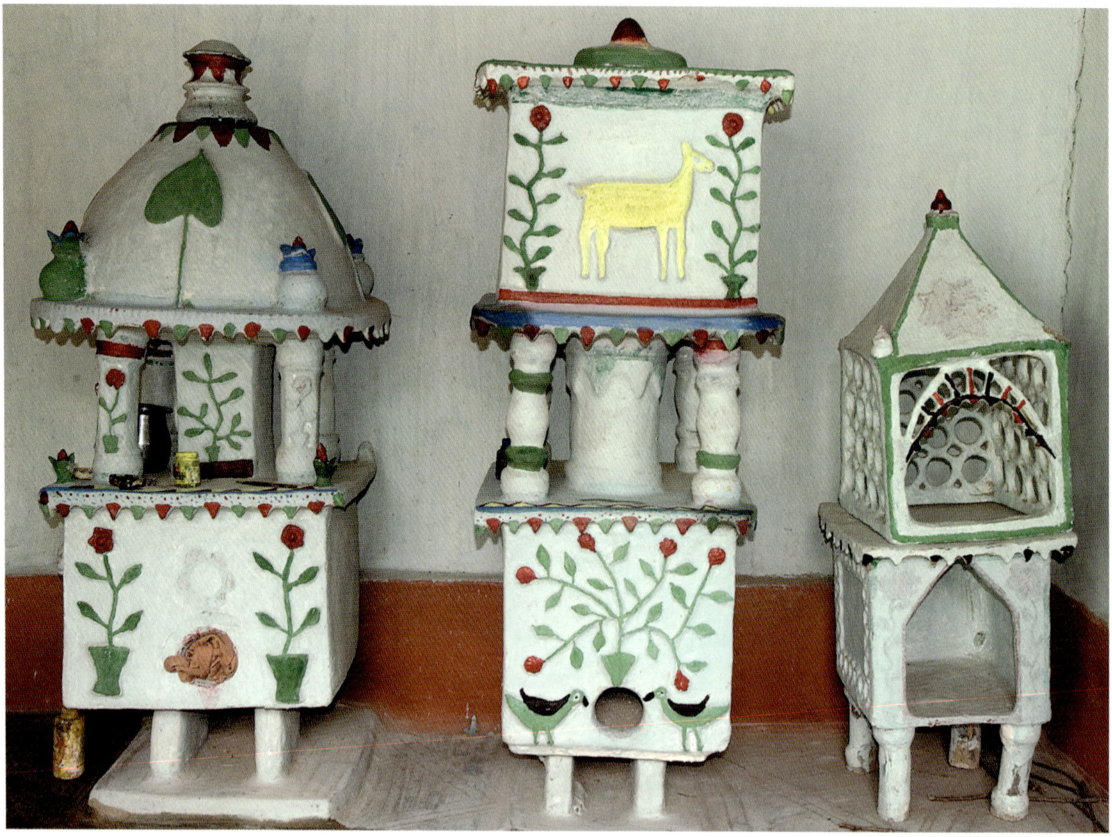

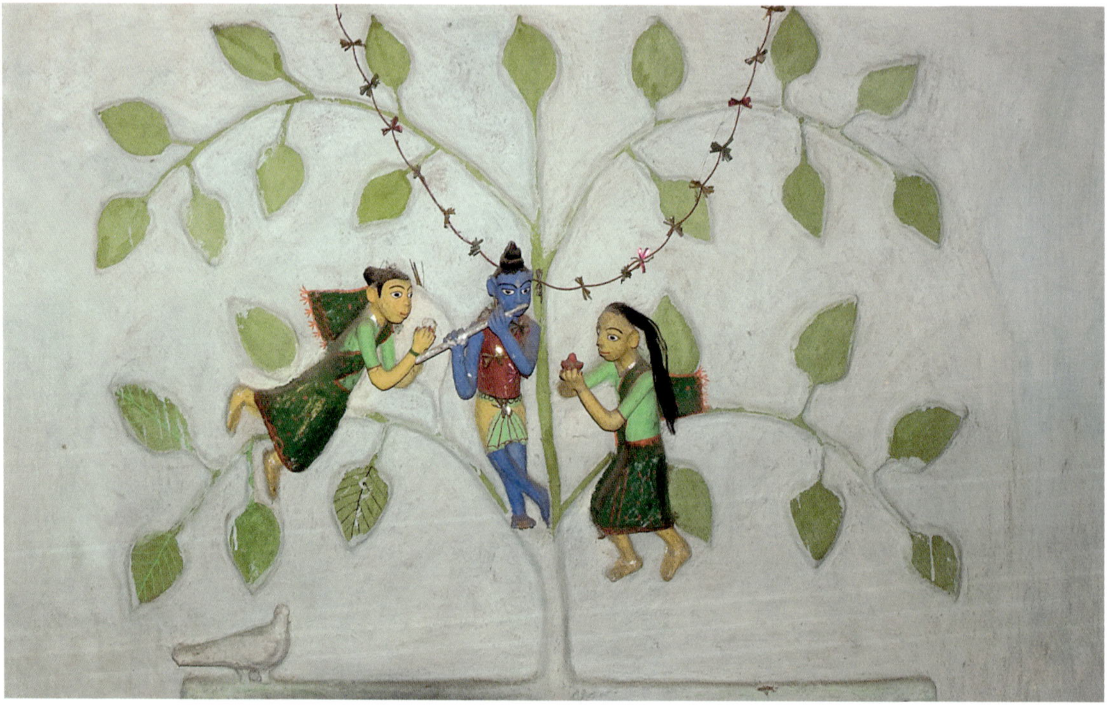

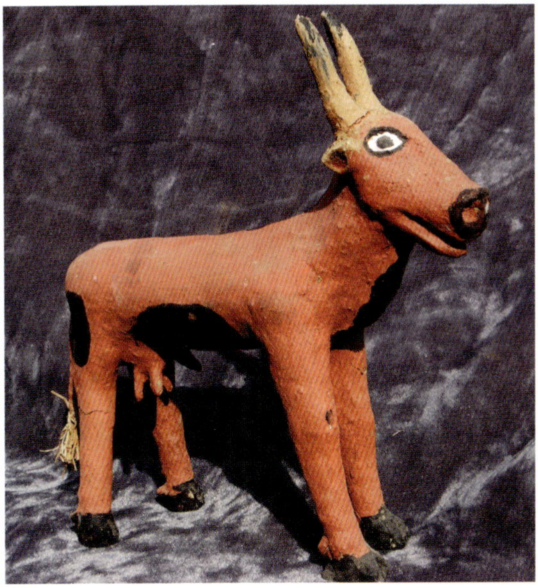

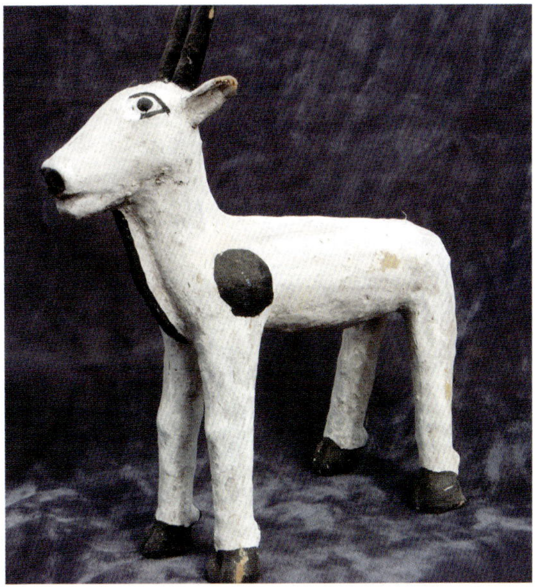

of unique sculptures she had created herself. These collectors were impressed with the high quality and imagination of her work and bought them for the museum. This acquisition was the beginning of an impressive career.

In the decades after Sonabai was discovered, featured and awarded, Sundaribai was determined that her own work should also receive attention. She did not take either of the government workshops that Sonabai taught. She correctly felt that she had learned enough of the technique through her own initiative. Sundaribai succeeded in garnering commissions to create important installations in the administrative city of Raipur that was to become the capital of the new state of Chhatisgarh in 2000. She sculpted part of the State Assembly building, an entire room at the Ghasidas Museum and an installation at the residence of the governor. Sundaribai has continuously experimented with techniques and methods, introducing new materials into her clay to make it more stable and durable. Like Sonabai, she expresses humor and whimsy in her art that has great public appeal. Dr. Jyotindra Jain, Director of the National Handlooms and Handicrafts Museum, the same brilliant scholar who had championed Sonabai's art, was deeply impressed by Sundaribai's artistic vision. In 2002, Jain arranged for her sculptures to be represented in an exhibition of twenty-one Indian folk artists at the Manchester Art Gallery, in Manchester, England. In preparation for this show, Sundaribai created a true masterpiece: three ascending tiers of box shapes formed of light and graceful sculpted *jali*. Through the center was a sculpted tree whose leaved boughs spread over the top, under which sat a blue Krishna playing his flute. The entire sculpture was Sundaribai's invocation to the Karama festival that she remembered celebrating as a child in Puhputra. This masterpiece was so popular that Jain arranged a solo exhibition for Sundaribai in Birmingham, England, the following year, complete with a full-color catalog of her work. Sundaribai rose to the occasion and created many new works, although much of it was directly derivative of Sonabai.

Subsequently, Sundaribai has had several other exhibitions in the U.K. in Nottingham, Bradford and a second in Birmingham. Her work remains popular with the public. She is a superb artist deserving of accolades. Sundaribai's increasing acclaim might yet encourage her to publicly acknowledge the one person to whom she owes her creative inspiration: Sonabai Rajawar, an artist who didn't want any attention at all.

BHAGAT RAM RAJAWAR

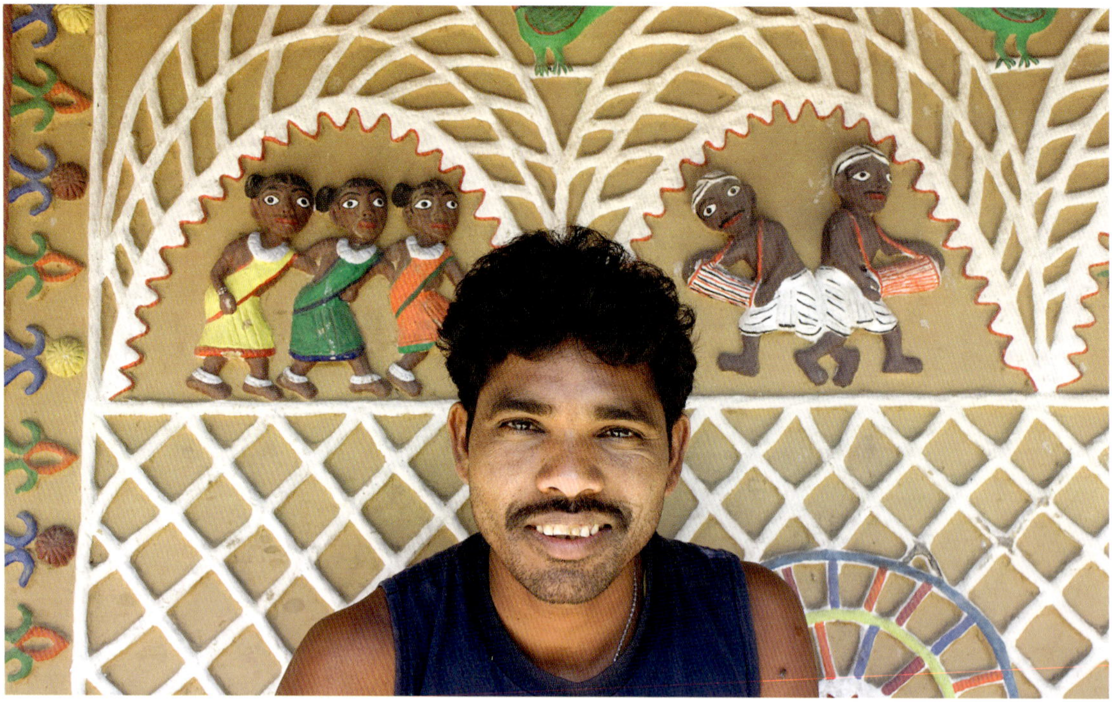

BHAGAT RAM is an engaging young man in his mid-thirties. He is married with two small children and they all live in a large extended family with his parents, his older brother and sister-in-law, and their children. As a distant, but much younger cousin of Daroga Ram, Bhagat Ram grew up visiting his Aunt Sonabai's house. It was always a part of his life. His own home is only a five-minute walk away. As a young child, Bhagat Ram showed artistic promise. He was fascinated by his auntie's artworks. She gave him clay and encouraged him to play with it. He loved making small toys and sculptures and Sonabai would tell him how to improve them. He attended elementary school in Puhputra and higher classes in Lakhanpur, but, in 1991, when Bhagat Ram was just nineteen, he was invited to take Sonabai's first government-sponsored workshop. This experience changed his life. Over the next twelve months he learned the techniques of building and adorning wall structures, constructing and sculpting *jali*, and forming three-dimensional bas-reliefs. Bhagat Ram was one of the few students who

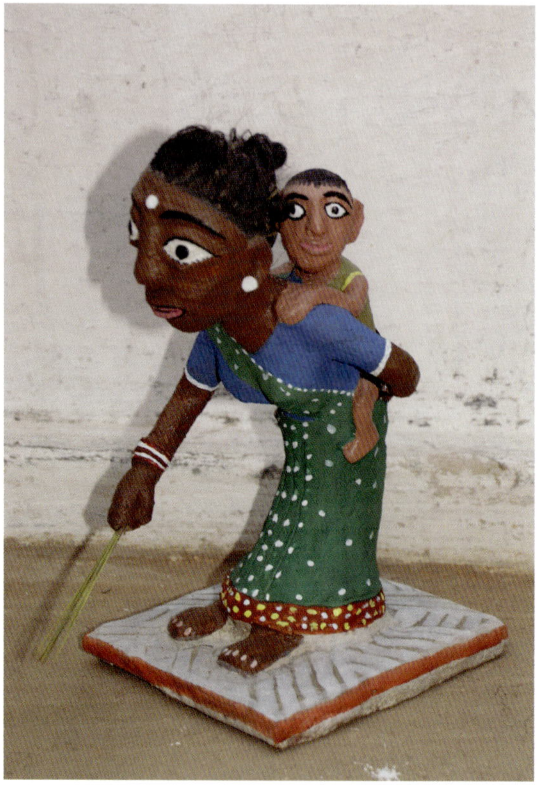

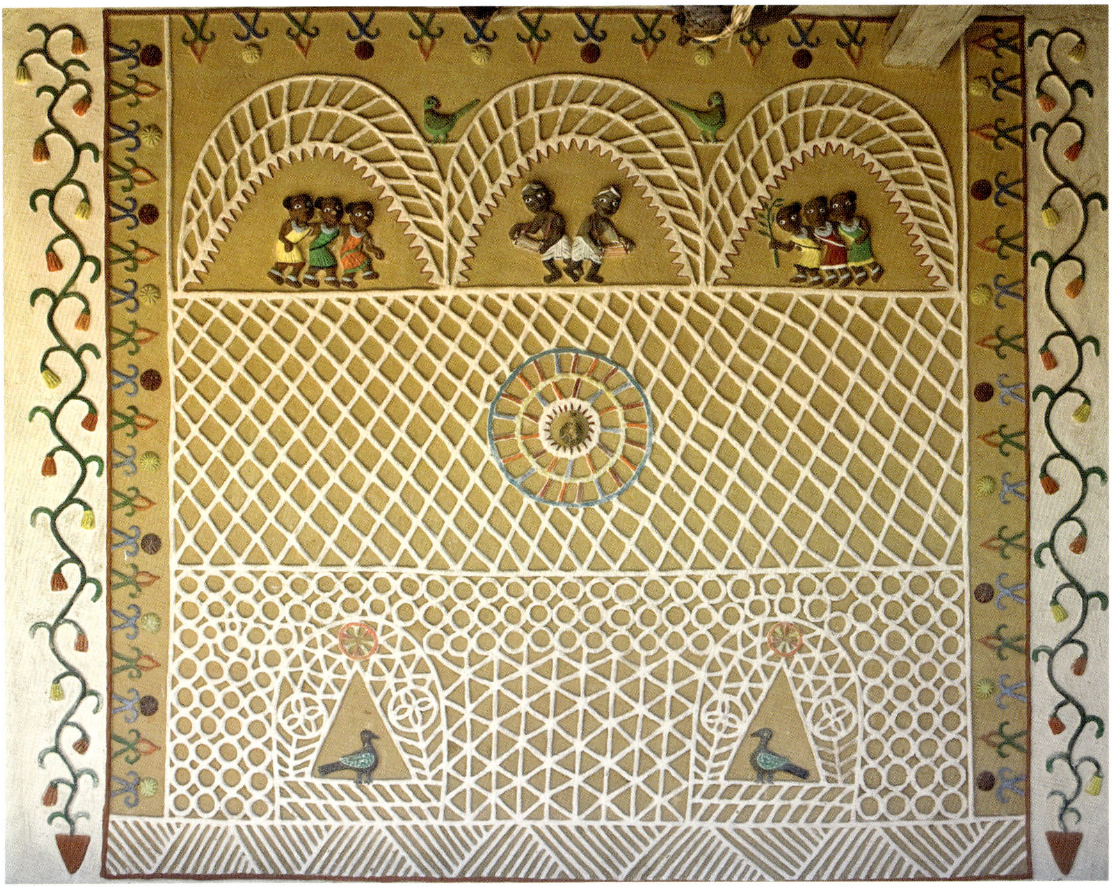

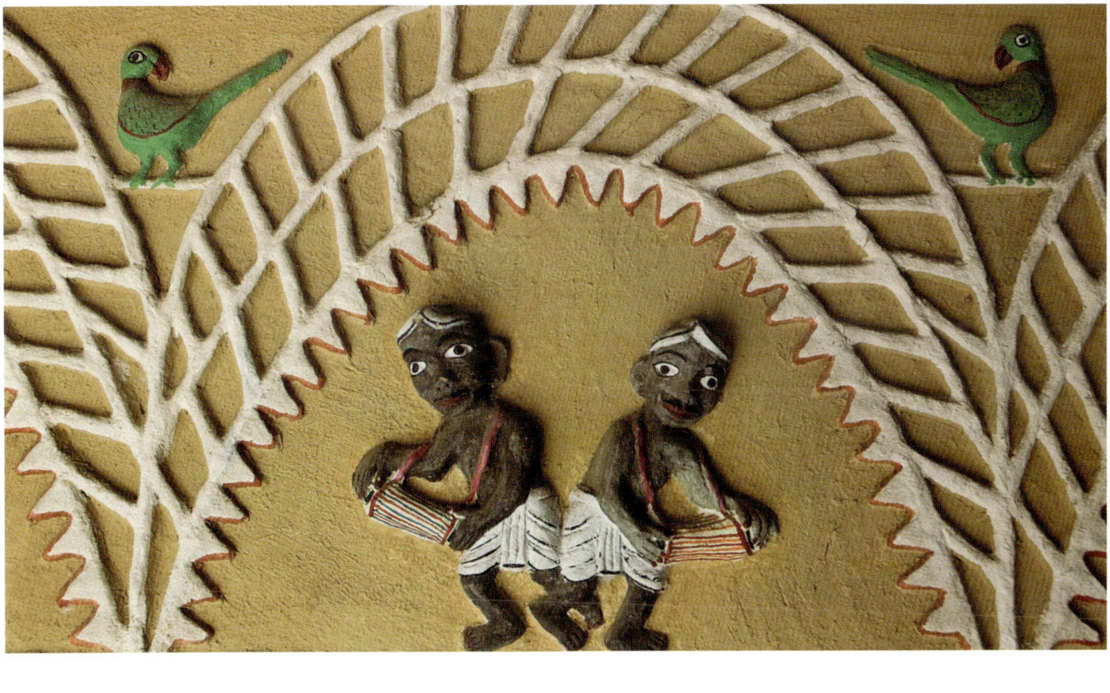

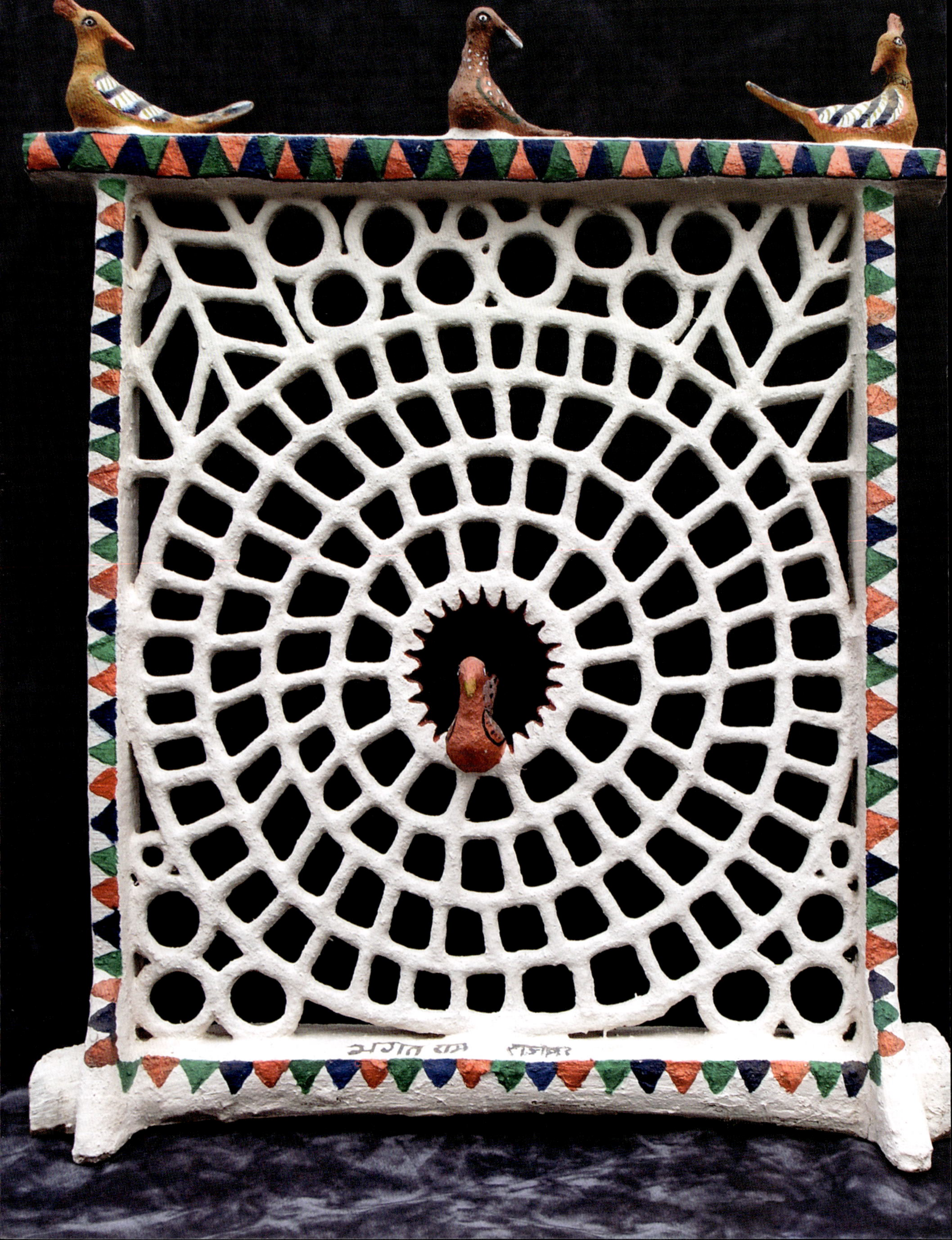
भगत राम

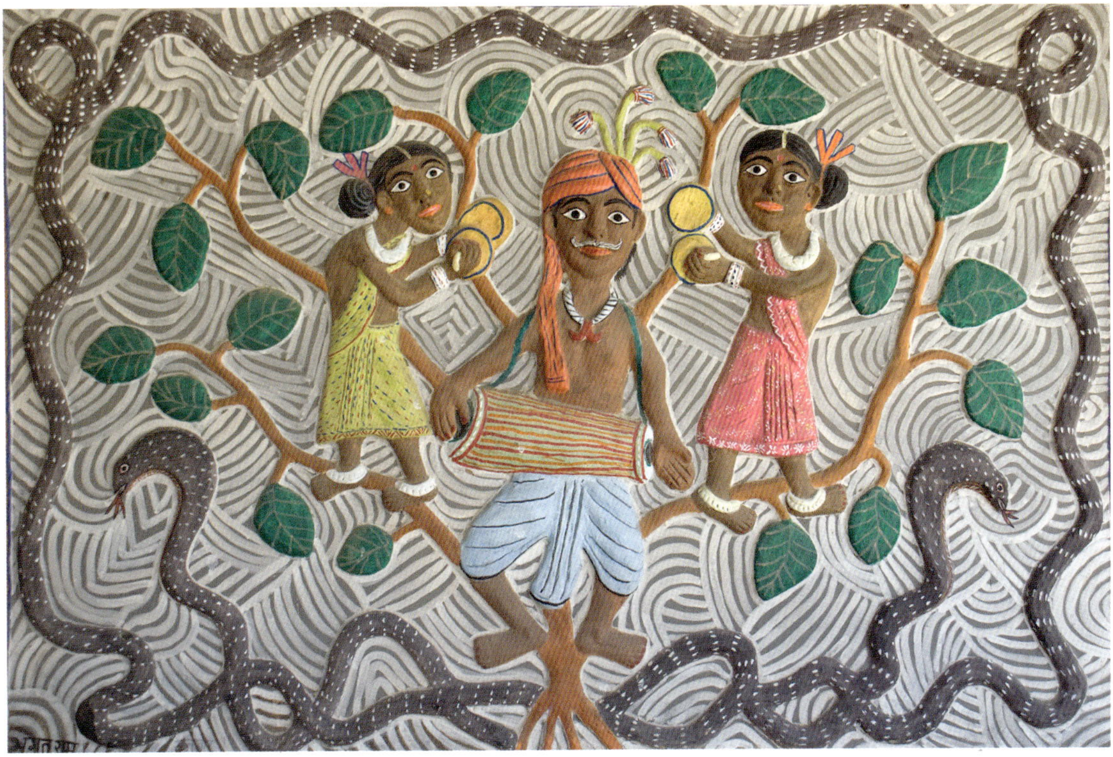

truly excelled in these classes. He immediately applied his new craft to the interior walls of his family home, entirely transforming their appearance. Initially as a young man, Bhagat Ram had no other outlet for his art. As his family were poor farmers, he had to spend most of his days laboring on the family land once the government art scholarship was over. Although Bhagat Ram could only sculpt when he had spare time, his enthusiasm for art never diminished. When, in 1996, Bhagat Ram was invited to join Sonabai's second government-sponsored workshop, he was elated. He knew his dreams would materialize and he would become a professional artist.

The thirteen years since the workshop have not been easy for Bhagat Ram. He has had to leave his young family often to travel to Raipur and other cities in order to sculpt. But his work is in demand. Bhagat Ram is a masterful artist, capable of sculpting precisely in styles reminiscent of either Sonabai or Sundaribai. He is also creative and inventive in his techniques, always attempting to stretch the boundaries of his sculptures in new ways. For example, Bhagat Ram has reinterpreted the concept of shallow bas-reliefs, recognizing that the deeply three-dimensional works pioneered by Sonabai and still created by Daroga Ram and Sundaribai are self-limiting in that they are particularly fragile to transport. Bhagat Ram's shallow wall sculptures combine humor, movement, color and composition in excitingly innovative ways. Recently he and his close friend, the artist Atma Das Manikpuri, were commissioned to completely design a new rural hospital in Ganiari, near Bilaspur, a town about five hours by bus from Puhputra. Together they are sculpting waiting rooms, halls, patients' rooms, operating theatres, a dining facility, and offices. This commission is a remarkable testimony to the trust that the hospital administrators and architects have in the value of Bhagat Ram's and Atma Das's work. They obviously recognize that both artists are not only accomplished and capable, but that their products will create an atmosphere conducive to healing and wellbeing. There can be no higher accolade.

ATMA DAS MANIKPURI

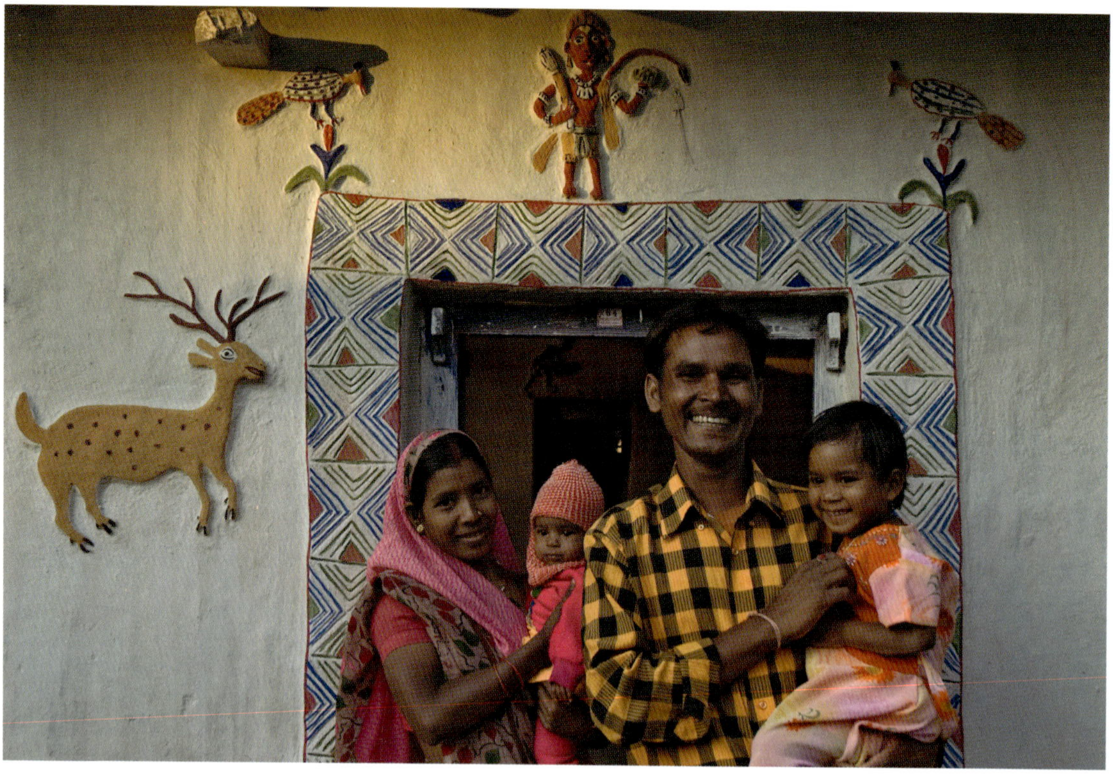

OF ALL THE ARTISTS in Surguja District directly influenced by Sonabai, Atma Das Manikpuri is the most broadly educated in art. In a country where hereditary customs govern most professional choices, it is particularly rare in rural villages to discover such an independent mind as his. Atma Das is fascinated by art, by learning everything he can about it, and by experimenting in different styles and mediums. He is constantly stretching the boundaries of his work.

Atma Das was born in 1972 in the village of Bitthikala, twelve miles from Puhputra. His family's traditional occupation was weaving, although in the past two generations their major income has been from farming. Atma Das was fourteen when Sonabai and Daroga Ram returned from America as local celebrities. Determined to see what it was all about, he walked the mile to the main road, took the bus as far as the Puhputra stop, and then walked the three miles into Sonabai's house. Atma Das was dumbfounded by what he saw. Sonabai's figures, *jali* and door decorations transfixed him. "If an illiterate woman could do all this," he remarks, "I thought, why could I not do it too?... When I saw Sonabai's art in her home, I wanted to know three things: How did she make the faces so expressive? Where did she get her colors from? How did she sculpt the hands and feet and create the hair?"

Atma Das's interest became a compulsion. He had to know more about art. He continued in school through the twelfth standard (grade), and in his last four years (the equivalent of high school in the U.S.A.) he began to paint on paper. Bitthikala was a remote village and Atma Das was lucky to be encouraged in his artistic pursuits by a perceptive teacher. This mentor borrowed books for the young student on the history of world art, and practical guides to drawing, painting and print-making. Atma Das desperately wanted to study art formally at the urban school in Ambikapur, but his family could not afford the tuition or room and board in the

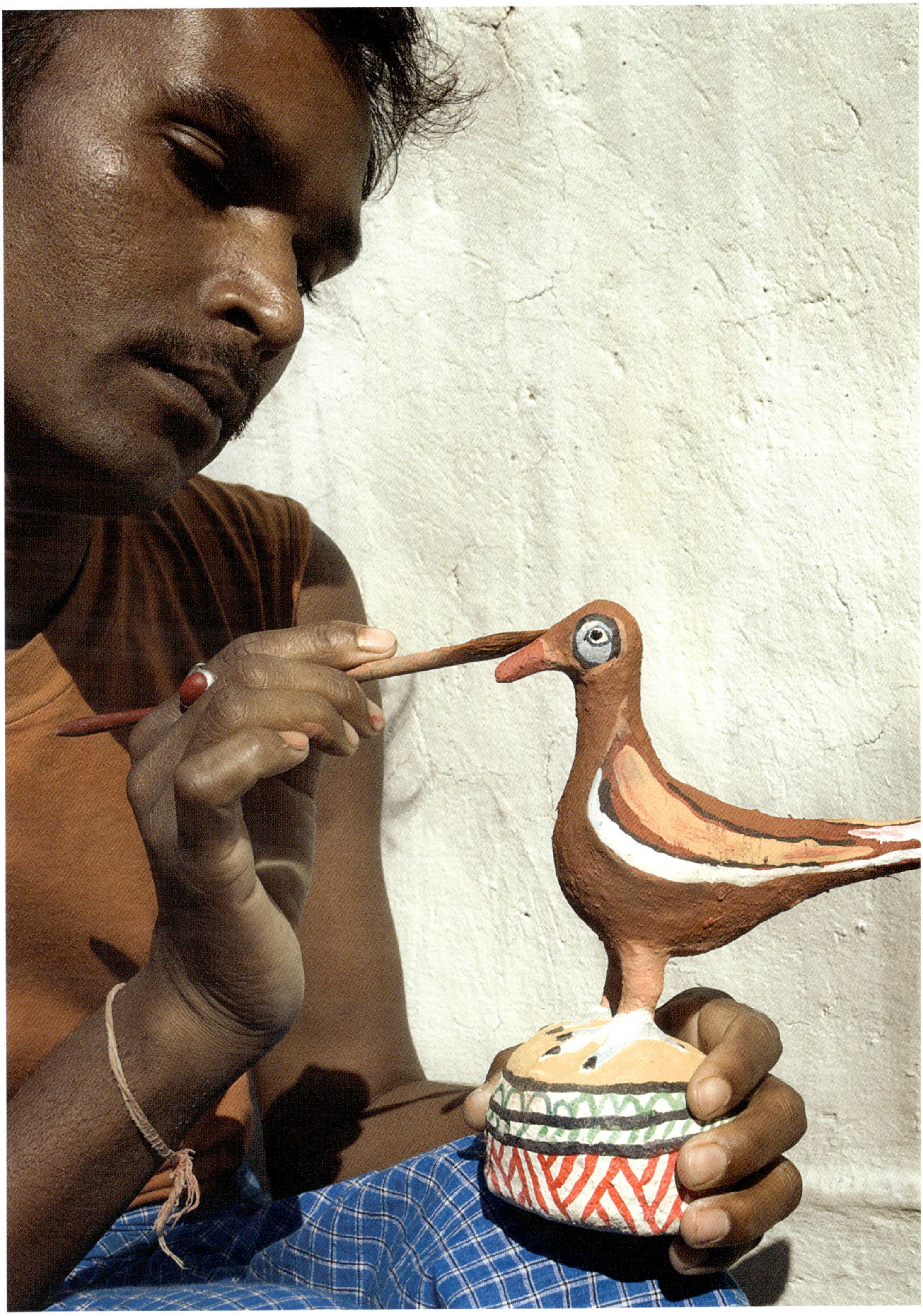

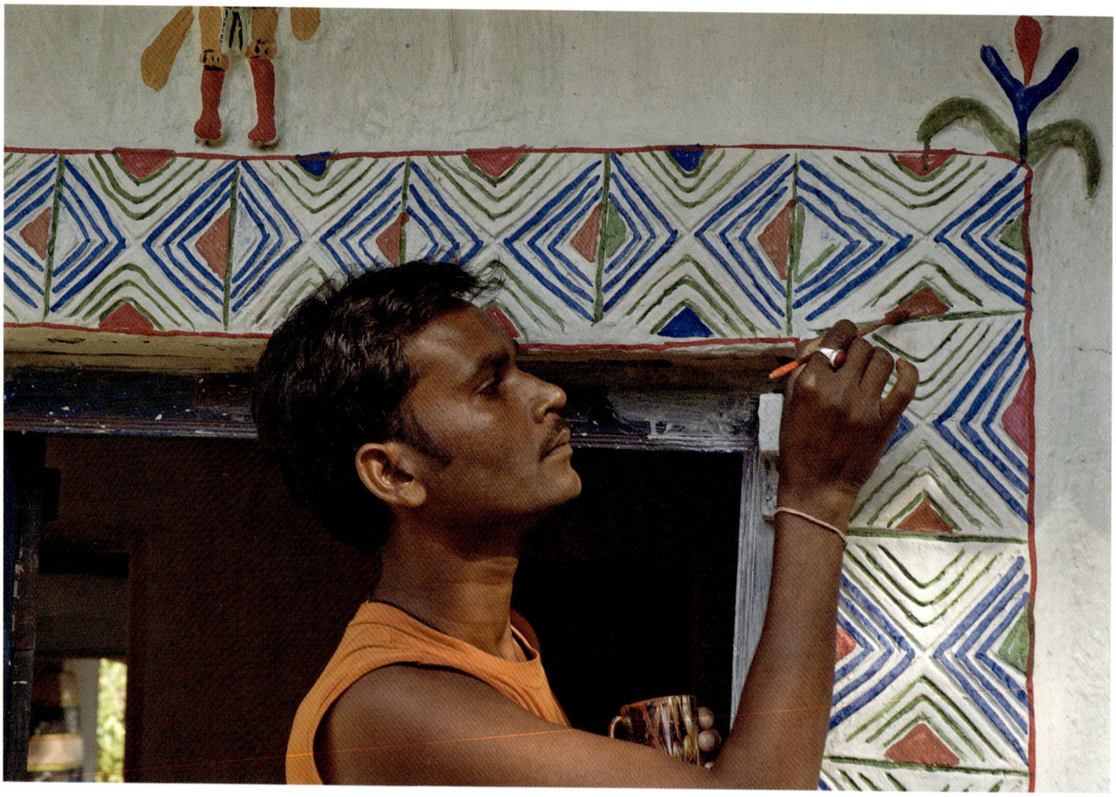

large town and his home was too far to commute. Instead, his teacher arranged for Atma Das to read on his own all the textbooks for the art courses. The boy's appetite for learning was insatiable. Atma Das was particularly fascinated by ancient Indian art (he cites the paintings and sculptures in Ajanta, Ellora and Jaipur) and the contemporary art of Picasso, M.F. Hussain and Ram Tinker Baij. Although Atma Das was not allowed to sit for the examinations when he had completed his courses in 1994, his teacher was able to arrange for him to take the tests privately, knowing that the results would never be accredited. Even without the benefit of formal schooling in these subjects, Atma Das scored the sixth highest marks in the entire Madhya Pradesh state!

When he left school, Atma Das was determined to support himself with his art. At first it was not easy. In 1996, he applied for and was accepted as a student in the six-month-long Sonabai workshop sponsored by the Madhya Pradesh government. This experience answered Atma Das's life-long dreams. It gave him the practical knowledge of how to build structures and sculpt in clay. It gave him the opportunity to translate ideas into form to learn first-hand from working directly with other artists rather than solely from books. Atma Das excelled in the workshop. He was spellbound by Sonabai and Daroga Ram and avidly noted everything they told him. And he became close friends with his fellow student, Bhagat Ram—a camaraderie that would prove invaluable to him in developing his career.

The government organizers of the workshop were looking for the best students to create a series of sculpted installations in Raipur. Atma Das and Bhagat Ram were their obvious choices out of the twenty students in the class. The two joined Sonabai and Daroga Ram on two different occasions at the Raipur Museum, first for twenty-two days and then for thirty days to sculpt panels for a long boundary wall and the *jali* and walls of a model house. Atma Das remembers fondly how seminal the

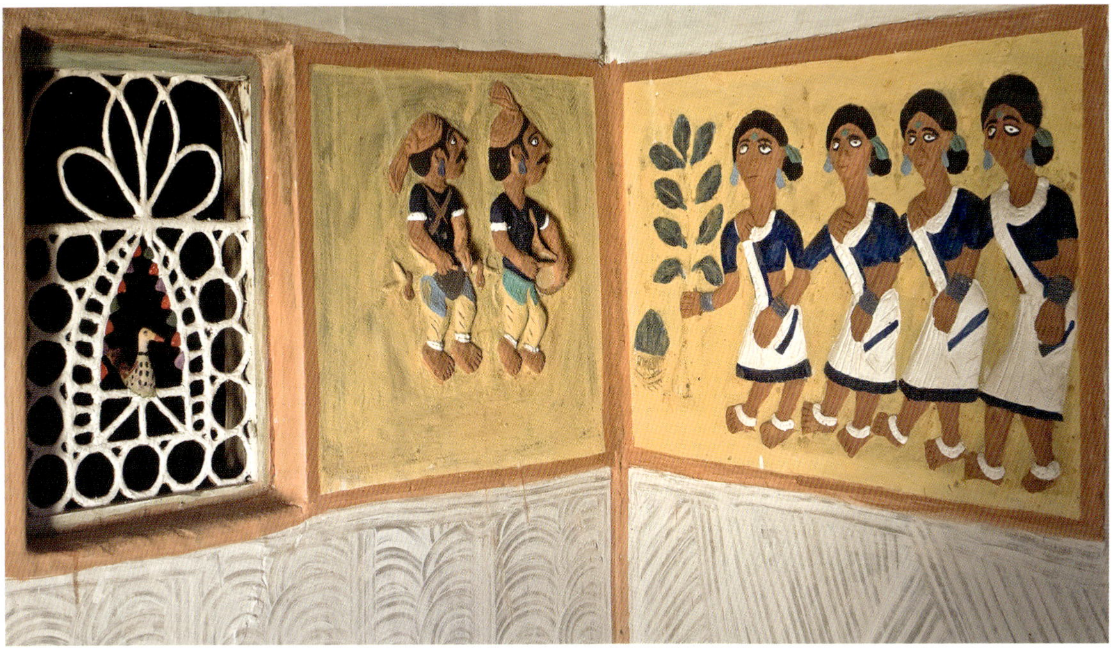

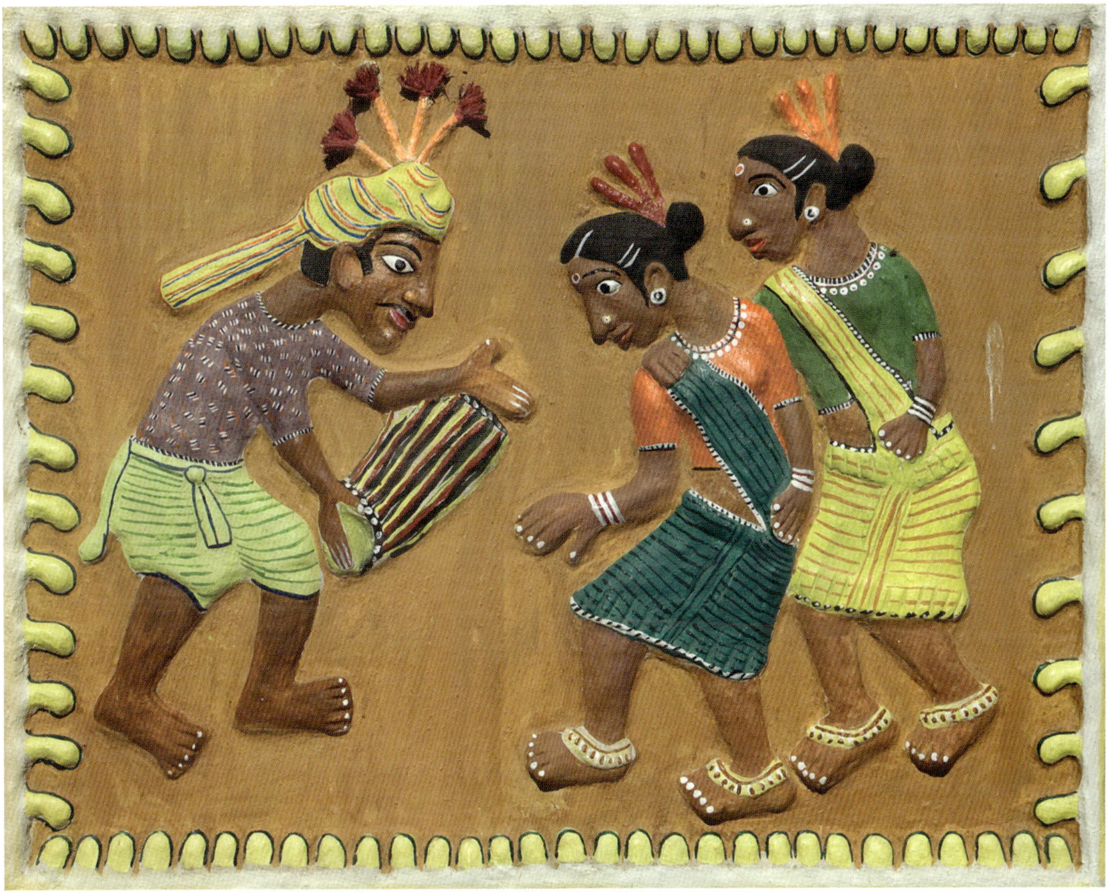

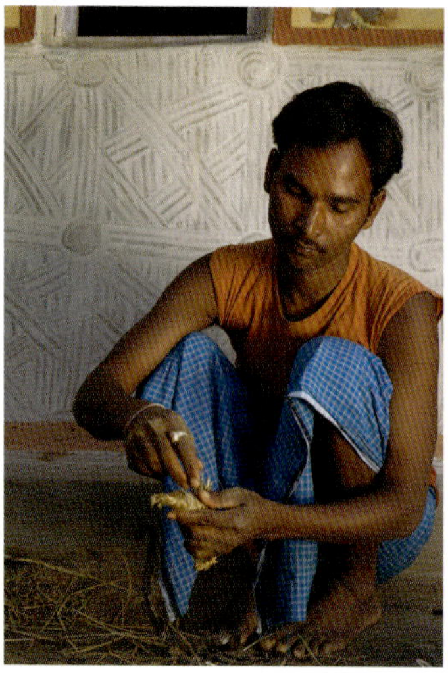
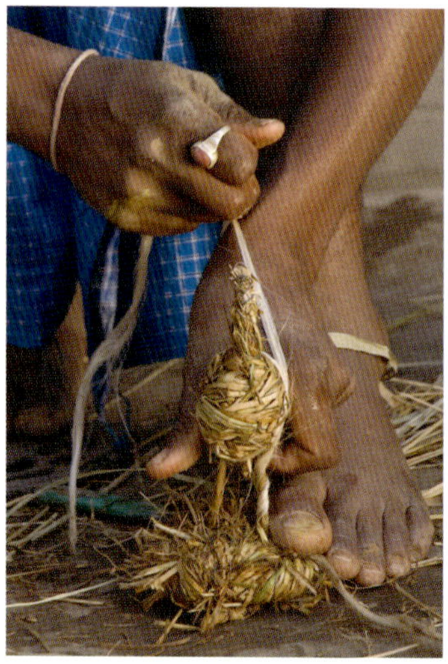
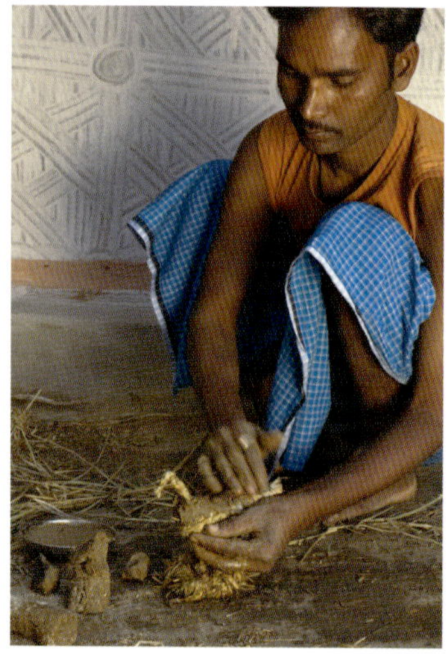
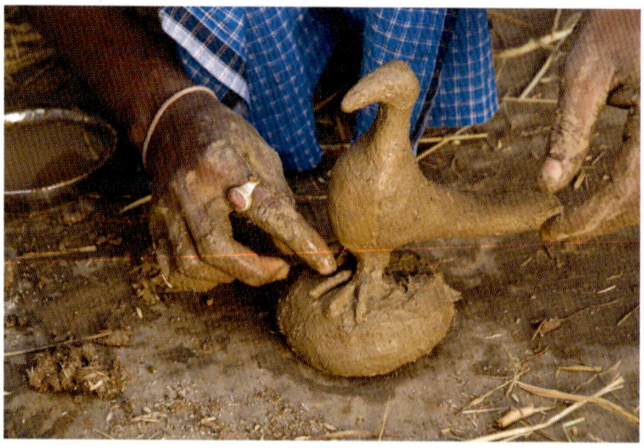
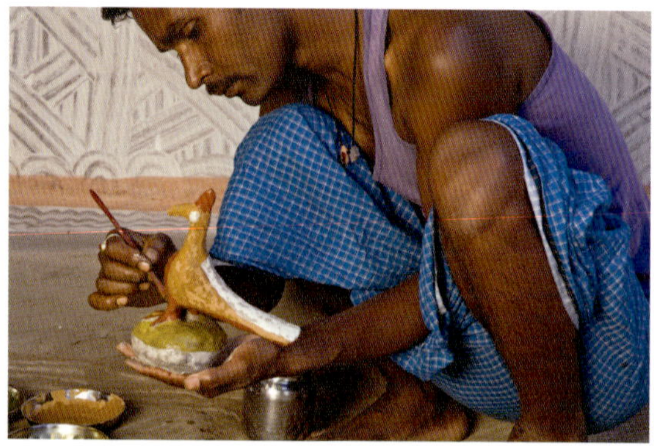
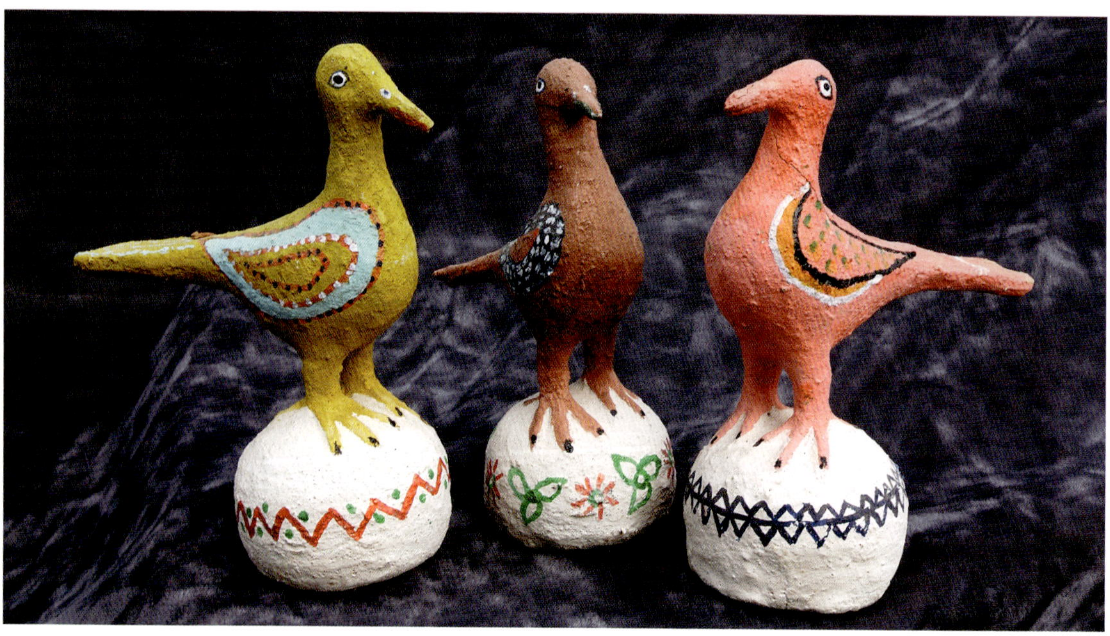

experience was for him to work alongside that great yet humble woman, observing and absorbing her methods of sculpture.

The two young sculptors were able to utilize their new reputations to find smaller jobs in Raipur and other towns. The income was modest, but they were able to practise an art they found fulfilling. When the new Chhatisgarh state was founded in 2000 with Raipur as its capital, they were hired to build fresh installations at the museum and elsewhere. In 2002, when Atma Das was thirty, his family arranged for him to marry Rukmanibai, a lovely twenty-two-year-old woman from a neighboring village. Although they did not know each other until shortly before their wedding, they rapidly fell in love. Atma Das credits his marriage as one of the sustaining strengths of his life. His home is remarkable. Although it is tiny, its doorways, window frames and walls are enlivened by Atma Das's sculptures. He lives with supportive, caring parents who express deep pride in his achievements. His sister and nephew live with them and occasionally help Atma Das with sculpture orders. Rukmanibai and Atma Das have two small children, both girls, upon whom they lavish affection.

Atma Das remains true to his education and is constantly trying out new sculptural concepts. Although some of his work is faithful to Sonabai's style, much of it has simply used her work as a basic medium from which Atma Das explores blends of many different stimuli. Of all the artists working in this field, his sculptures are the most durable. Like his friend, Bhagat Ram, Atma Das finds shallow bas-reliefs more reliable and he is constantly experimenting with different substances to mix with his clay to keep them from breaking. An example of Atma Das's creative enterprise was his response to an order from a museum shop for fifteen small plaques and fifteen sculpted birds. He might have created one prototype for each and then made fourteen more copies. Instead, Atma Das sawed fifteen pieces of plywood (ten squares, twelve inches on a side, and five rounds, twelve inches in diameter). Using a mixture of clay and glue, he sculpted a completely different bas-relief on each panel, molding the edge with decorative ornamentation and painting the background with a linear design reminiscent of local wall paintings. The result was fifteen distinctly different panels, five round and five square, that expressed many aspects of Surguja life: a mother and child, a girl on a swing, two dancers, musicians, a farmer and plow, monkeys in a tree, etc. For the second part of the order, Atma Das created fifteen three-dimensional birds by beginning with a bunch of tightly wrapped rice straw in the manner he was taught by Sonabai. On top of this base, he added clay mixed with glue and carefully sculpted the specific characteristics of one species of bird, which he then painted individually. Each of the fifteen birds represented a different species. Together they created an entire menagerie.

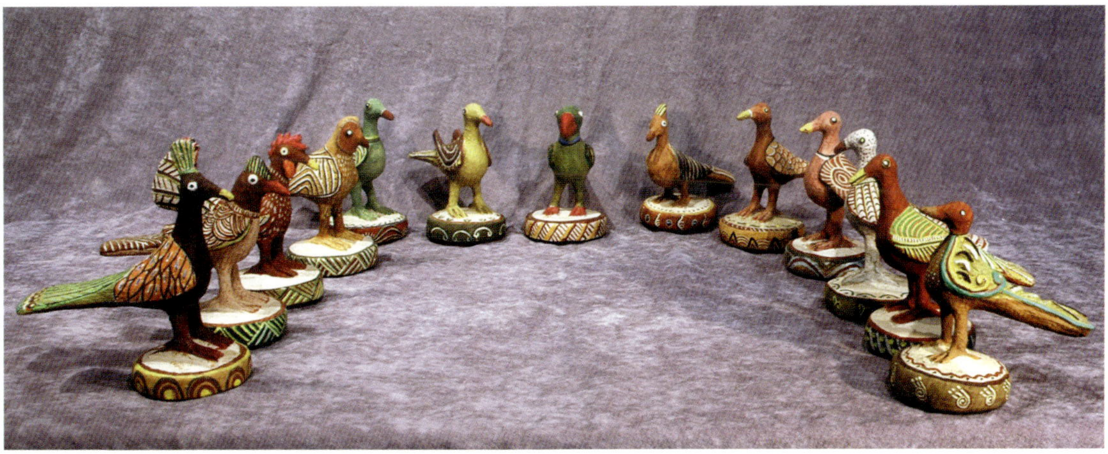

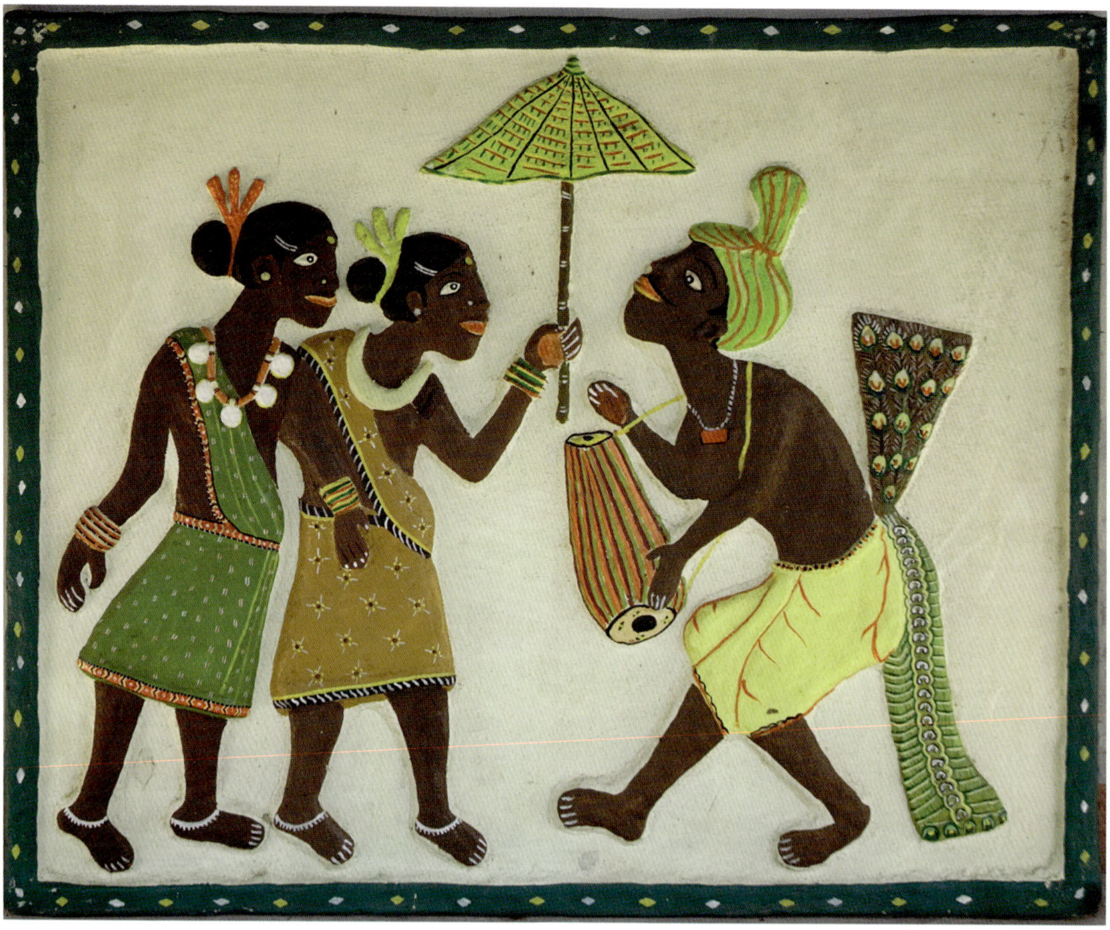

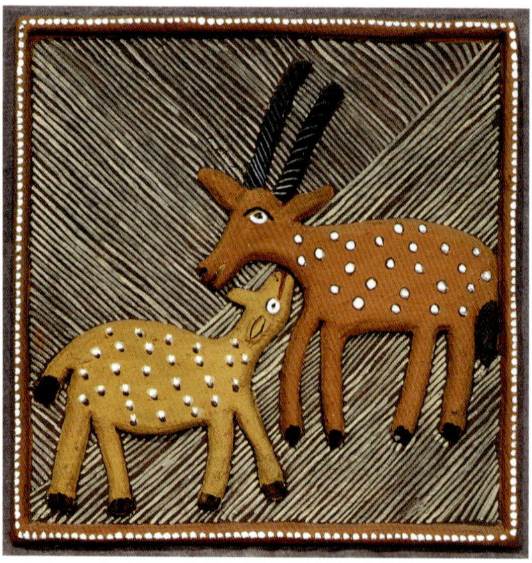

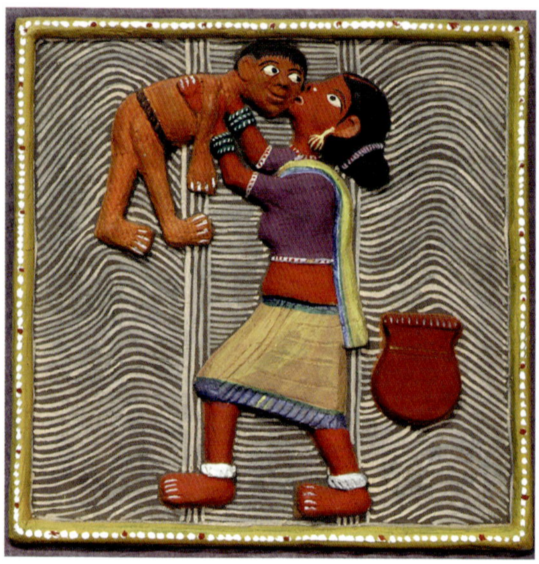

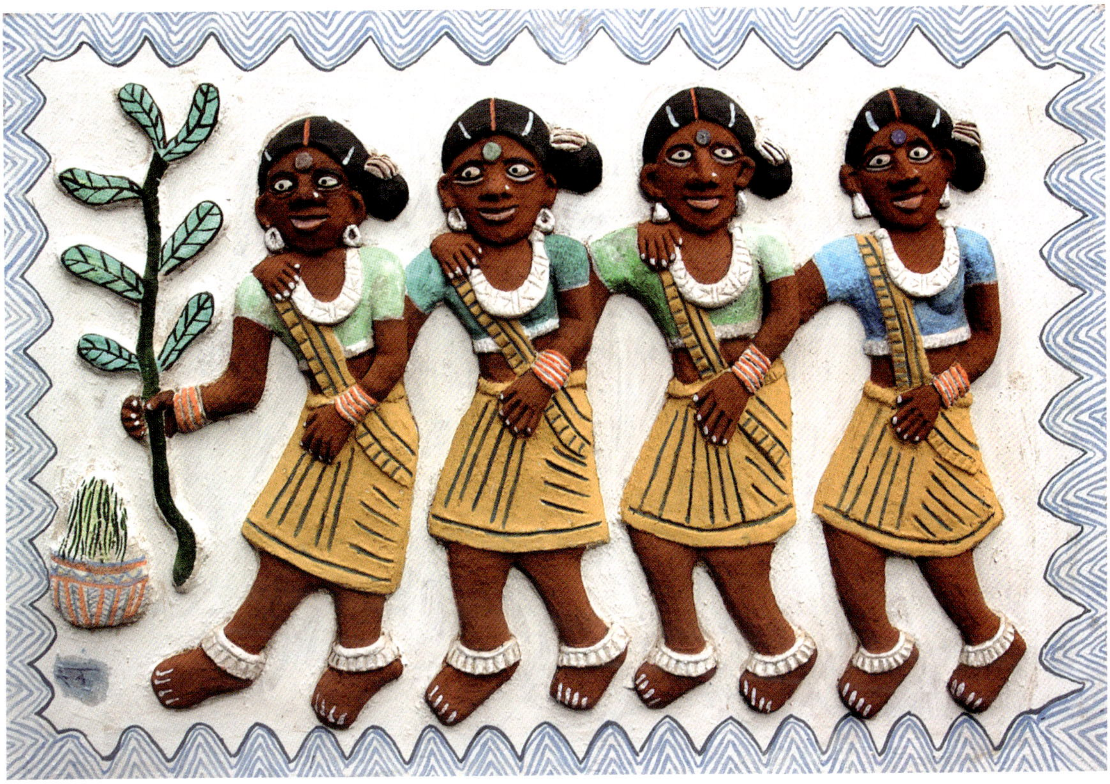

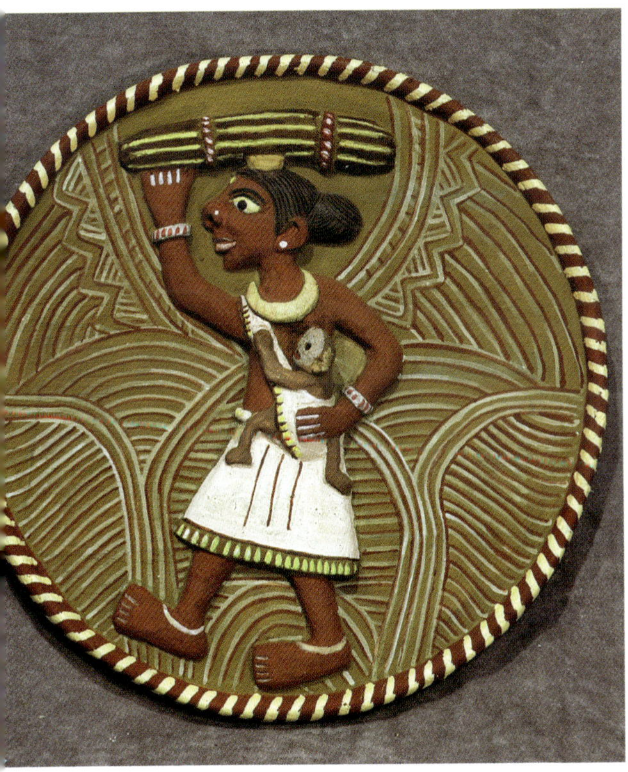

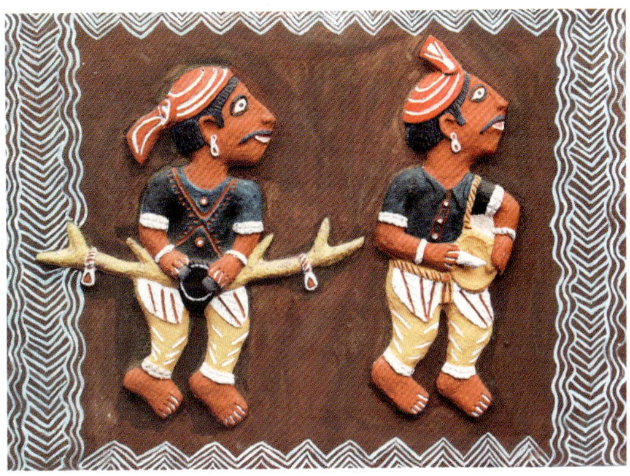

A thoughtful, kind man with a generous heart, Atma Das readily honors his many mentors and those who have influenced his work. There is nothing disingenuous about him. Atma Das epitomizes self-reliance and creative initiative based within a secure and well-balanced life. His artistic talents are remarkable and his future is wide open. His career will be worth watching.

PARBATIBAI SARTHI

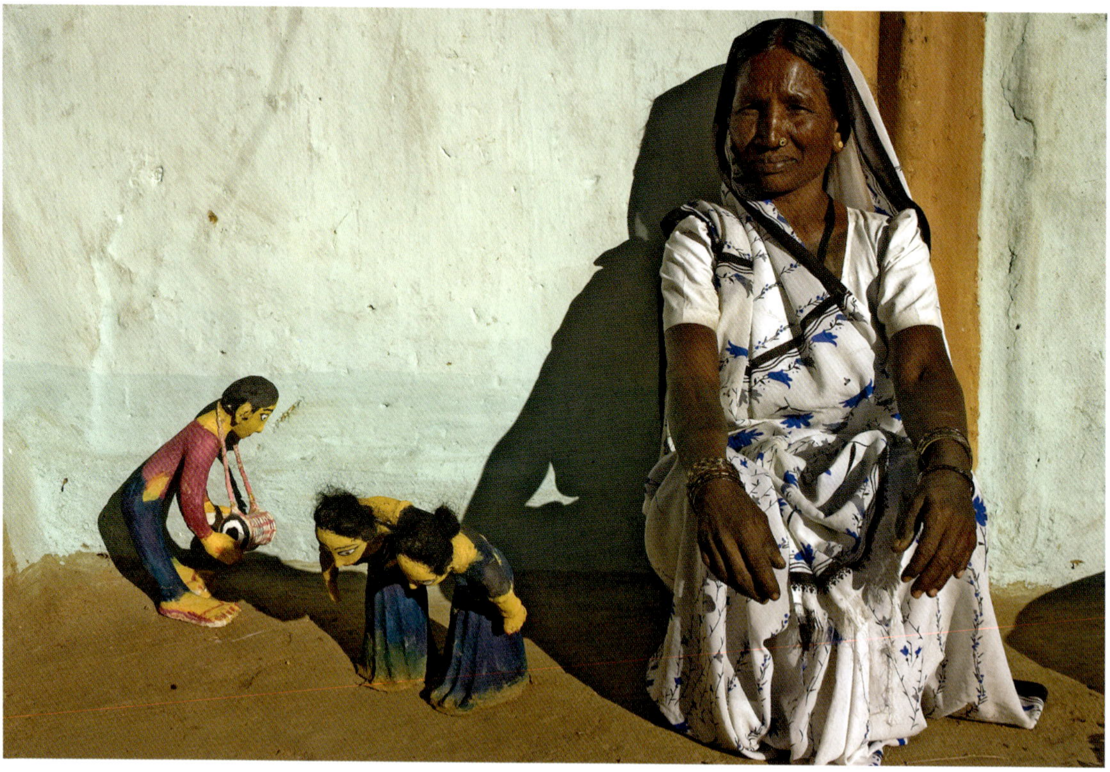

PARBATIBAI is a determined artist too—but her determination has a completely different basis from that of Sundaribai or Atma Das. Though the families of all the other artists profiled in this book were originally poor, they nevertheless owned their own farmlands and could usually sustain themselves by working it. Parbatibai and her husband are members of the Ghasia tribe, a social order of landless grass-cutters, horse tenders and musicians that prior to Indian independence were treated as outcastes or "Untouchables". The Ghasia are only one small portion of this class of people who comprise hundreds of millions spread throughout India today. Early in the twentieth century, Mahatma Gandhi renamed them "Harijans" (Children of God), but in recent decades they have preferred to be known by the generic term of Dalits. Dalits account for one-fifth of the entire Indian population! Although discrimination by caste is illegal in India and many government and private programs exist to offer Dalits reserved jobs through affirmative action, in fact prejudice still limits the opportunities of most Dalits and the injustices perpetrated towards them are pervasive. Puhputra, as was stated earlier, has only a few Dalits in its population—Parbatibai and her family among them. They work for low wages on other farmers' lands. Some of Parbatibai's family have been forced to work as servants, sweeping and cleaning homes. They state that generally the villagers ignore them. It is as if they are not even there. When she and her family are acknowledged, it is often with a slight air of distaste or disdain, although contemporary Indians are all aware that open hostility towards Dalits is now frowned upon. Parbatibai has good reason to want to succeed as an artist. She is desperate to improve her income and her family's reputation in the community.

Born in about 1955 in the village of Rakhara, four miles from Puhputra, Parbatibai was married to Mohan Ram when she was thirteen and he was fifteen. The young couple lived in his parents' house in Puhputra with Mohan Ram's many brothers and their families, but when his parents died, they moved into their present small house. They had three sons and two daughters and initially supported their five children as musicians at festivals and marriages and as wage farmers through the *jajmani* (barter) system. This ancient feudatory arrangement for rural management meant that the Sarthis almost never received cash for their work, other than occasional gratuities at weddings. Their payment was usually rice and sometimes lentils. To supplement these staples, they had to grow a small crop of vegetables behind their house.

Parbatibai began to sculpt in clay in the period between 1990 and 1995. "I had been to Sonabai's house," she said, "and saw all that she had made. It was so beautiful and so many people were coming to see it. But they gave me no instruction. I had to learn all by myself. I started trying to make things out of mud. I couldn't even eat or finish my meals while I was working on a sculpture... My family did not understand what I was doing, but I had to continue... They (the sculptures) would break and I would keep working without eating until I got it right." Parbatibai sculpted small horses, deer, bullocks and human figures. In comparison with Sonabai's art and the pieces created by the other artists, Parbatibai's figures were crude, and yet—after about five years, she says—they began to attract some attention. When the author arrived in Puhputra in 2001, Parbatibai came to Sonabai's house to meet him, requesting that he accompany her the two miles to the other side of the village to her small home to see her work. The relative poverty of the living conditions of Parbatibai's family was humbling. While her sculptures lacked finesse, they exhibited a simplicity and uninhibited strength that was captivating. Parbatibai's own courage in facing adversity and resolving to somehow be recognized as an artist was inspiring. She blended the infectious excitement of new creativity with a yearning that her work might make a substantial change in the future of her family.

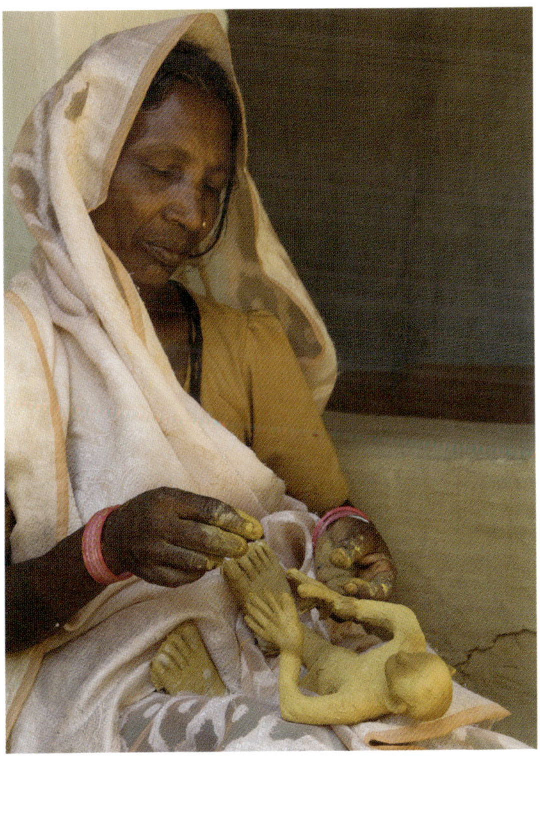

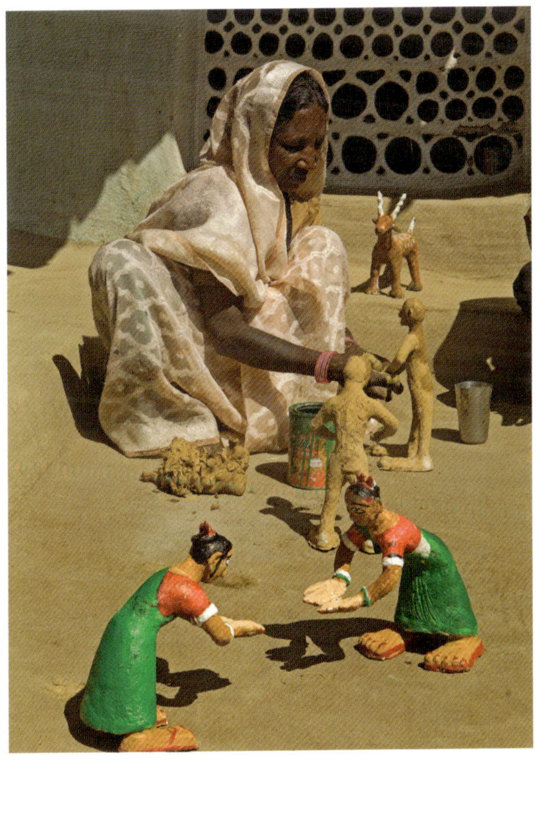

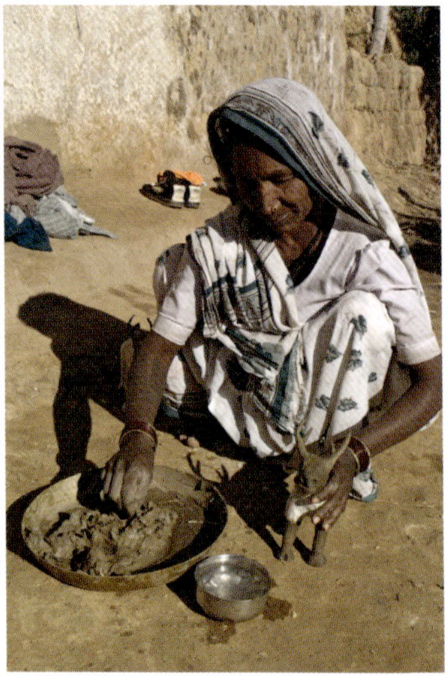

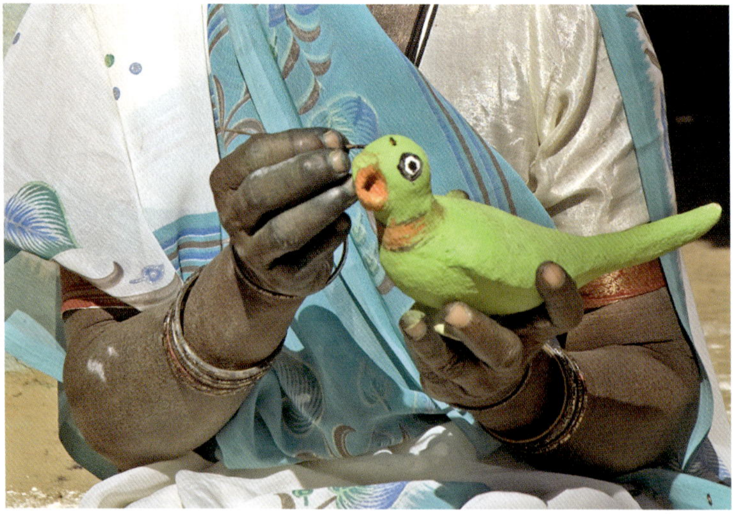

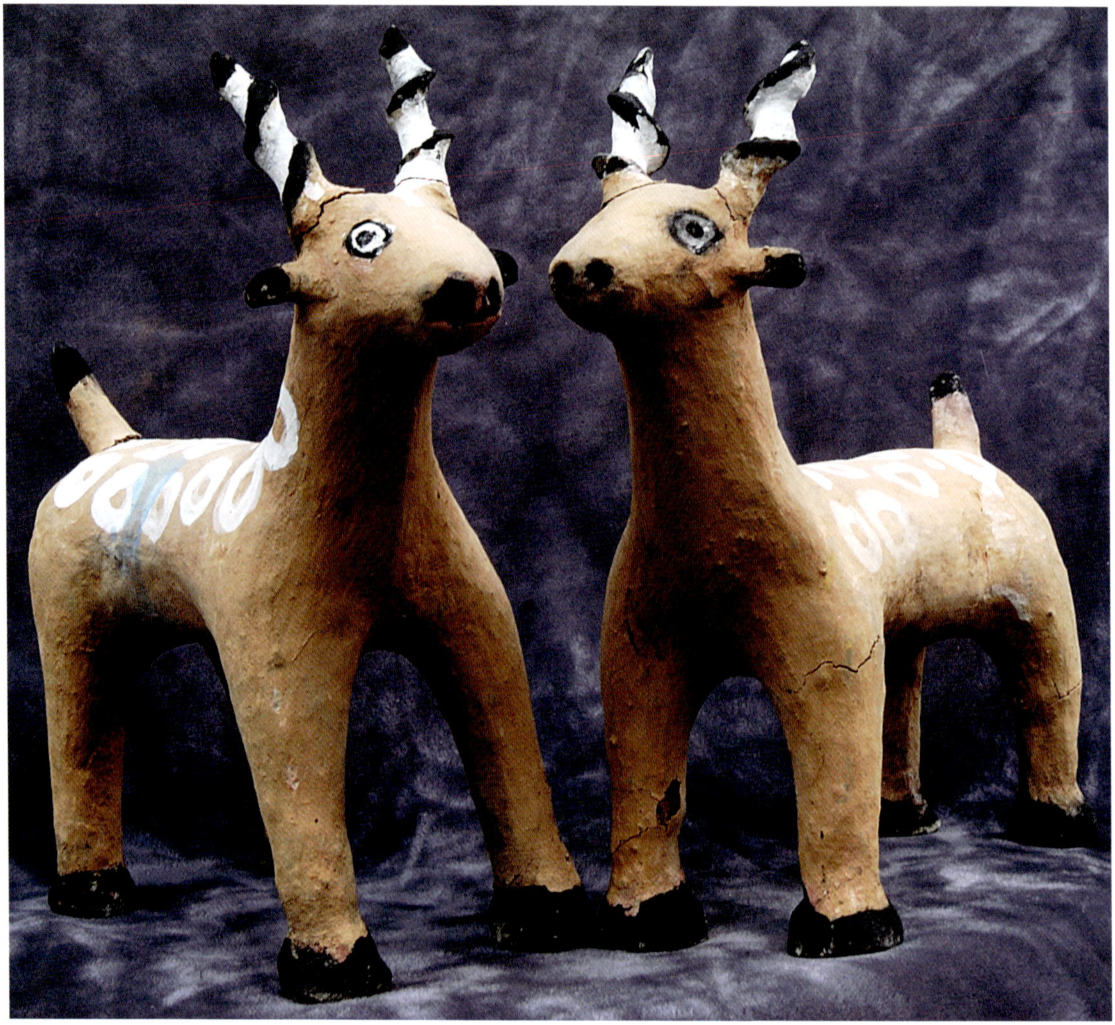

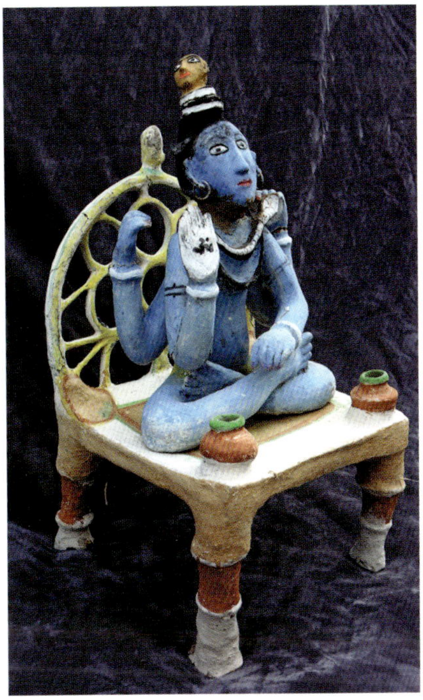
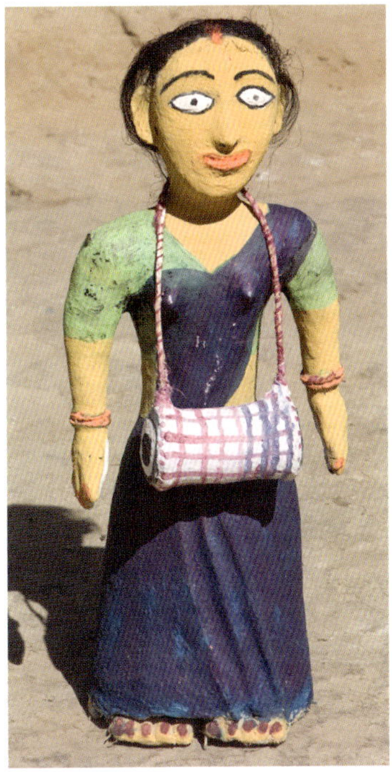
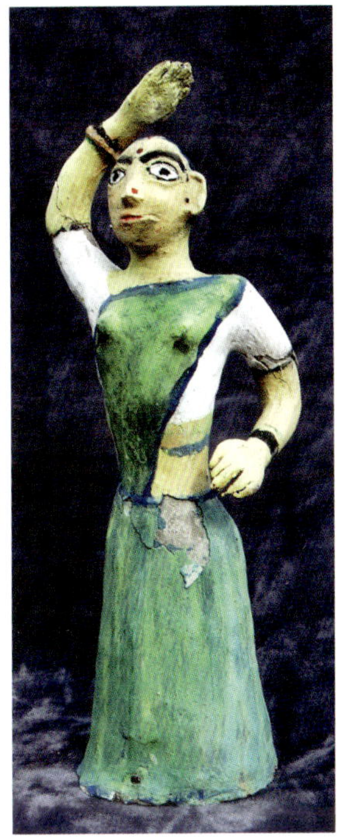

Although Parbatibai has not yet drawn the same level of critical recognition that some of the other artists have achieved, she has also been invited to sculpt in the museums in Raipur and Bhopal. Over the past few years her self-confidence as an artist has grown and she has begun to express herself more boldly. Recently she created an entire series of free-standing three-dimensional figures of harvest festival musicians and dancers that are true masterpieces. In order to balance the heavy weight of their upper bodies, Parbatibai was forced to give the figures disproportionately large feet; but the consequent effect is superb. Five male drummers and horn players dance around four male stick dancers while seven women, with arms around each others' shoulders, shuffle in a line dance. The complete ensemble is brightly colored and almost kinetic, so vibrant with raw energy that one can almost hear the music.

Mohan Ram, Parbatibai's husband, died in 2007. His death was a clear example of the neglect shown to the disadvantaged. He had a tumor in his leg that had to be surgically removed at the hospital in Ambikapur. He was released from the hospital before it was properly healed and sent home to Puhputra without enough antibiotics. The wound became infected and then gangrenous and Mohan Ram fell unconscious. When he was taken again to the hospital in Ambikapur, the doctors realized that they were poorly equipped to deal with this serious condition, so he was transported to the emergency hospital in Raipur where his leg was amputated. Again, he was not properly cared for and he died without either antibiotics or pain medication. Parbatibai was devastated. She felt as if her life force had been taken from her. Although she continues to work as a sculptor, Parbatibai has aged considerably in the short time since her husband's death. All of Parbatibai's children are married now. As a widow, she must defer to her three sons who live at home with their wives and children. The house is full, with fifteen family members living in a relatively small space. Her sons encourage Parbatibai's work, but she is now fragile. She is unsure that she will ever recover the artistic zeal she once had. Her determined future now seems uncertain.

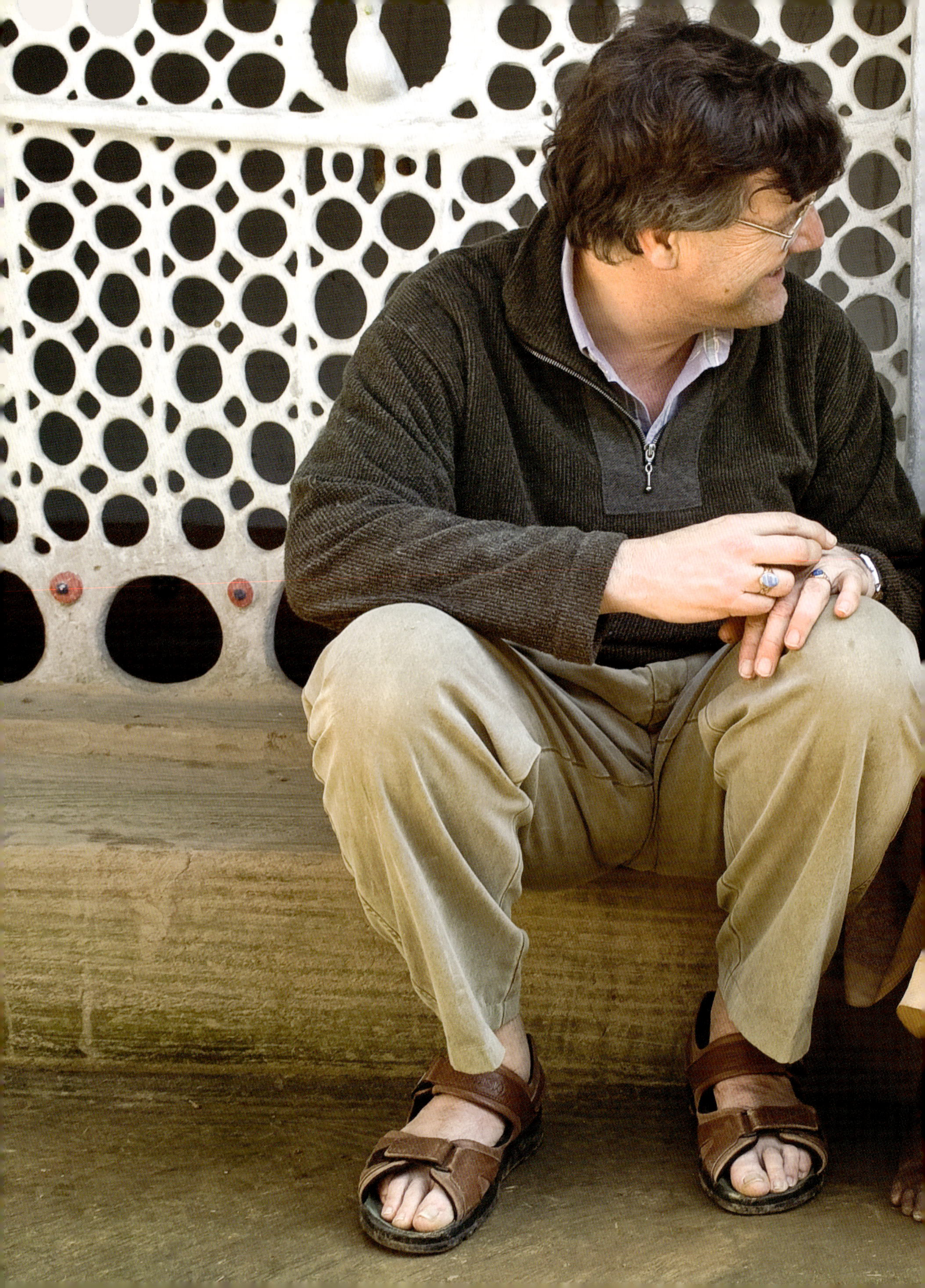

A PERSONAL VIEW

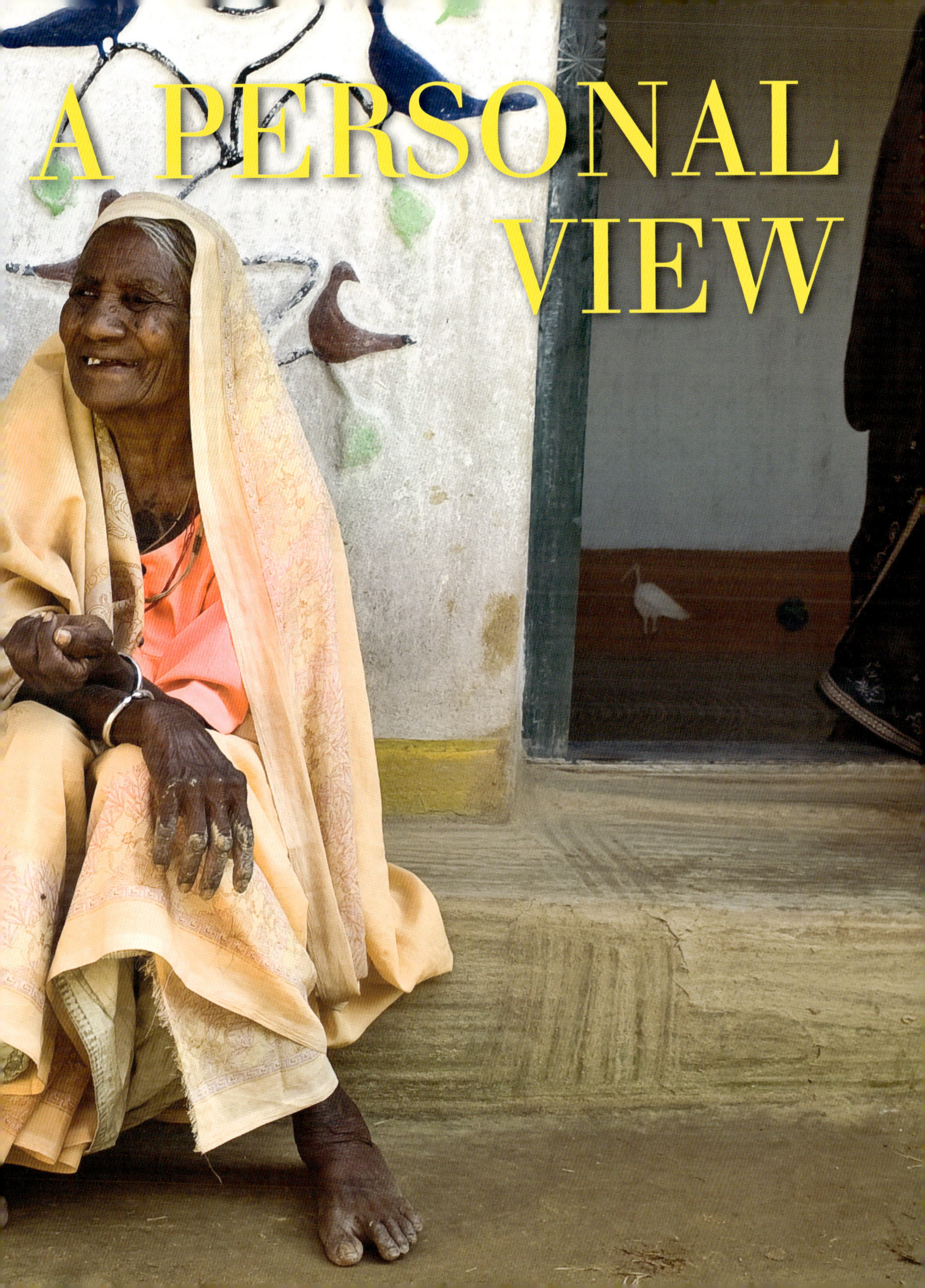

I STOOD SPELLBOUND WATCHING the nimble fingers of a tiny middle-aged woman in a blue sari manipulate clay into wondrous forms. She was intertwining the organic layers of a lattice with fauna, flora and figures in a manner completely unlike any art I'd ever seen during my fifteen years of travel in India. This was Sonabai Rajawar, and I was in the Crafts Museum in New Delhi in the late autumn of 1986. (Although I had never met Sonabai before, I had helped design and install the terracotta exhibition that had featured her work earlier that year at Mingei International Museum in San Diego.) I was to meet Sonabai and her son again at the Crafts Museum a number of times over the next few years. Each time, they invited me to visit them in Puhputra. I yearned to experience first-hand the house that Sonabai had transformed in her isolation. As a scholar, I needed to ascertain whether her sculptures were truly unique or whether they had evolved from a little-known wellspring of local traditions in Surguja District. Factual information about Sonabai was scant and I could find no scholars who had actually traveled there. I wanted to make an accurate photographic and written survey of the art of the region. Surguja District is one of the most inaccessible areas of India and, for one reason or another, my travel there kept being postponed. I was first able to visit Sonabai in her home in early 2001.

My friend, folk art curator Ute Stebich, accompanied me. Lacking good advice, we made the mistake of flying into Ranchi, an industrial city almost directly east of Surguja and geographically its closest airport. While waiting for our luggage, a fellow passenger expressed horror that we were planning to drive from Ranchi to Ambikapur: he said the roads were almost impassable and were riddled with bandits who might rob and even kill us. He recommended that we book the next flight back to Delhi. It had taken me so many years to get this far that I was hesitant to backtrack. Ute suggested we wait for a sign. Picking up our bags, we were met on the curb by my Indian assistant, Babu Mohapatra (*www.innerindiatours.com*), who introduced us to the Jeep driver he had hired for the job. The

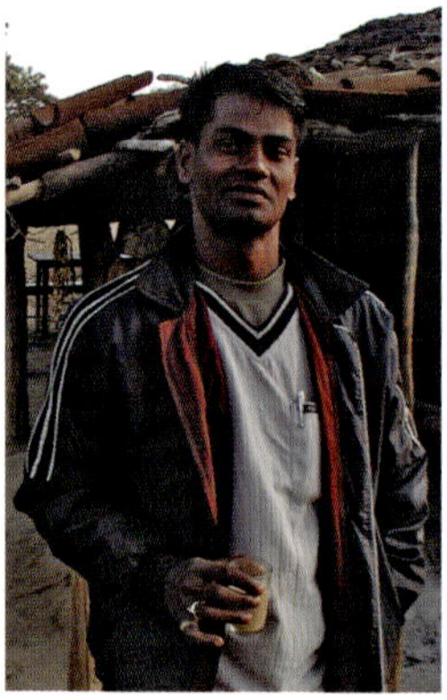

God, the driver

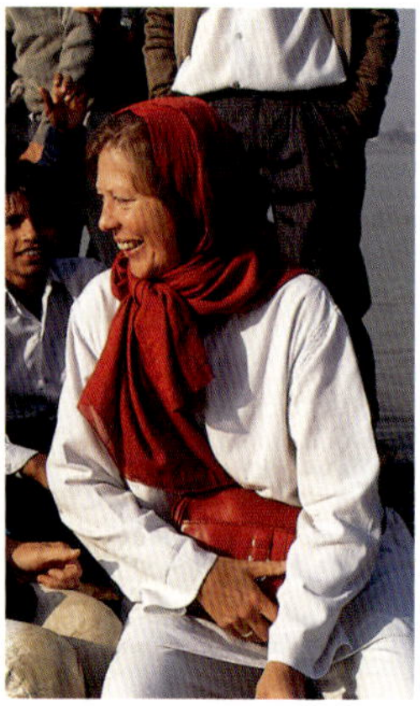

Ute Stebich

driver's name was God. His illiterate parents had heard that the British success in India was due to religion, so they had named their son for their conqueror's deity. Our prayers had been answered. God was in the driver's seat! Although the road was terrible and took us a day-and-a-half longer than we had expected, we had no major problems. God took us right to Sonabai.

Ute and I were tired and dusty. We had been traveling for days on bumpy roads worried about the possibility of bandits. (They are a serious problem in the district.) The closer we came to Puhputra, the more fascinating the architecture became. Time and again we stopped along the roadside to marvel at the bas-relief decoration on a house and were asked inside. We couldn't believe how a room would unfold into a courtyard carried on by a motif or a color or form in a minimal yet sophisticated style. We were captivated. But nothing we saw reminded me of Sonabai's work. We saw no *jali*. There were no three-dimensional sculptures. There was no use of whimsy or bright colors or figures. Finally, after stopping and asking and having the way pointed out, then stopping and asking again, we found Sonabai's house on the farthest side of the dusty village.

I will never forget my first experience of walking into Sonabai's home. My life has been changed by it. How can I even begin to explain? After passing the many extraordinary doorways and house fronts in the village, the exterior of Sonabai's house is very plain; the only hint is a little unassuming design over the door. Through that portal is a small, dark barn often containing a couple of tethered cows and a goat or two. Beyond it begins a world of bright imagination. On the right of this first courtyard is a long covered porch sculpted on one side with dancers and on the other with monkeys climbing a tree. As we first entered, Rajenbai was just covering the entire floor with a fresh layer of *gobar-mitti* (clay mixed with cow dung), spreading it with her open hand in a design of broad sweeping arcs. Daroga Ram was there to warmly welcome us further into the house, through the next, more elaborately sculpted doorway, past the long, dark rice grinding and storage room and into the space I regard as the sanctum sanctorum: the inner courtyard. This is Sonabai's world: a large area about eighteen by thirty feet with a wide surrounding verandah covered by an overhanging roof. Everywhere around us was art. The columns, the walls, the doorframes, the windows, the beams, and the baseboards—all alive with Sonabai's humor, wit and remarkable eye for balance and form. My eyes wanted to dart in all directions at once, entranced by the way the *jali* were anchored into place by strong columns and offset by the branching limbs of bas relief trees, birds, animals and human figures. All was filigreed light and shadow, a balanced chiaroscuro of shapes and colors. And here was Sonabai herself, a little more wizened than I had last seen her, wearing a yellow sari, smiling shyly, her hands together in a *pranam* to invite us to sit down. Did she recognize me? Probably not. Were we welcome in her home? Indubitably. We were the first foreigners ever to visit them. No one else had come, even from Delhi, in years. It was too far. So with typical generosity, Sonabai, Daroga Ram, Rajenbai and their family accepted us into their hearts, shared their food with us and let me begin to document their lives and their art. We were invited to join in the family's activities, to watch as they sorted vegetables, cooked, cared for their children, and sculpted. Ute and I were in bliss. Within a couple of days Ute made a comment I have

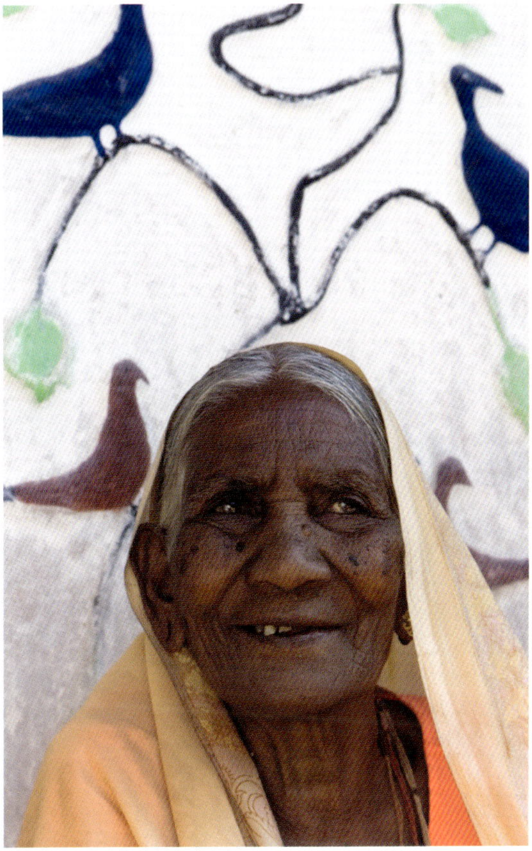

never forgotten: "Being in Sonabai's house is like living in the Sistine Chapel!" Of course, the style is completely different, but Ute meant that we were immersed in a sacred experience that entirely transformed our perceptions.

I was in India to gather material for a new book about Indian women, *Daughters of India: Art and Identity,* and I had come to interview Sonabai with a specific intention: to profile her as one of twenty featured women. Ever since my introduction to India in 1971 by my major mentor, artist Beatrice Wood, I have conducted a broad survey of Indian peoples, cultures, arts and crafts. In those thirty-seven years, I have traveled the length and breadth of India pursuing field research in rural India and taking hundreds of thousands of archival photographs. As a surveyor, the definition of my career is to compare and contrast the attitudes, customs and creativity of one region to those of another. In my initial exposure to India, I had observed that a great wealth of scholarship is focused on the documentation of individual subcultures or on surveying a specific discipline over a wider region, but few are attempting to document Indian culture laterally as a broader cross-cultural interdisciplinary survey. I have traveled in India months each year for decades in pursuit of this elusive goal. I have met hundreds, perhaps thousands of fascinating individuals whose stories are compelling, and yet I have always eschewed spending a very long time on one specific facet in deference to the general. Sonabai Rajawar changed my resolve.

When I returned from Puhputra to the United States and began to review my notes and edit my photographs, I could not get Sonabai out of my head. As I wrote the initial chapters for *Daughters of India* and worked successively on two exhibitions on Hinduism that I was curating in the U.S. and the U.K., I dreamed of Sonabai. As I talked about her to friends and colleagues, I realized that I could not tell enough of Sonabai's story in just one chapter of a book about Indian women. I began to visualize a larger project that contradicted my earlier cross-cultural approach: a monograph accompanied by an exhibition on Sonabai and the artists she had influenced—and possibly even a film. It took a few years to be able to arrange.

In January 2004, my talented American assistant, Kathleen Brown, flew with David Wright and me to India. David is a gifted filmmaker who had expressed a wish to work in rural India. We three were joined in Varanasi by my adaptable Indian assistant, Babu Mohapatra, and by two close friends: Sushmita and Shunia Tandan, an open-minded and versatile mother- and -daughter duo who were to be our interviewers on camera. Although I had occasionally led tours to India for the Smithsonian and other organizations, I had almost always worked solo or with just one assistant when conducting field research. This time, with another driver and without God at the wheel, six of us drove a mini-bus on the back roads from Varanasi to Ambikapur. It took ten hours rather than two days. We had made arrangements to stay at a hotel in Ambikapur town, a forty-five minute drive away from Puhputra. Months before, I had informed Sonabai and her family that we six would be coming. They were as prepared as they could be and were as gracious as ever.

For twelve glorious days we virtually lived in Sonabai's home. We usually arrived in Puhputra before sunrise to photograph and film the first light, reaching the house for early morning tea. Sonabai arose while it was still dark, as did Daroga Ram and Rajenbai. The latter two were already busy preparing for the day's activities while most of the rest of the family still slept. The others slowly straggled in to sip hot cups of tea while they grinned at us sleepily. We usually brought fresh vegetables

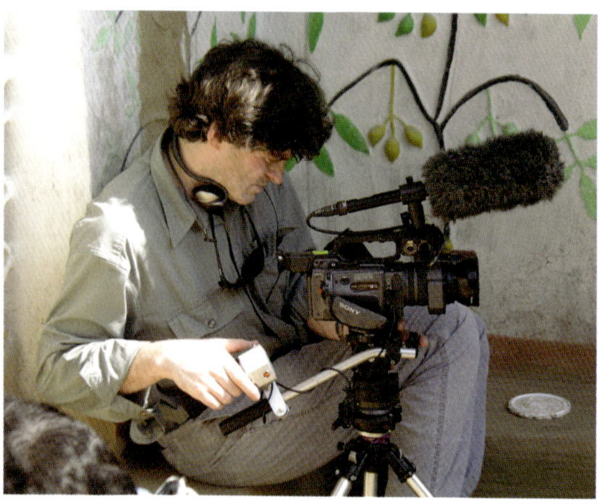

David Wright

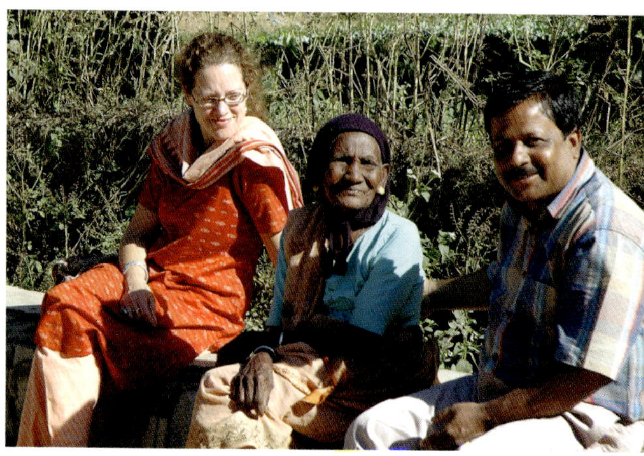

Kathleen Brown   Babu Mohapatra

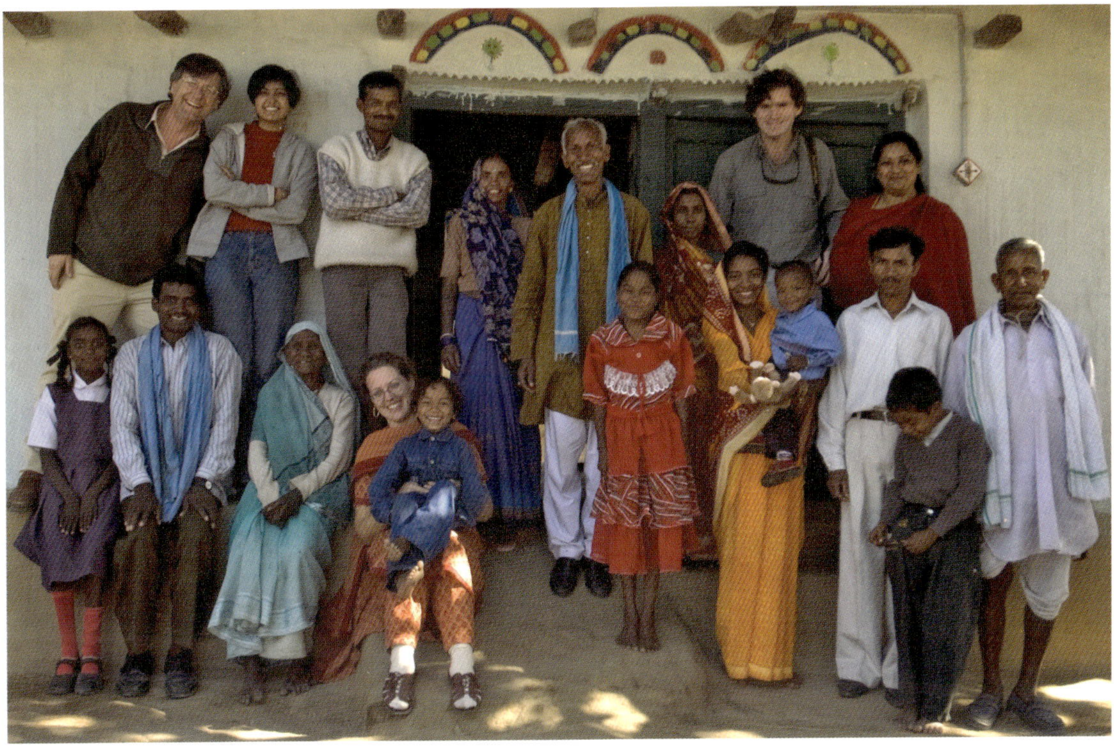

The family and team in January–February, 2004.

with us from the town market, choosing varieties not easily found in the fields of Puhputra. (Decades before, I had discovered this means of contributing openly to a host family's nutrition without undermining their dignity or self-pride.) On most days we were invited for breakfast and later for lunch, the food deliciously prepared by Rajenbai, Munita or one of Sonabai's two granddaughters still living at home. We ate dinner back at our hotel. Sonabai squatted for hours in front of a cow-dung-patty fire, warming her hands above the flames, musing. Her eyes were mostly rheumy now, her mind beginning to fail. Lucidity was illusive. As the day wore on, she would sometimes perk up and become talkative. Sonabai was always sweet-natured, but by 2004 much of life was passing her by. It made our documentation, particularly the film, a challenge. She was difficult to interview.

All the others that had come with me were as in awe of this magical house as I. It was remarkable to settle down and get to know it intimately. We tried to stay out of the family's way as much as possible, spreading ourselves on mats in one corner of the verandah, partially veiled from their activities by our own set of *jali*. We even napped there, our dreams filled with the individuals who were now becoming our friends. We spent hours interviewing the young mother, Munita (Sonabai's granddaughter-in-law), about what it was like to live in this home: the family's expectations of her, her daily tasks and chores, caring for her two infant children, and how different it was from the family in which she grew up. We were particularly enchanted by Munita's sister-in-law, eight-year-old Sunita, (Daroga Ram's youngest daughter) and her little brother, Pradeep. They entertained us for hours with their games. I even began to take photographs of Sunita for a children's book just about her. Each of our group engaged in different ways with family members. We felt accepted and were fascinated to learn about their daily lives. However, one of the major reasons we were there was to photograph and film the process of sculpting.

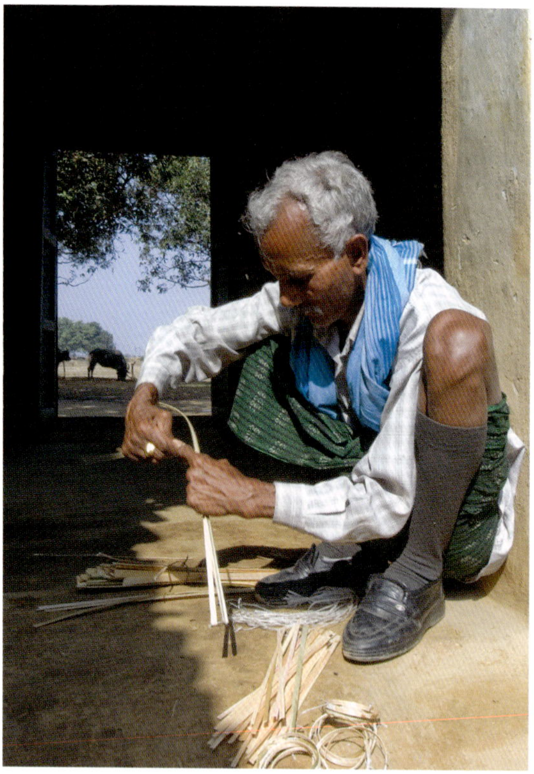
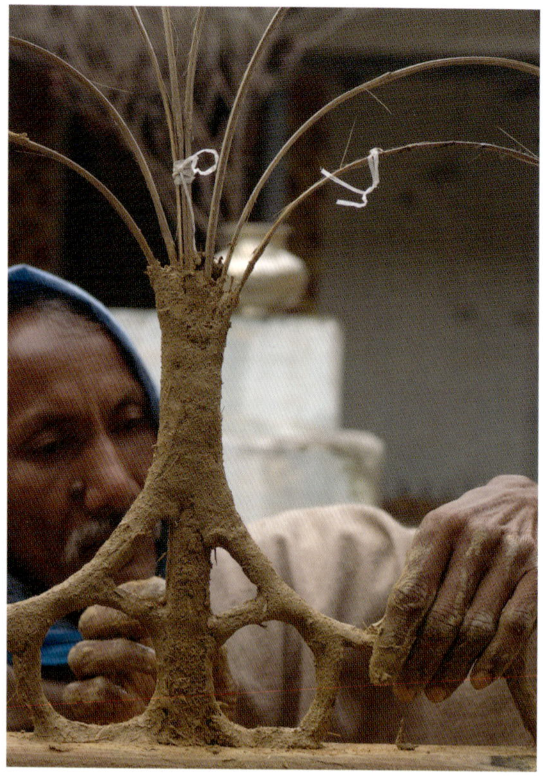
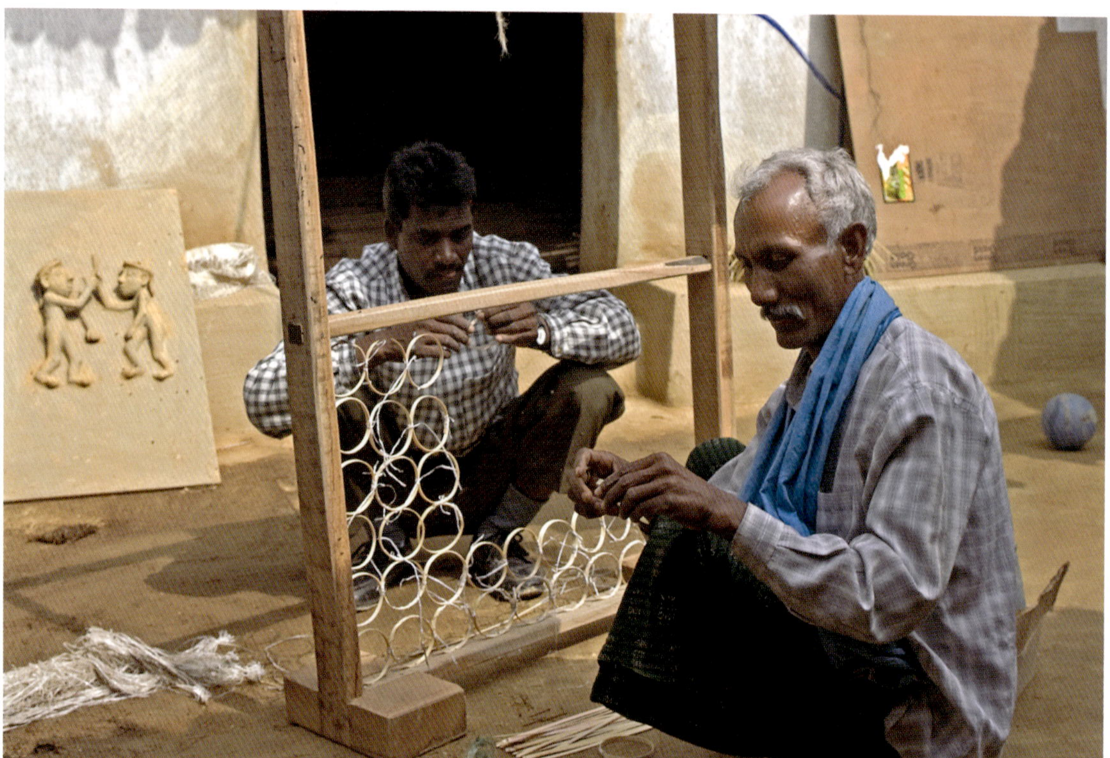

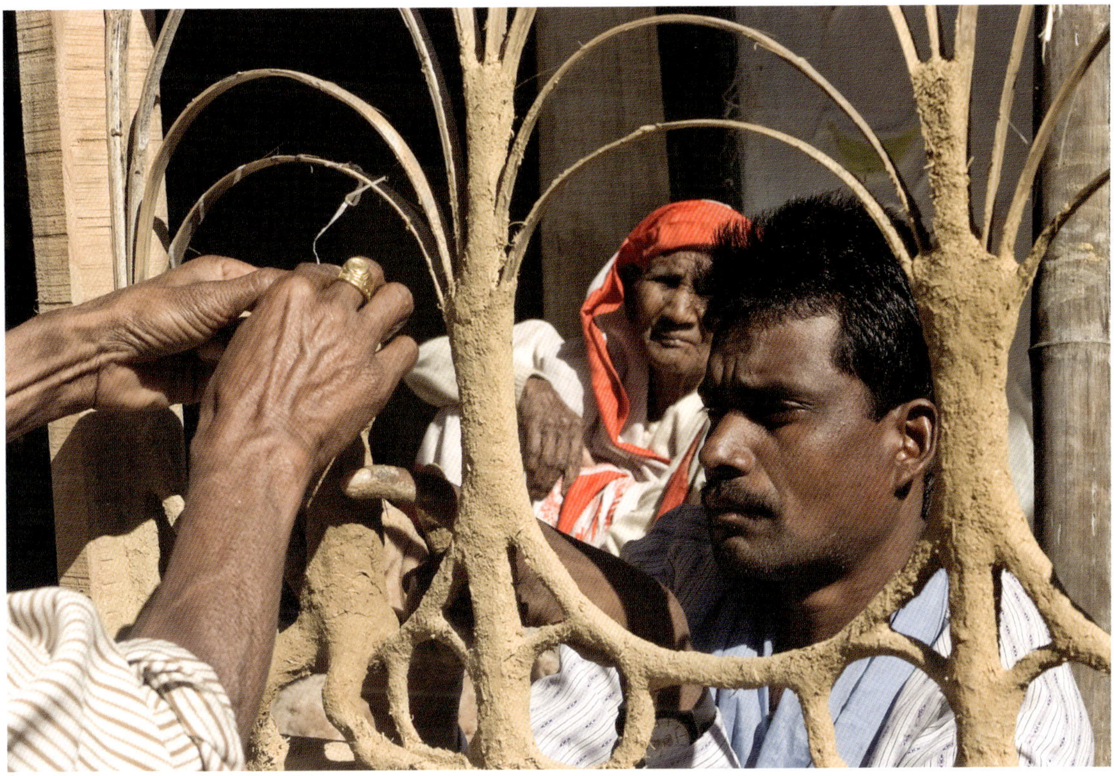

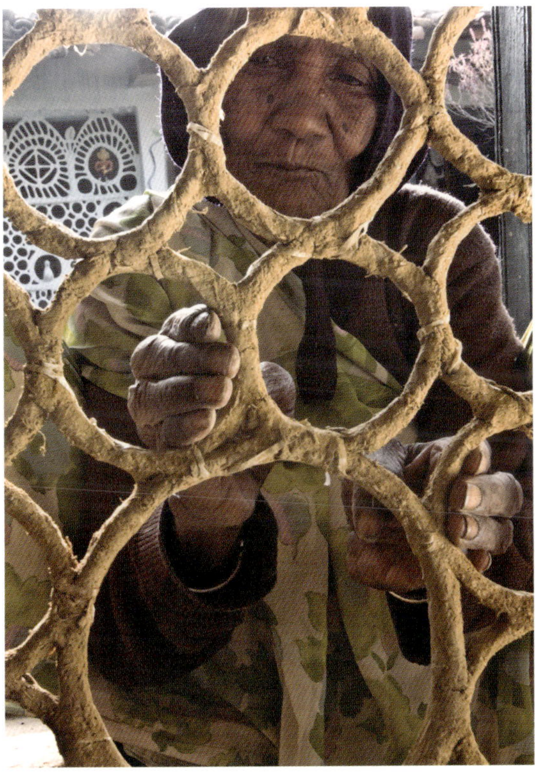

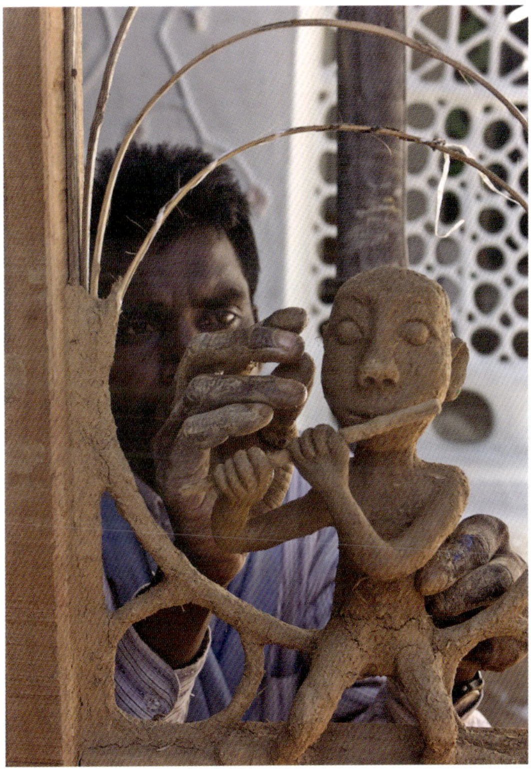

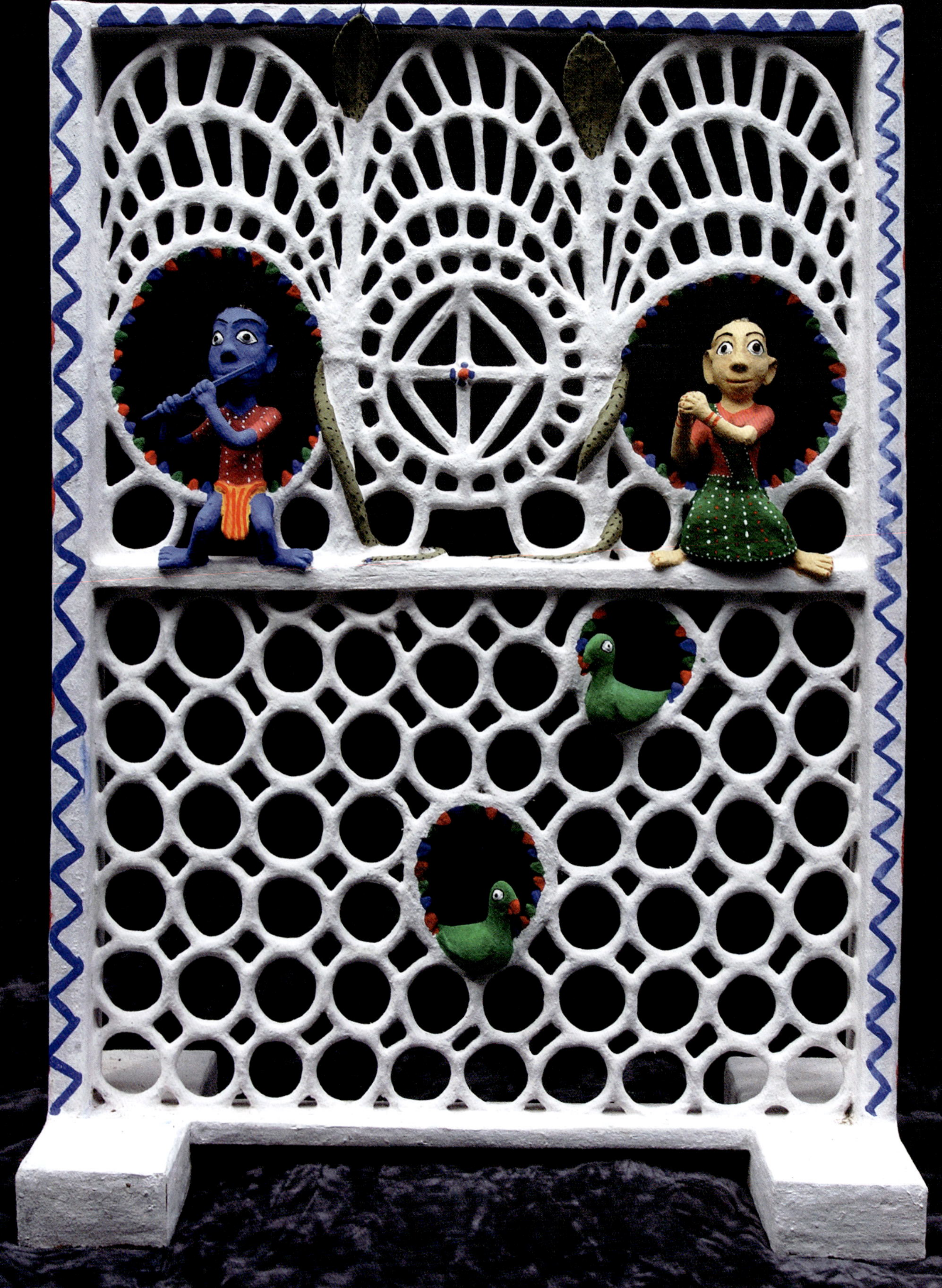

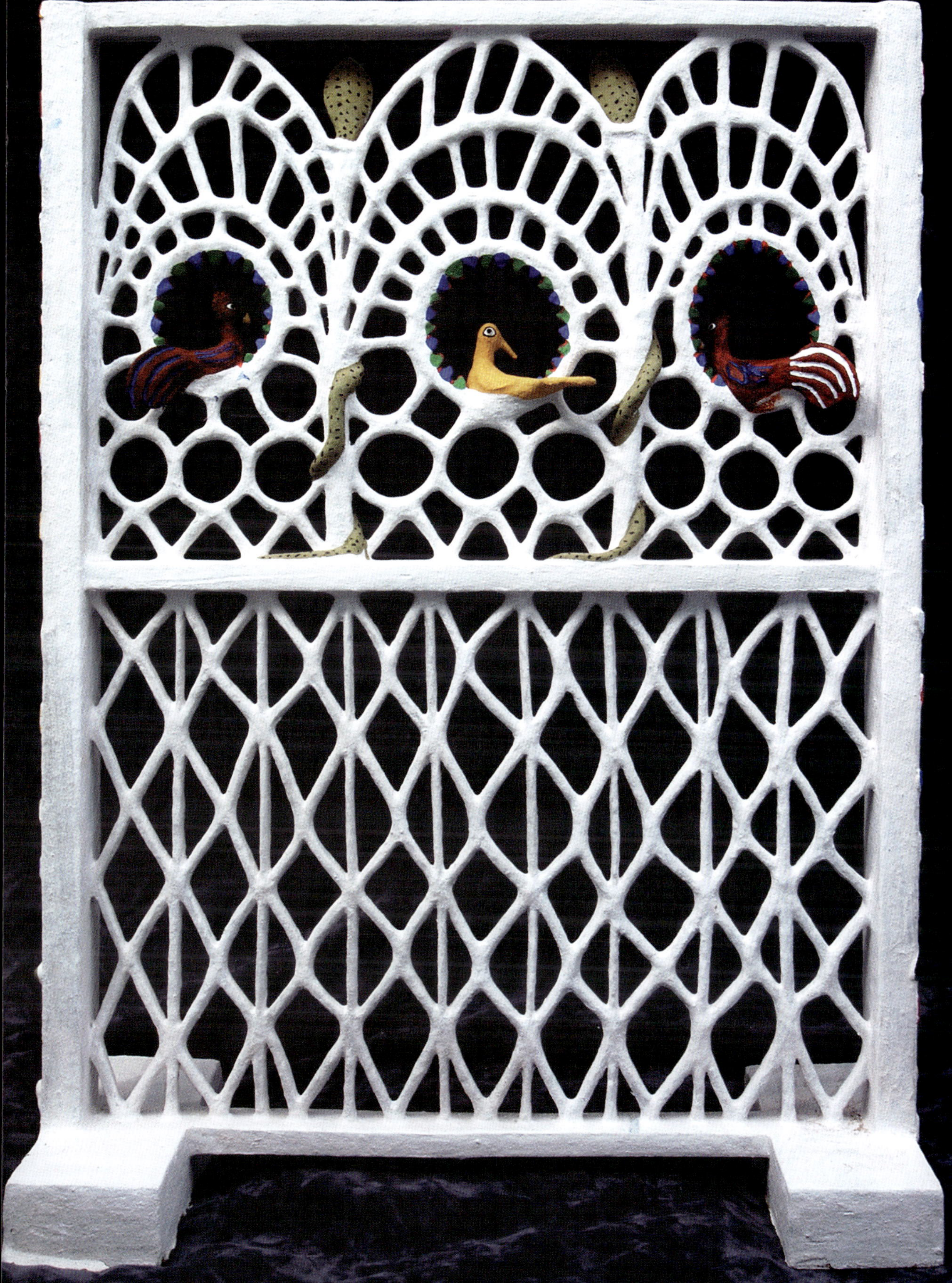

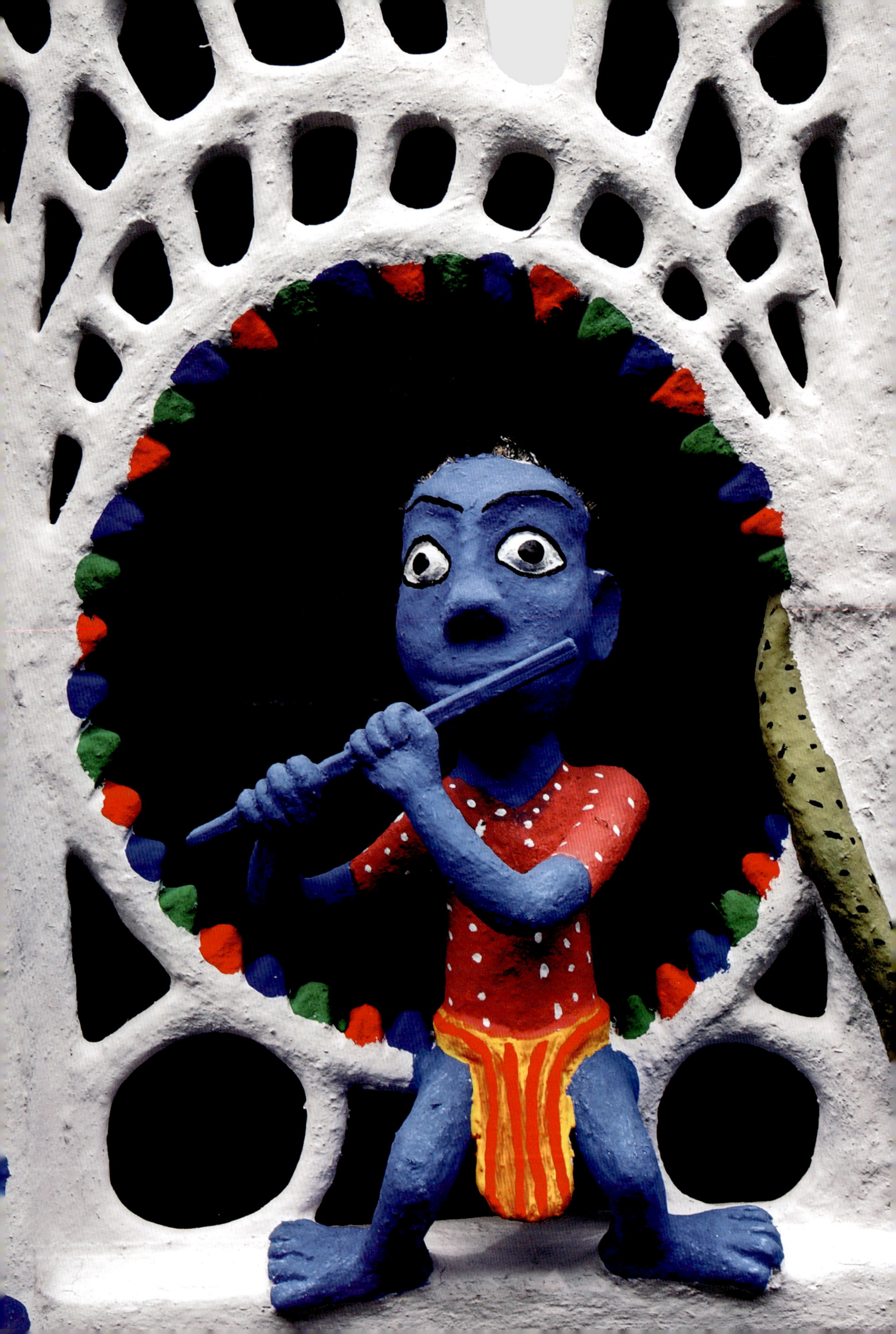

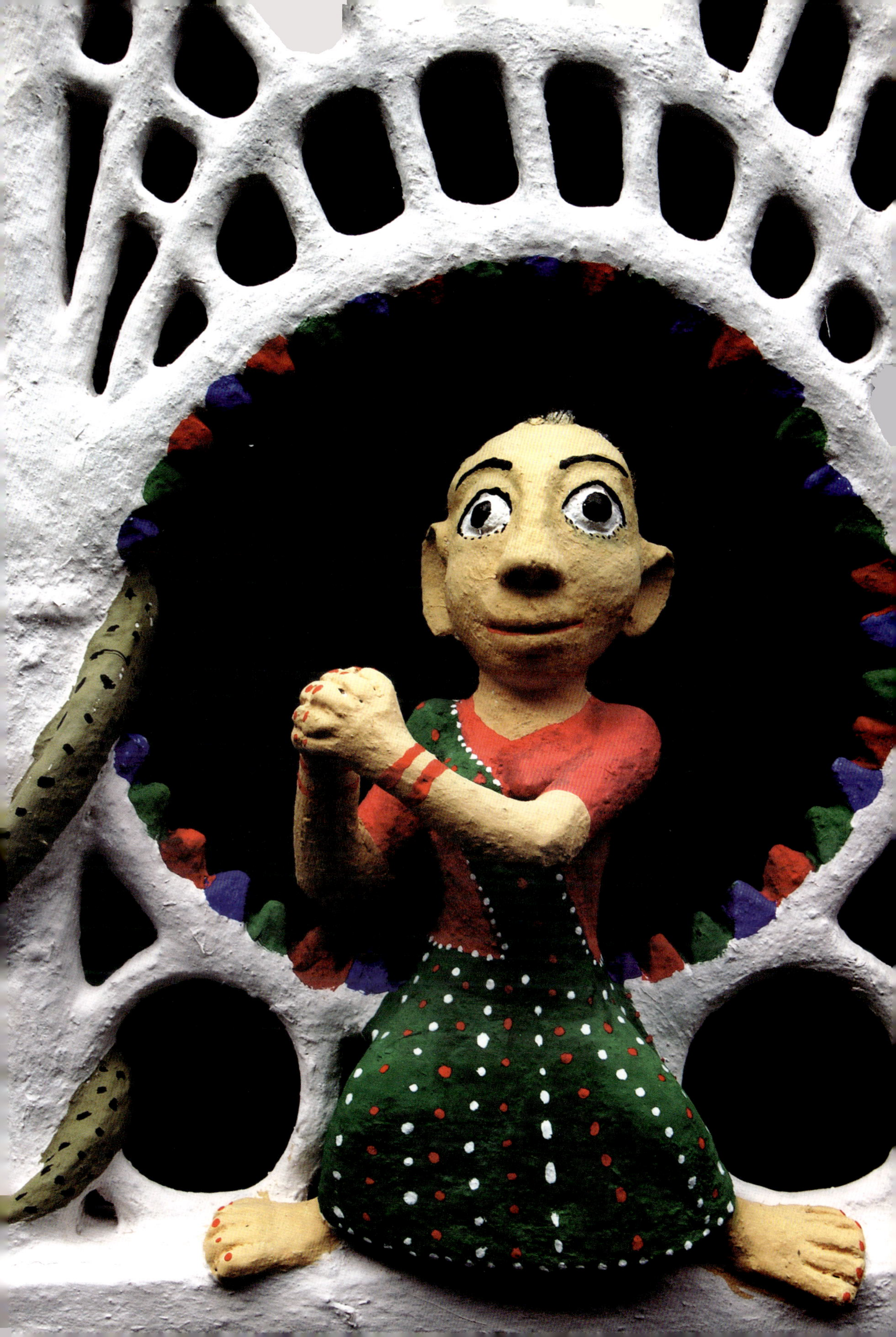

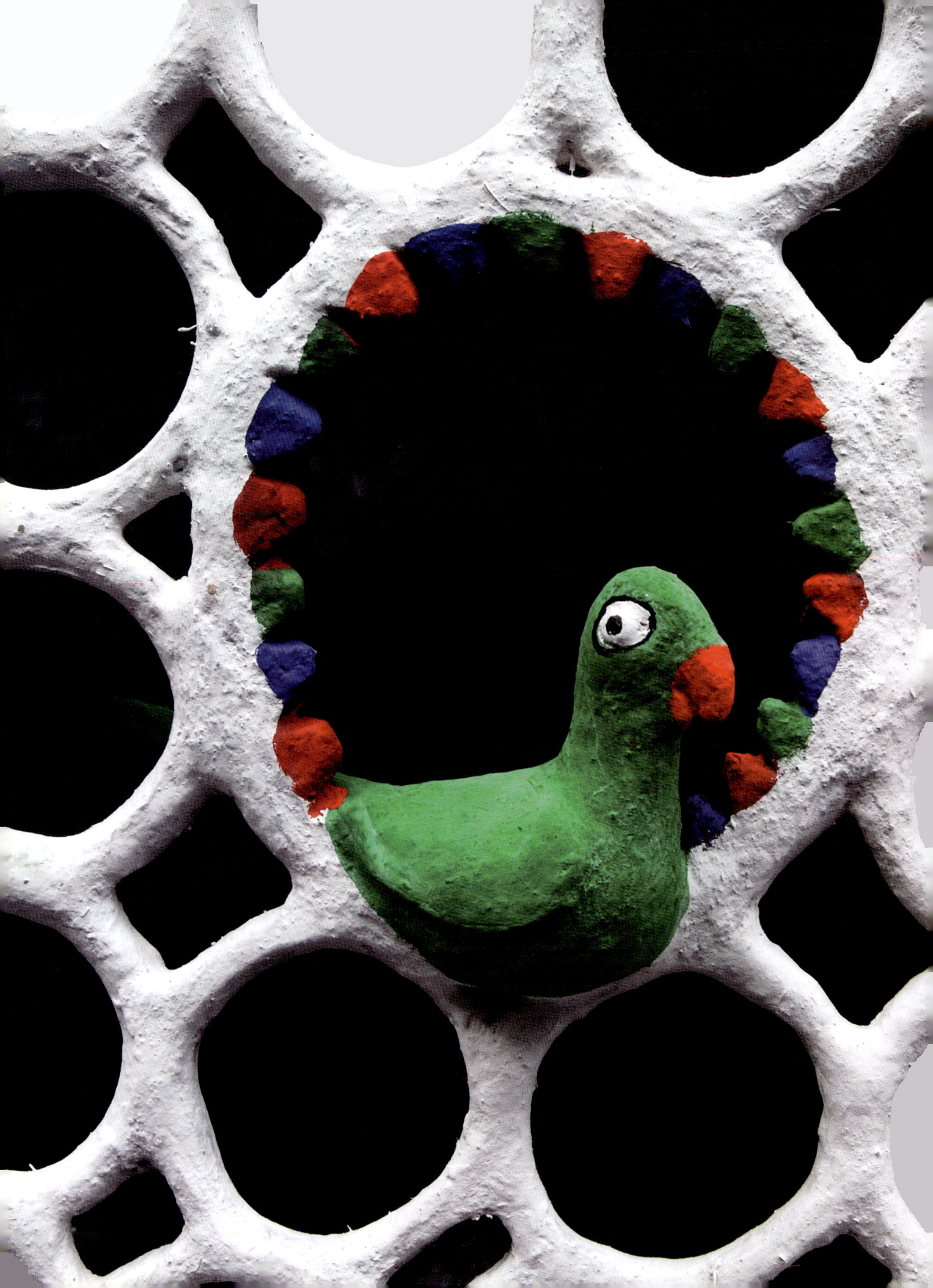

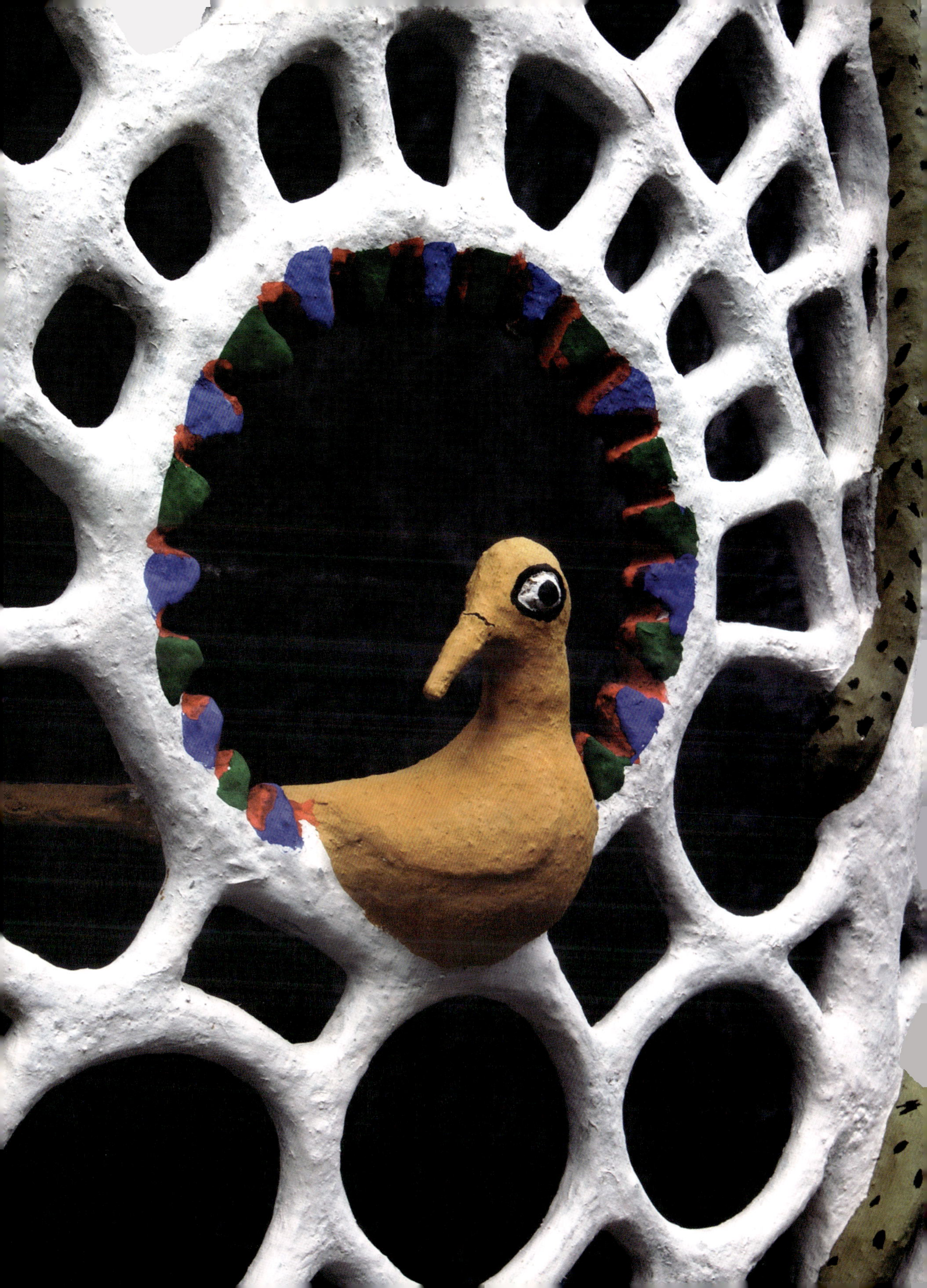

We started by asking Daroga Ram what he and Sonabai might create. (Sonabai was too old and disinterested to concern herself at this early stage.) Although he wanted my suggestions as to what I wanted them to make, I refused. The choice had to come from the two of them. We settled on a price: I paid them generously for twelve days of work. After all, not only were they giving up all other work to create sculptures for us, they were feeding and caring for six virtual strangers in their home. My only criterion was that if they were able to make their sculptures strong enough to travel, I would attempt to ship them to America for an exhibition. Daroga Ram then went into consultation with his mother and Buddhi Ram, his young assistant (a distant cousin who had taken both of Sonabai's government courses).

Sonabai, Daroga Ram and Buddhi Ram chose to create five large pieces for our exhibition: three bas-relief panels, two jali, and one small sculpted grain storage box. First Daroga Ram contacted a carpenter, ordered plywood that was delivered to the house, and supervised the sawing of it into the required dimensions. The three artists began by sculpting the two dance panels. At first it was all a surprise to us: we had no idea what they were creating until each piece unfolded. Sonabai and Daroga Ram bound five stick figures with straw and twine and nailed them in a line across the center of a panel. Buddhi Ram then joined in to help add clay to these figures, fleshing out their heads, bodies and legs. After the faces were pinched into place, coils of clay were added above them as turbans. Now we knew these five figures were men... Separate sticks wrapped with string were added for arms. Next, Daroga Ram spent hours putting small balls of clay onto the tips of thin strips of bamboo that he stuck into the turbans. We could not understand their purpose: they seemed odd and disproportionate! Finally, almost as an afterthought, Rajenbai added a surface of clay to the entire board, and the bas-relief was allowed to dry. As the complete forms began to surface on the panel, we so admired the earthiness of the clay color that we hoped without expectation that they would not be painted.

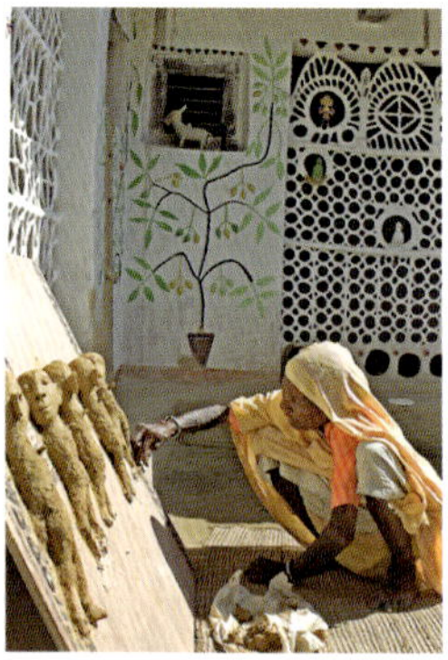

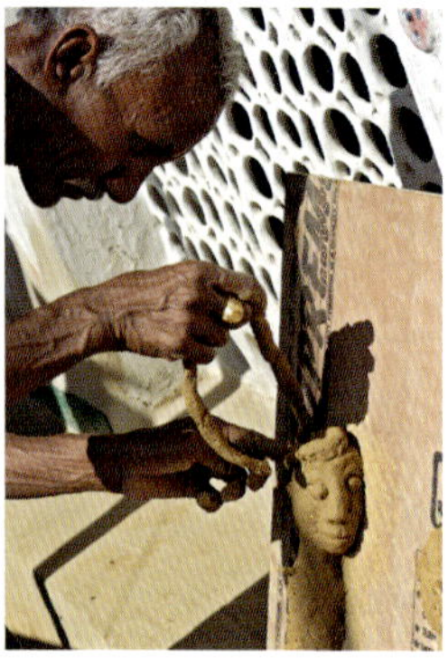

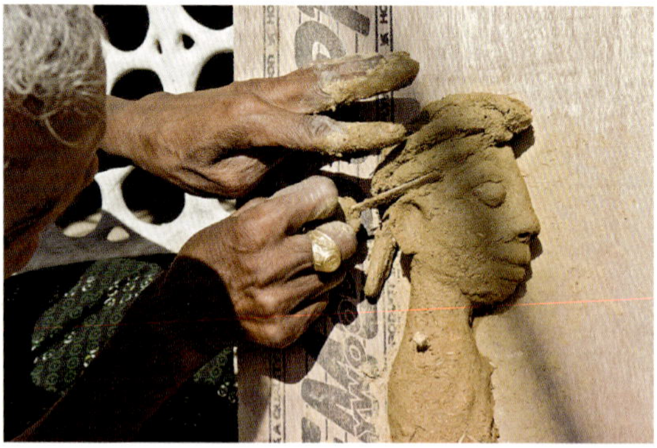

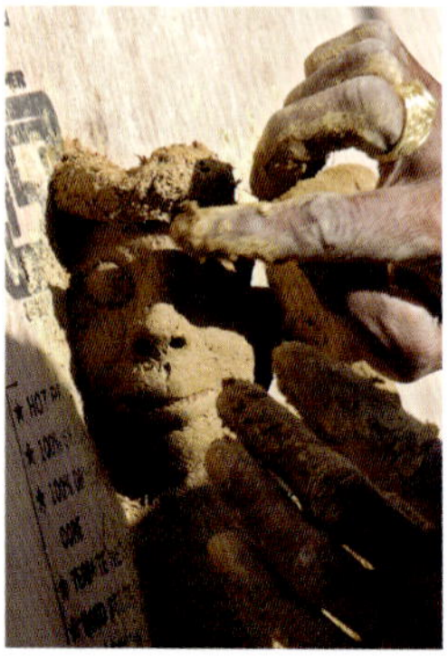

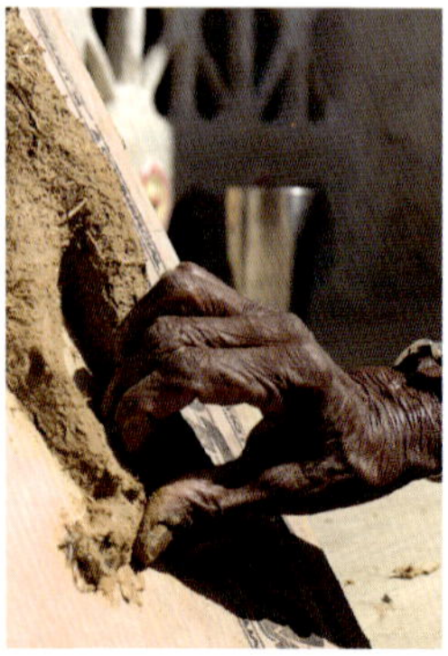

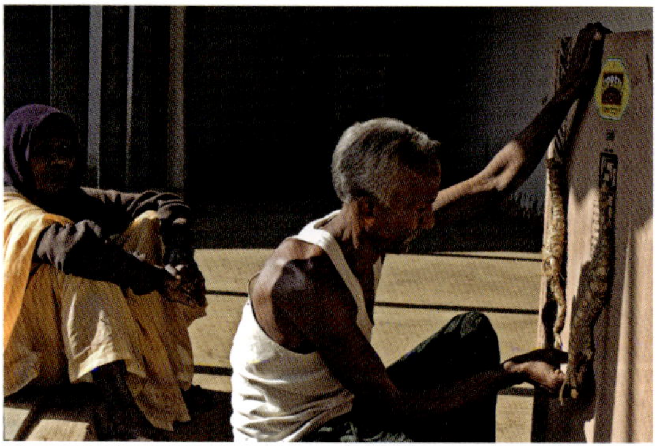

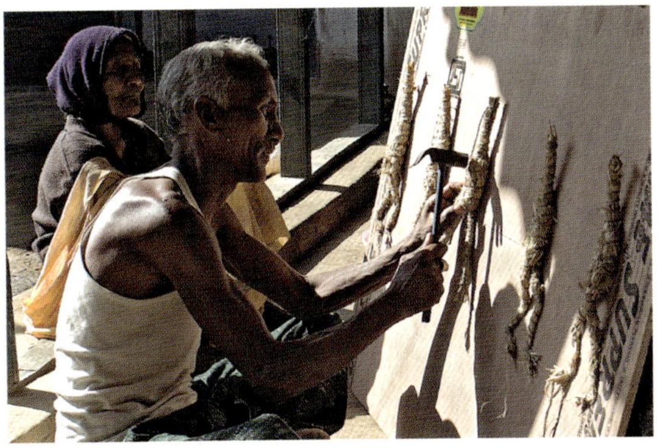
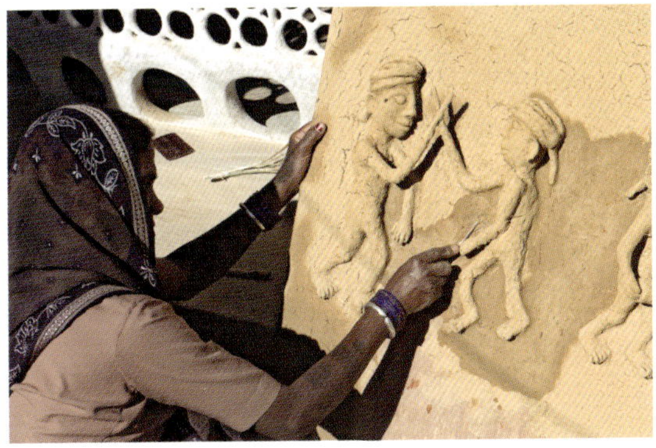
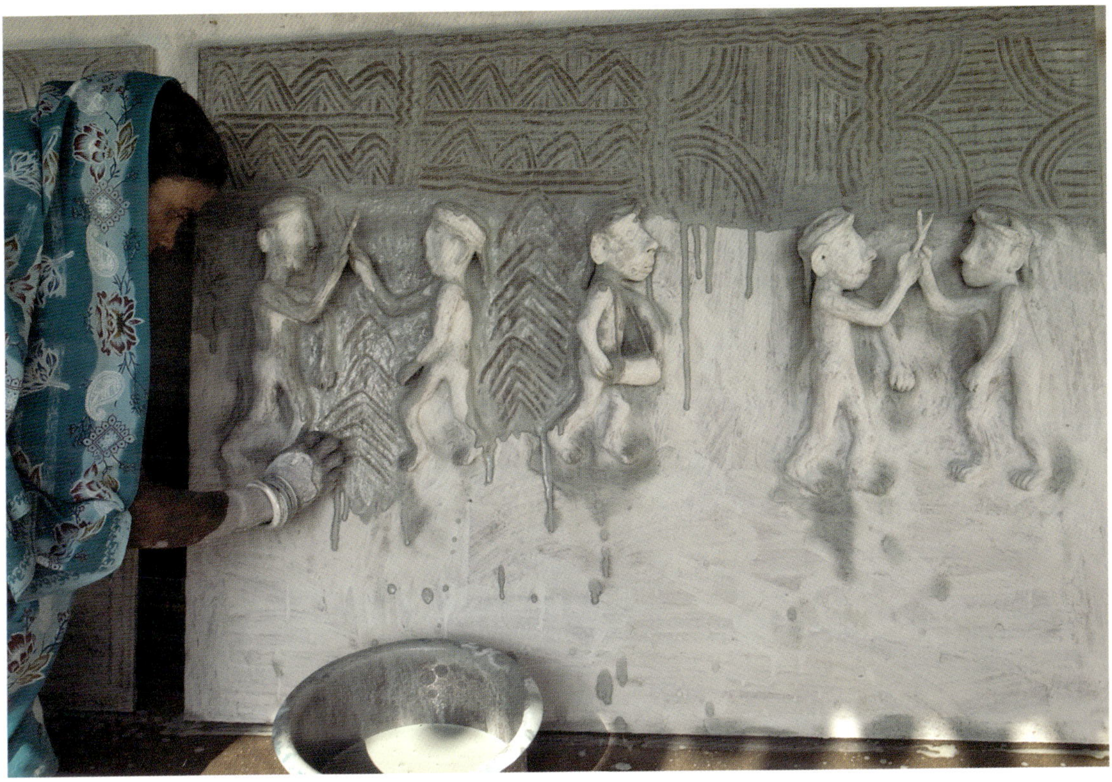
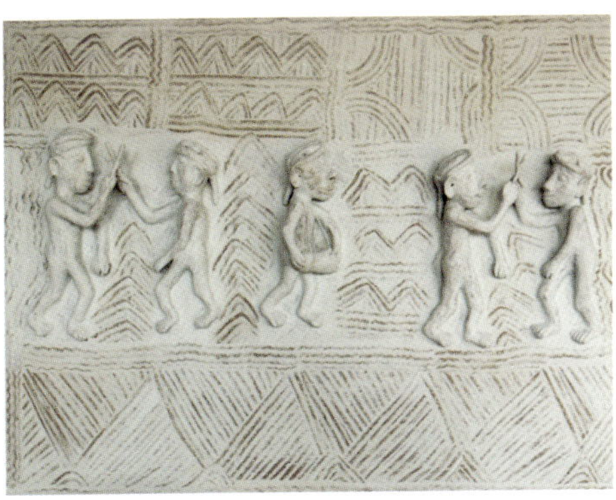
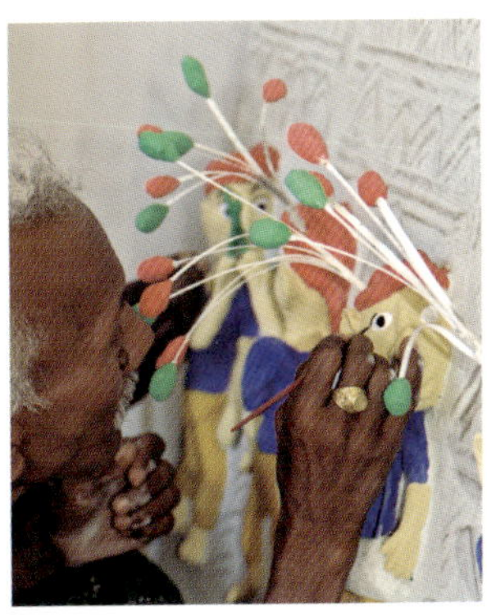
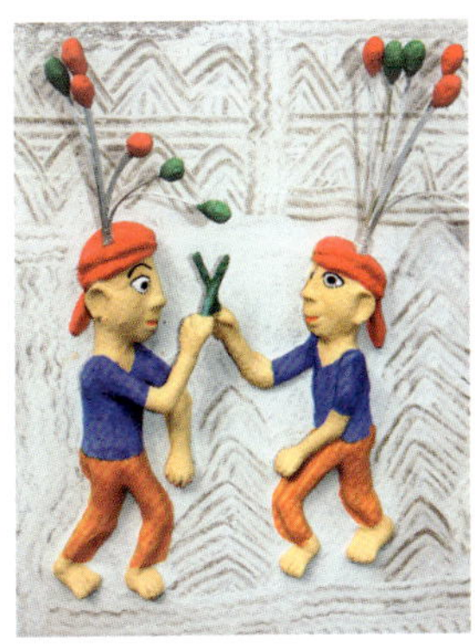

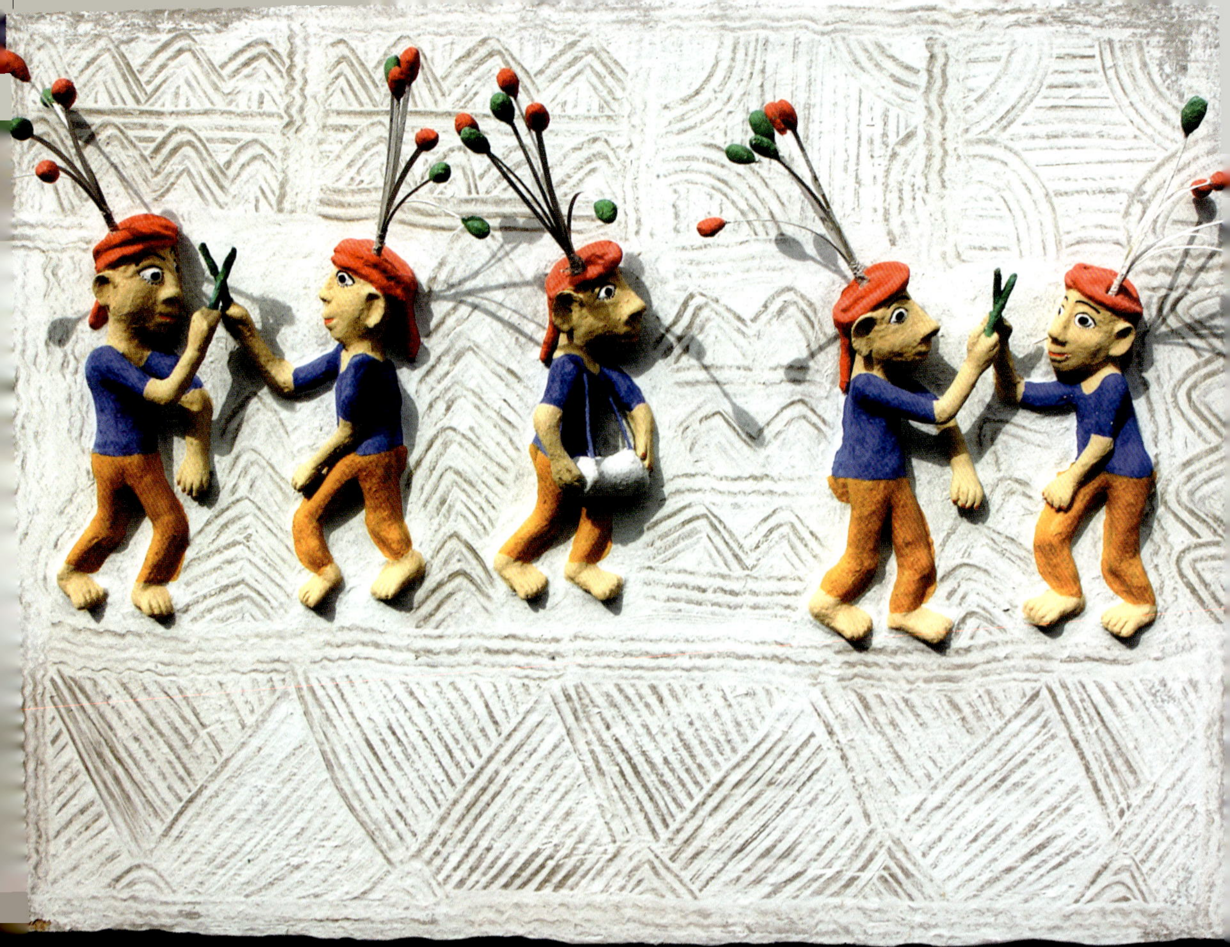

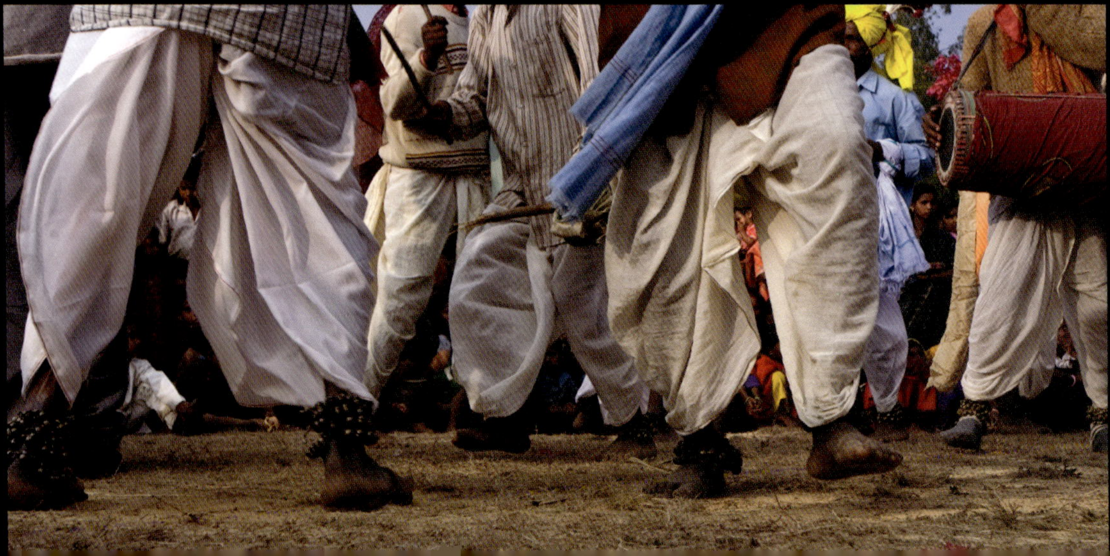

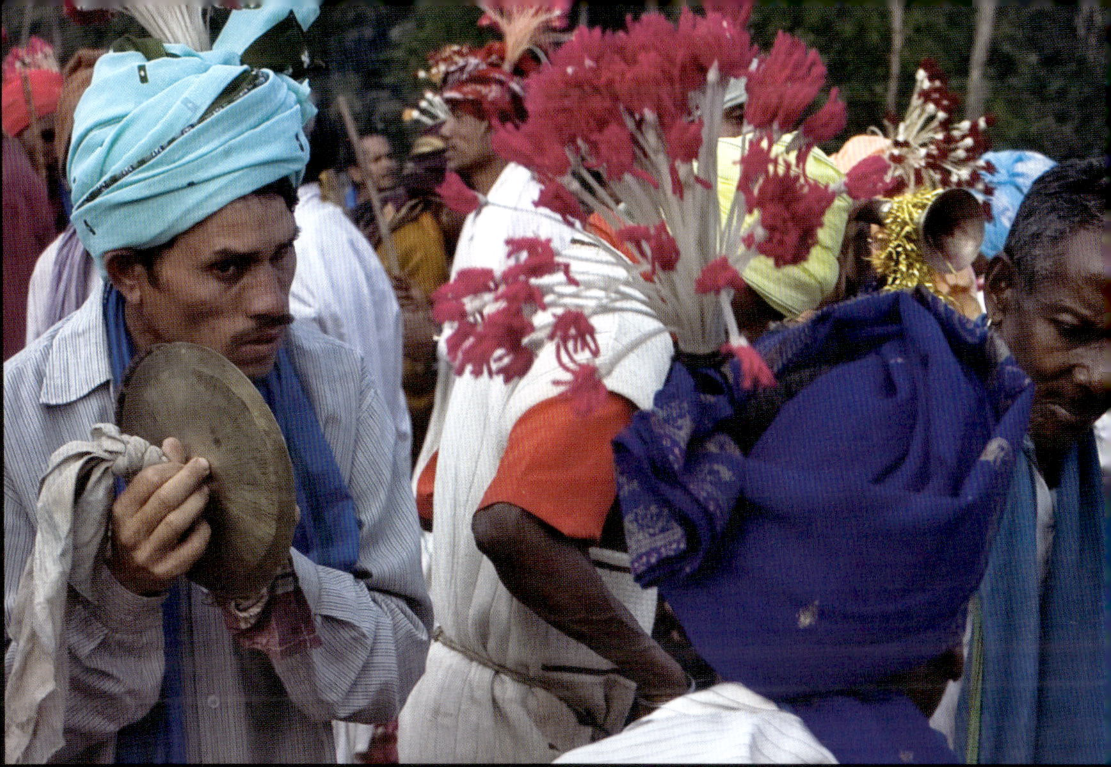
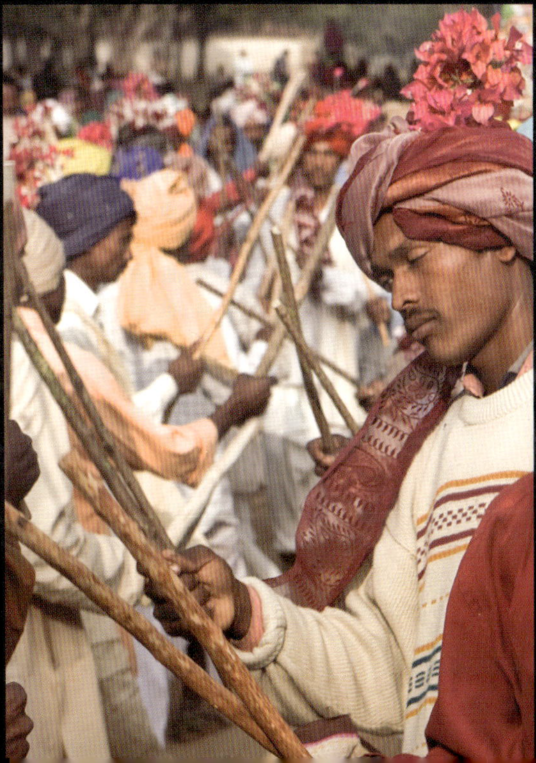
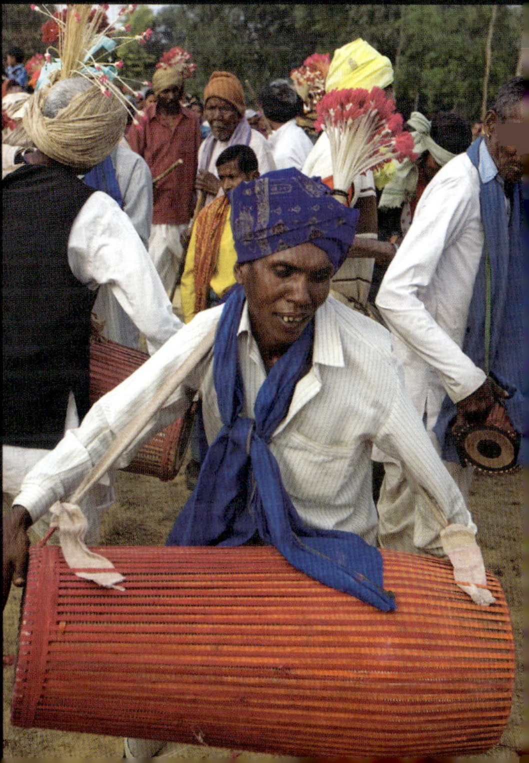

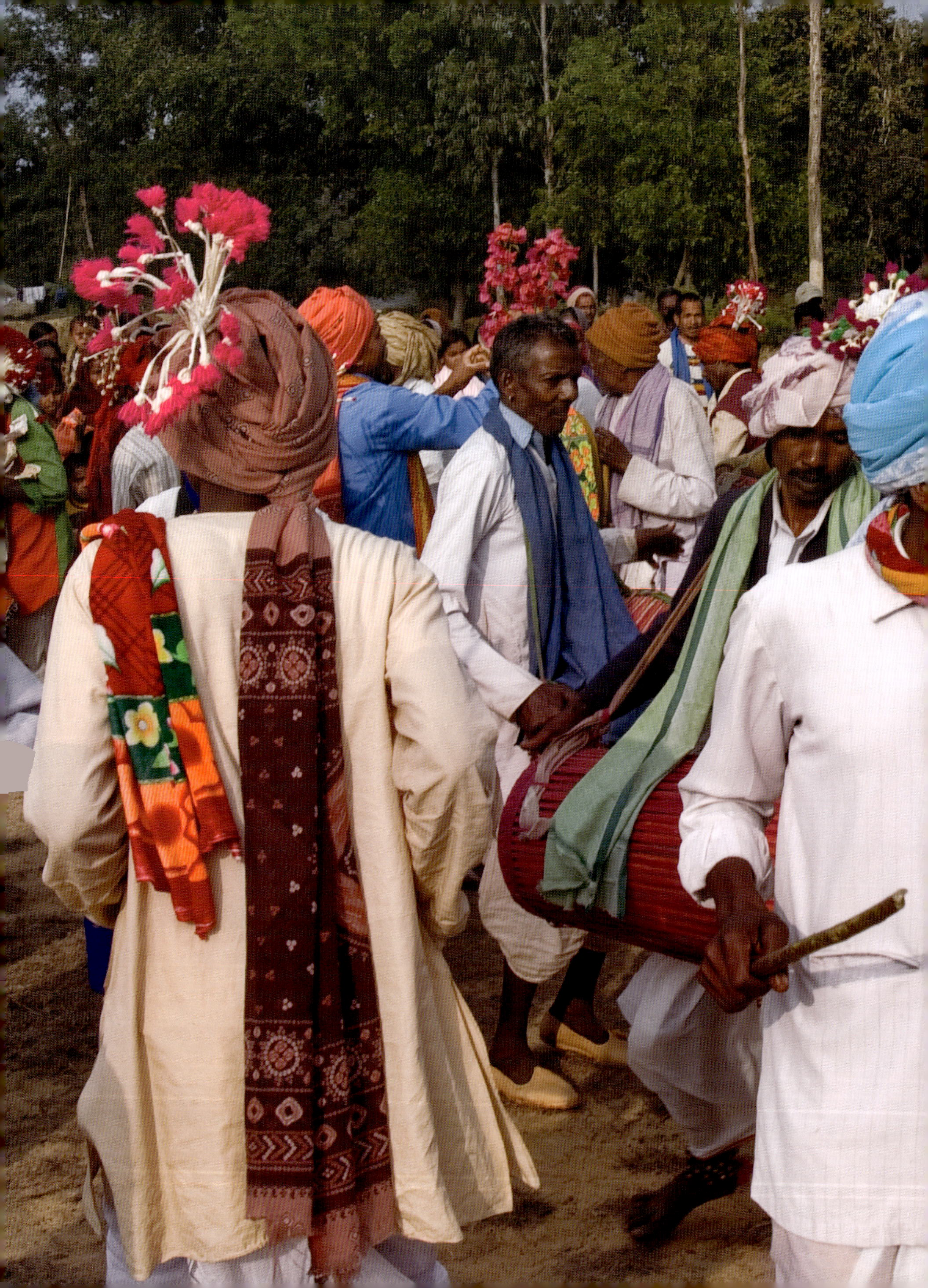

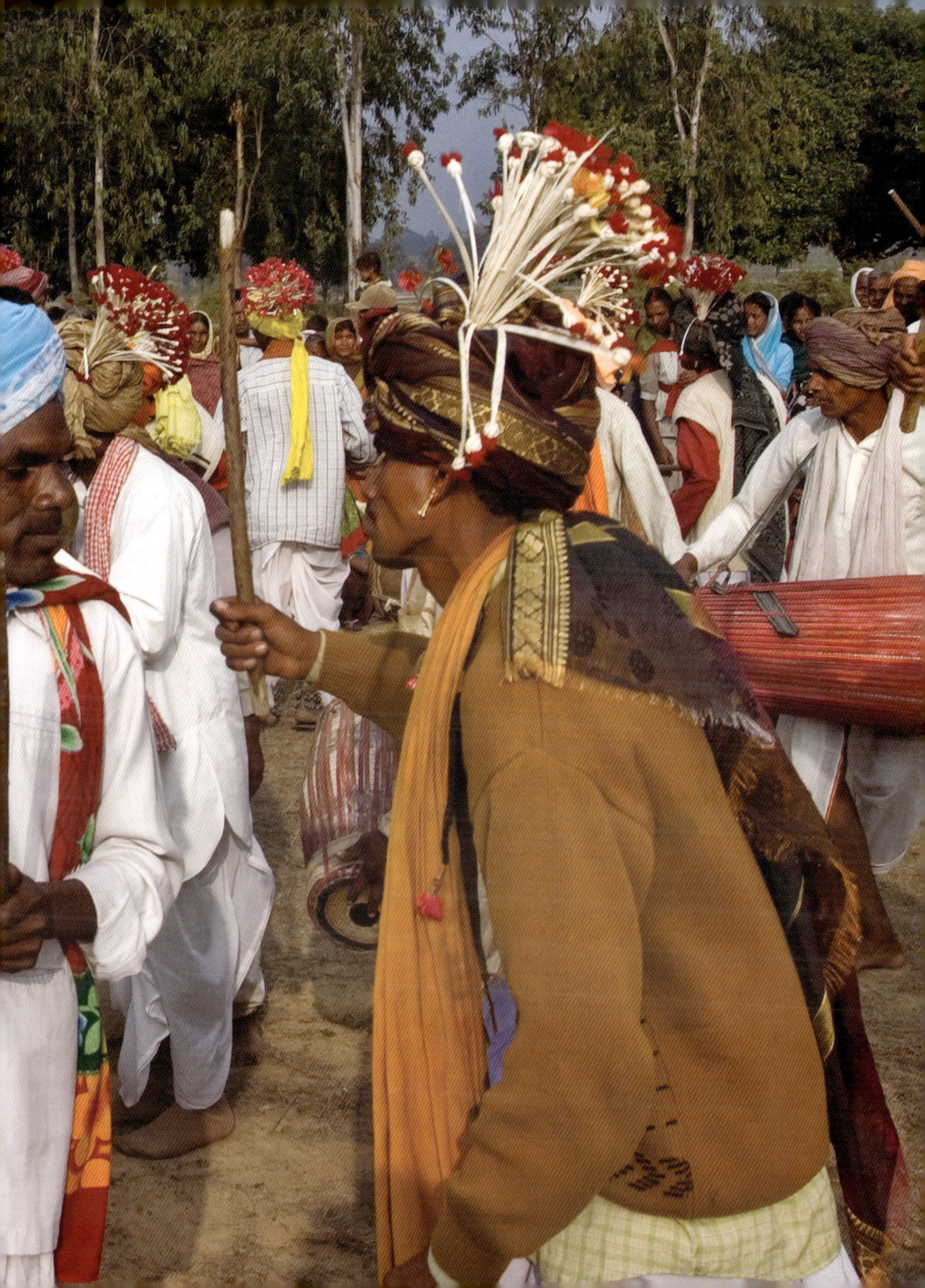

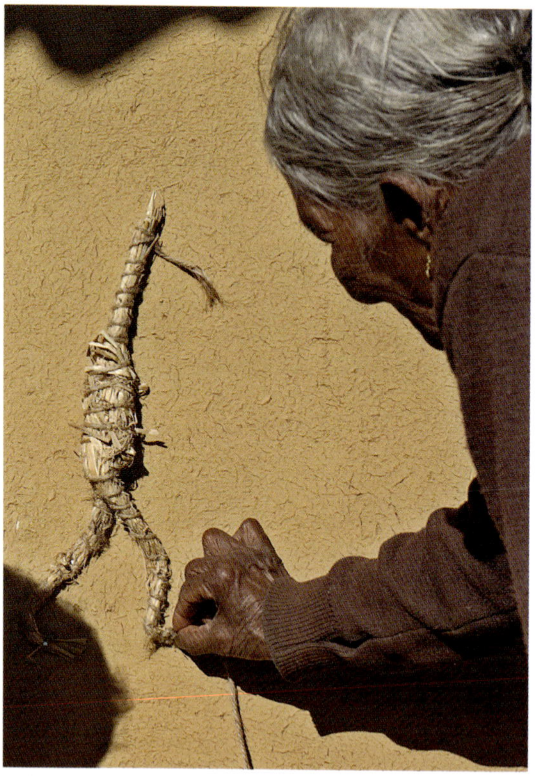

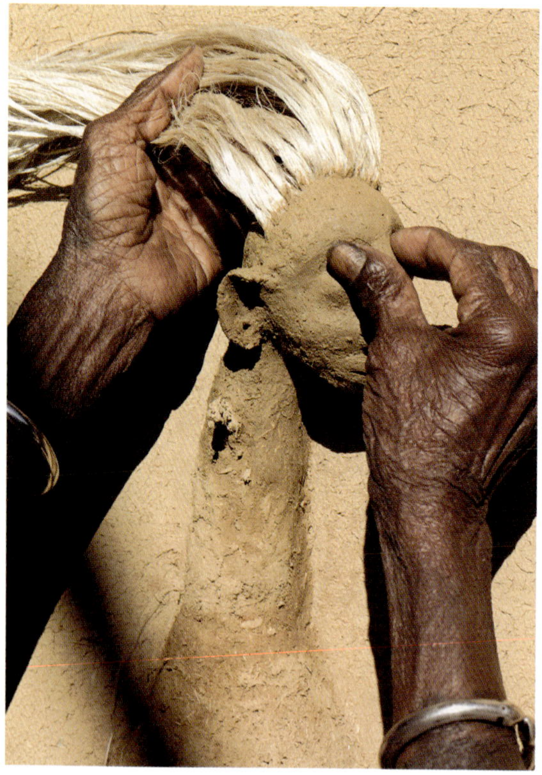

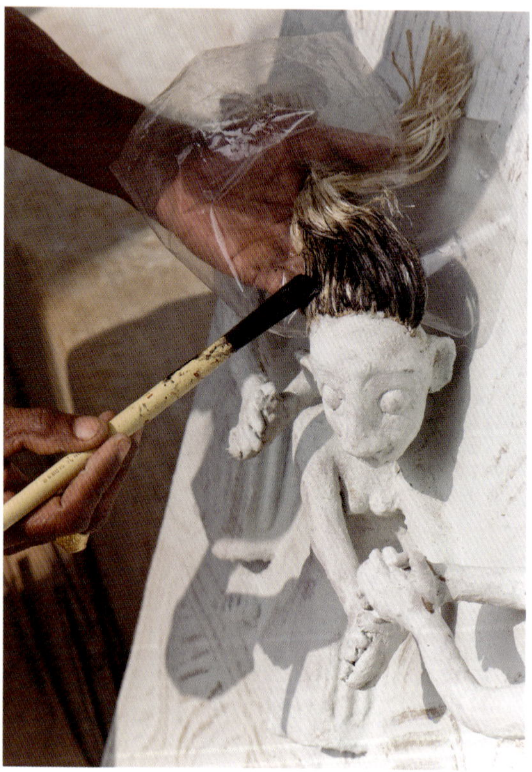

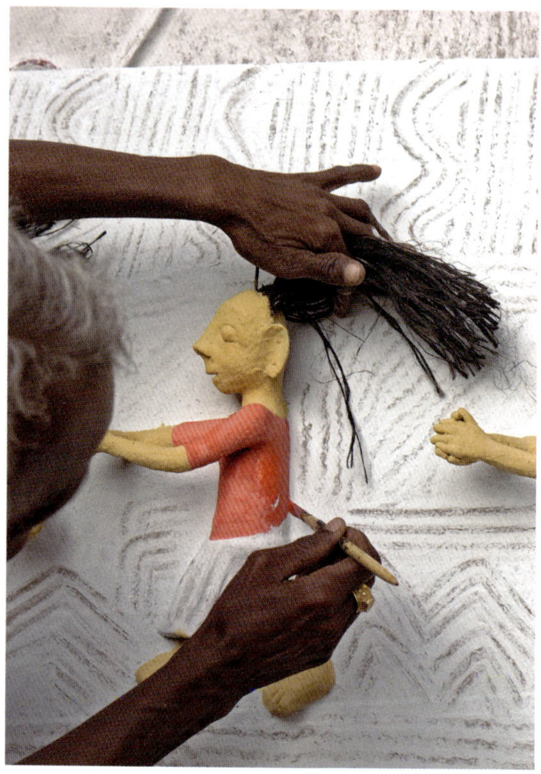

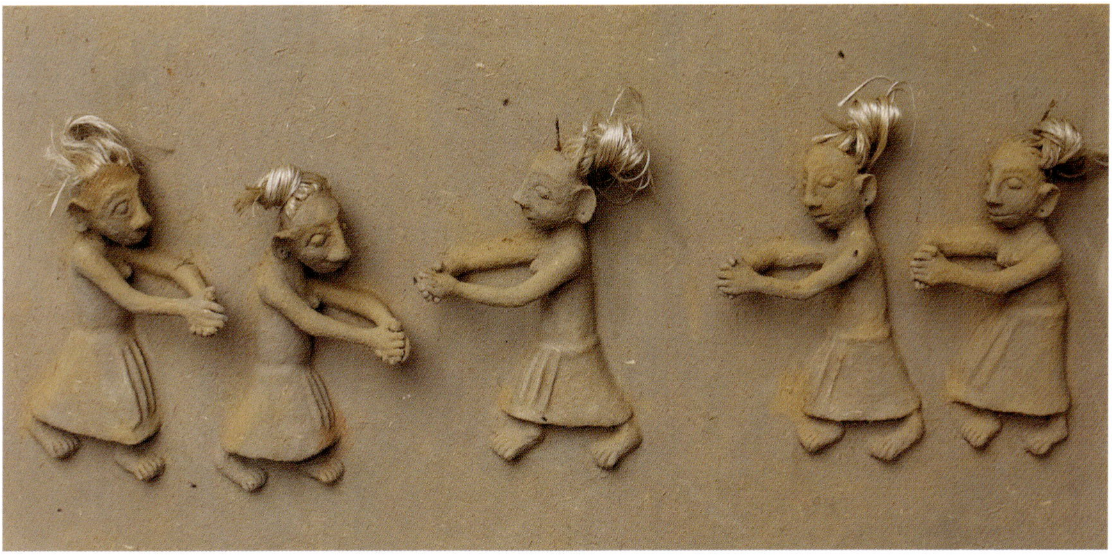

The artists immediately began a second panel that was similar to the first, only this time Rajenbai started by covering the entire surface with clay before the straw figures were nailed to it. We soon saw that these five figures were developing different bodies: they were women dancers, their hands extended as if they were clapping. Daroga Ram spent a long time creating a small clay basket with two tiny birds in it that he placed on the center woman's head. He then cut lengths of hemp rope, unraveling it to create floss-like skeins that he embedded in the scalp of each figure as her hair.

We loved both bas-relief panels but were mystified by them. We were told that they depicted figures from the rice harvest dance usually held at the local Chherta festival on the full moon day of December. The sculptures were so lively that David and I longed to be able to film and photograph the festival itself as their complement. But the season was wrong: we had missed the festival by two months. When Daroga Ram saw our sad reactions to this news, he suggested that he ask the villagers if they would be willing to re-enact the harvest dances for us. They responded positively to his proposal and set the date for seven days later.

Every day for the next week we returned to the village. Each day we walked around it photographing, filming and talking to villagers. We often heard drums in the distance, but never once did we see anyone practicing the dance. They were, though…well out of our sight! When Sonabai's family was not sculpting, we would ask them questions about their lives and work. We occasionally walked to either Bhagat Ram's or Sundaribai's or Parbatibai's house to document their work and their lives.

In the meantime, the work in Sonabai's studio continued. While the dance sculptures were drying, the three artists began to sculpt a third panel (a marvelous tree filled with monkeys picking fruit), two free-standing *jali* and an elaborately sculpted three-tiered box that was a replica of a much larger grain storage container. We closely documented the details of each production.

When the panels were dry, Sonabai and Rajenbai evenly whitewashed the entire bas-reliefs and then, while they were still wet, Rajenbai took a cloth soaked in whitewash, letting it drip through her fingers as she drew intricate finger designs on the back walls of each. Daroga Ram then masked the area around each female dancer's hair with plastic and used a brush to paint it with commercial black pigment. He used other brushes to paint each figure in bright colors and the panels were done. They were superb and well worth exhibiting in the U.S.

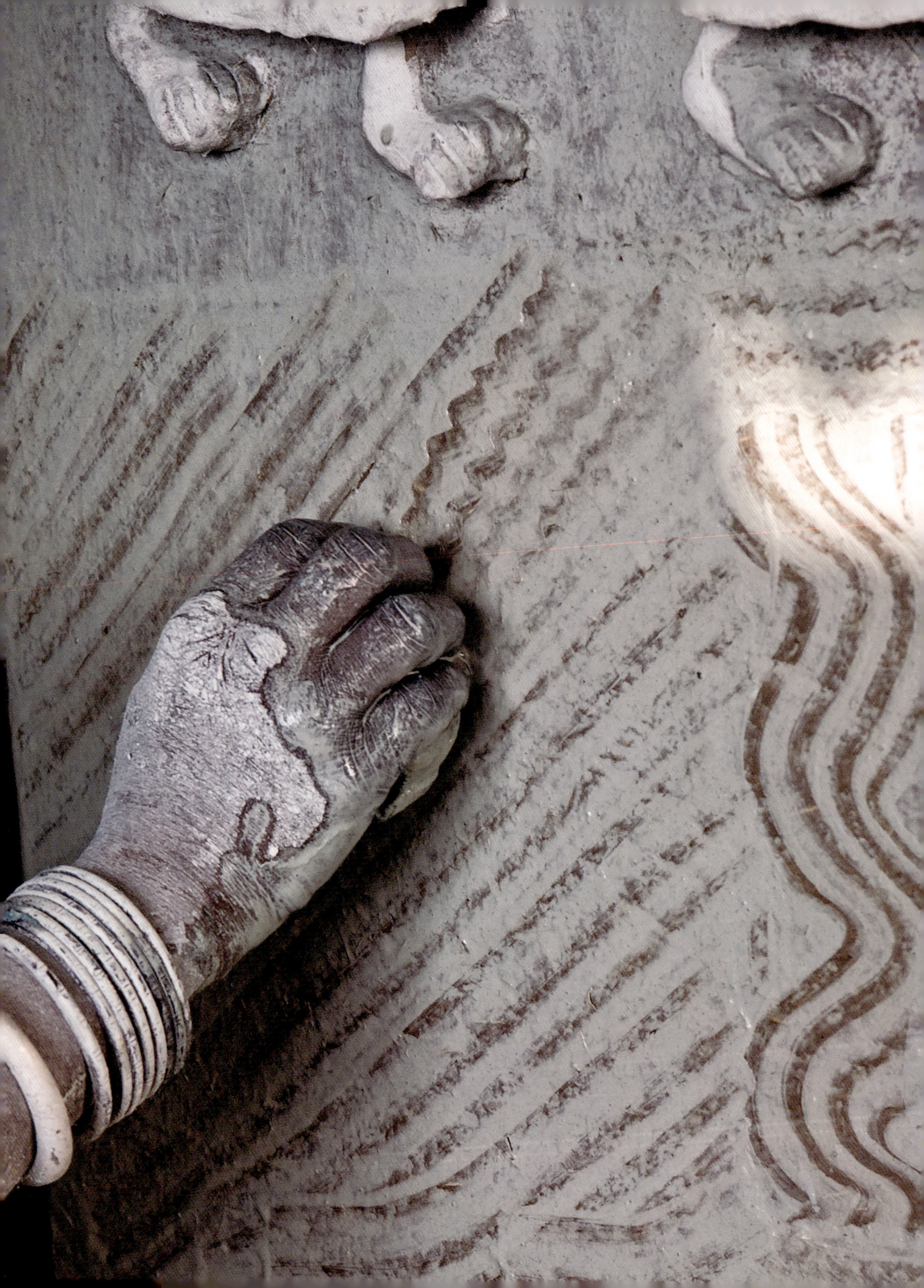

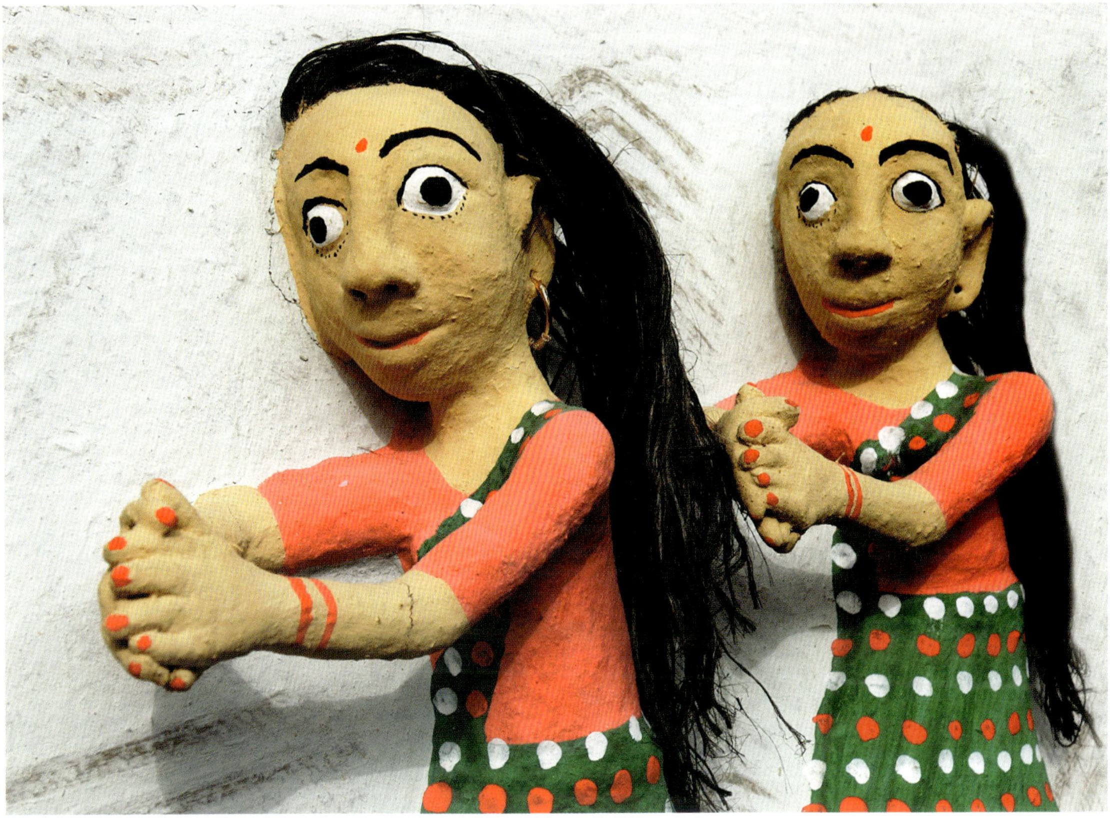

At noon on the seventh day after Daroga Ram had spoken to the villagers, we heard drums approaching Sonabai's house. Hundreds of people were slowly coming down the road from the last village houses. In the center we could see swirling flashes of bright color that, as they drew closer, turned out to be a line of about sixty men, all wearing brilliant turbans, each carrying a stick with which he would twirl and beat rhythmically against the stick of the opposite dancer. Men no longer habitually wear turbans in Surguja District. The custom completely died out several decades ago. So, for this dance, each had made his turban out of one of his wife's saris tightly wrapped around his head. Each turban was completely different: one block printed, one flowery, another striped, many solid and some brocaded. In each turban were suspended brightly colored pompoms on the ends of painted peacock feather quills or bamboo strips that bounced and twirled as the men danced. The music was percussive, cacophonous. There were drums of every size from small hand-held tom-toms to large pot drums, long horns, short horns, whistles and flutes. Each man had rows of small bells tied to his ankles.

Surrounded by their laughing, clapping families, the men whirled, pranced, cracked their sticks, and danced down the lane, past Sonabai's house, and around into a large threshing field about seventy-five yards beyond. These were the figures in the first dance panel! Daroga Ram, Sonabai and Buddhi Ram had captured their movement, color and spirit precisely. Even those silly pompoms made sense. By this point there must have been more than a thousand locals joining in the spectacle! David and I were right in the middle of them, filming and photographing their turbans, their hands, their swirling motions. I even lay with my camera on the ground photographing their feet while they danced all around me! It was an extraordinary experience!

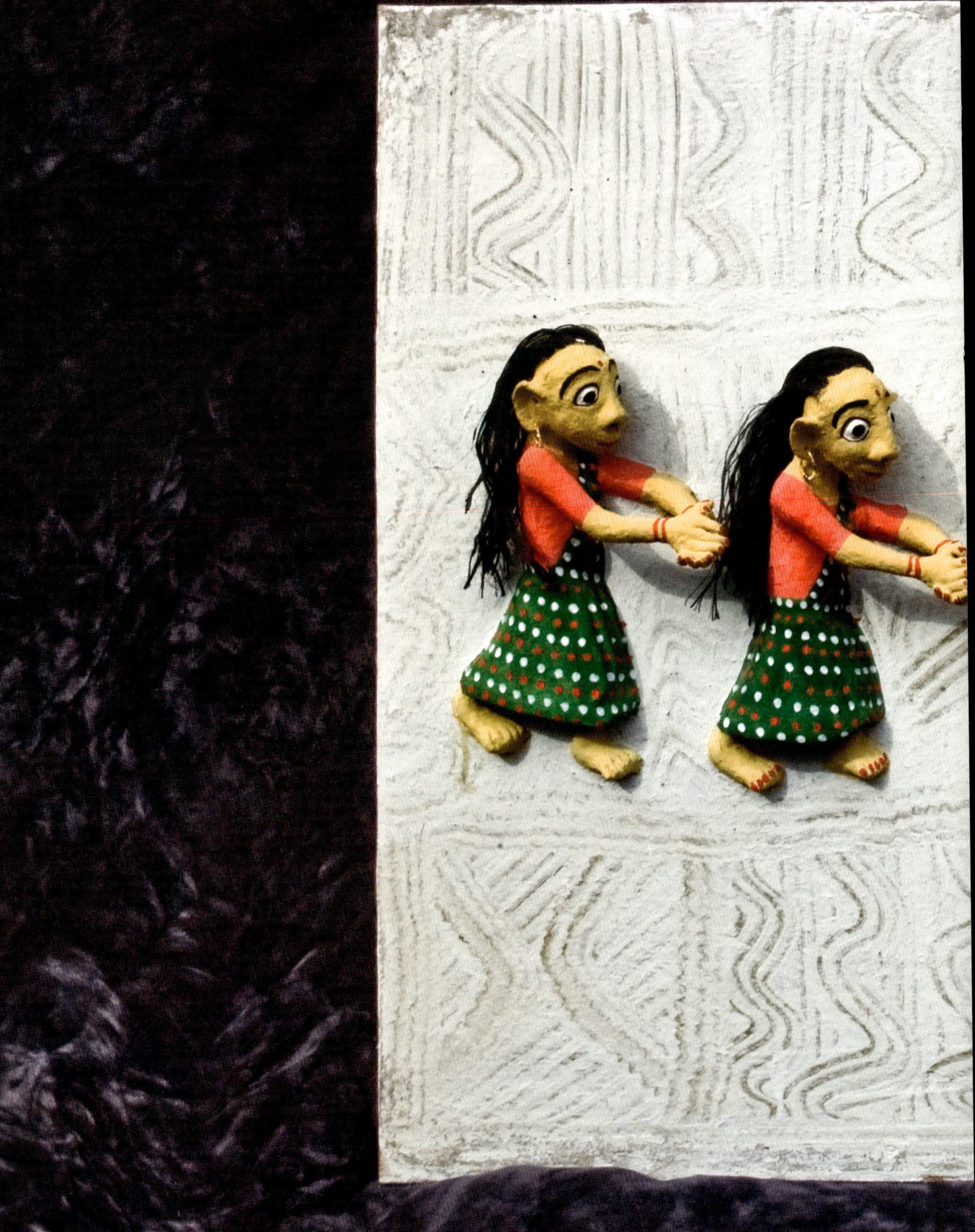

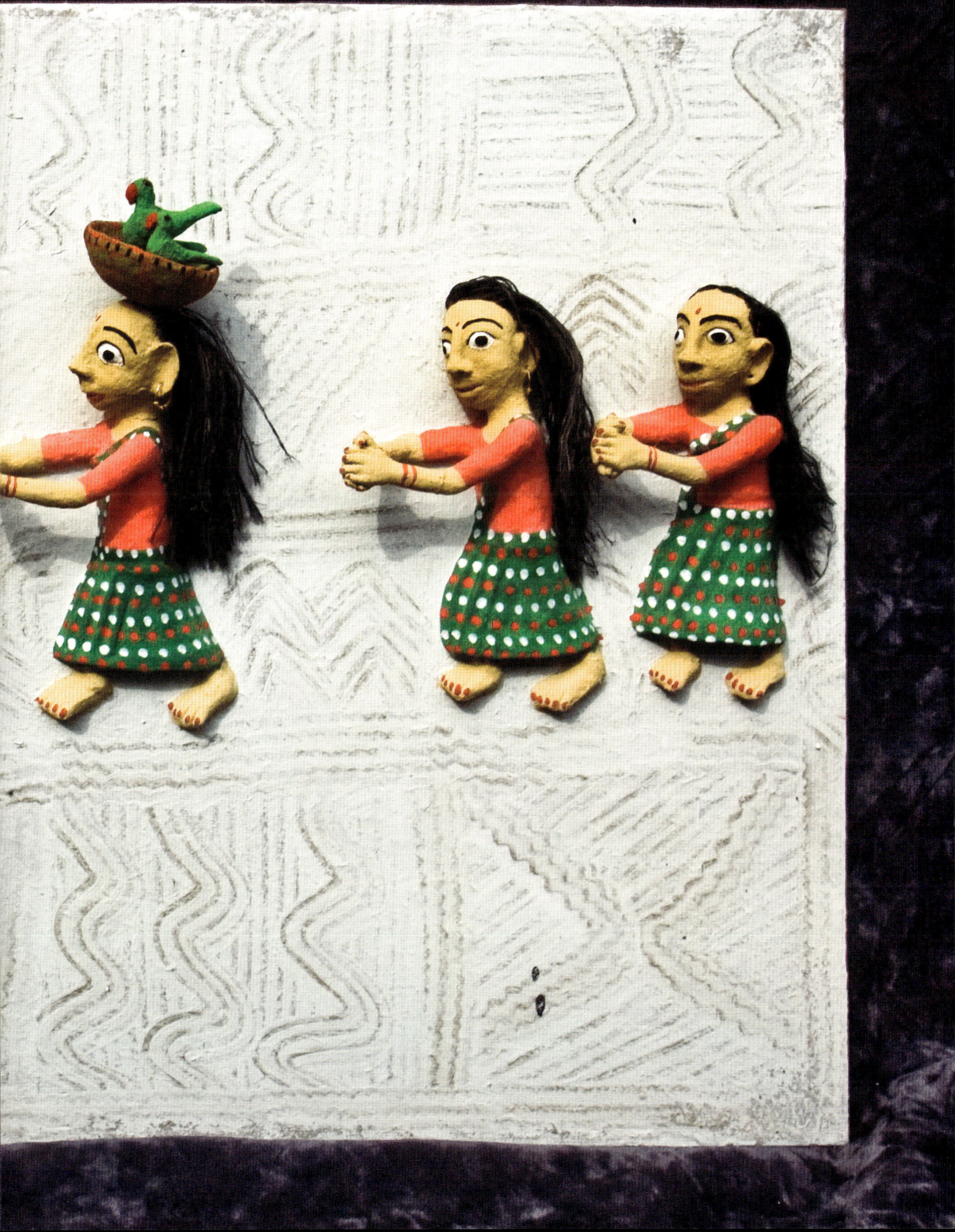

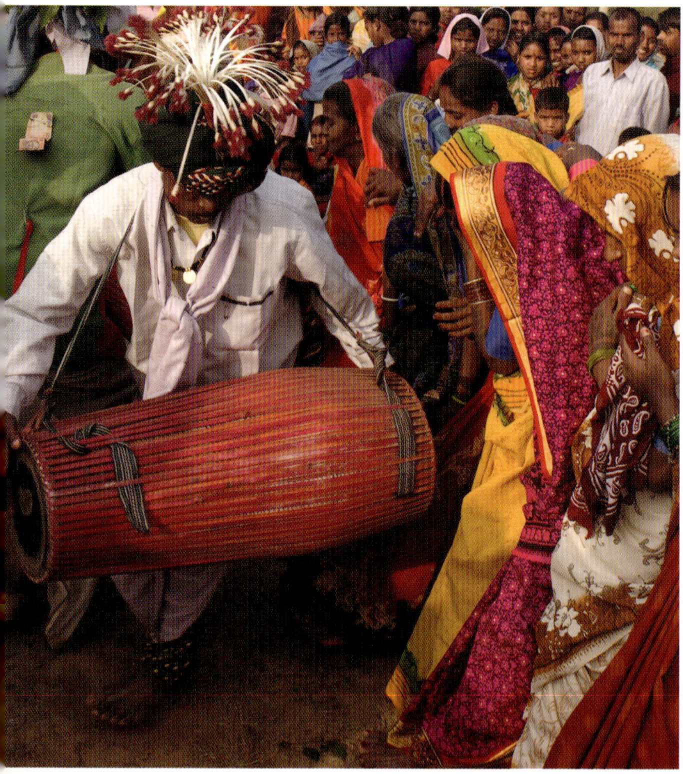

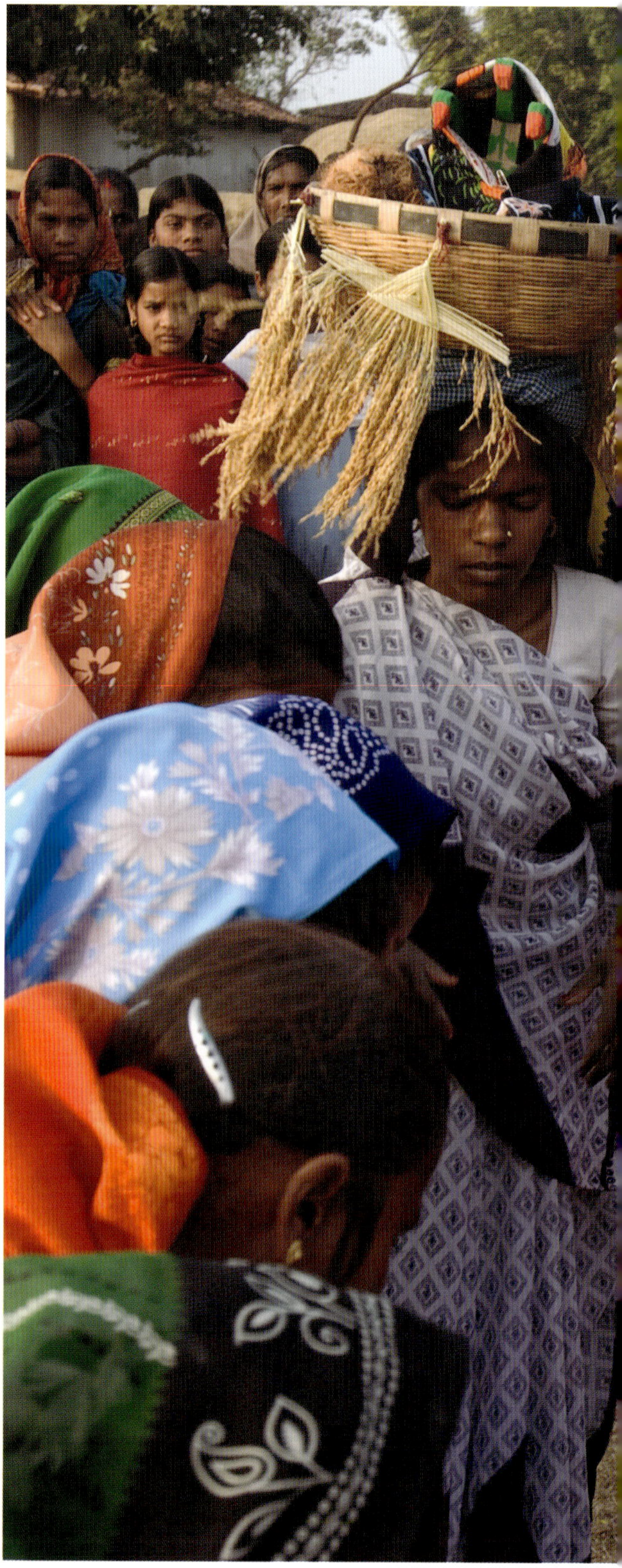

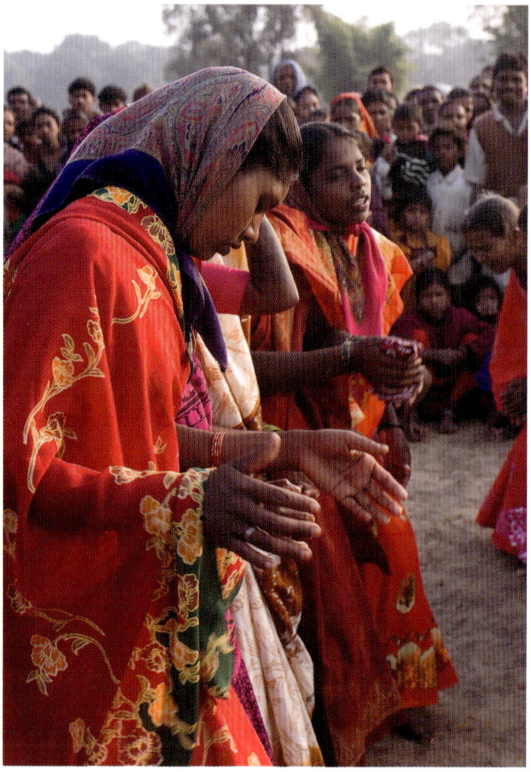

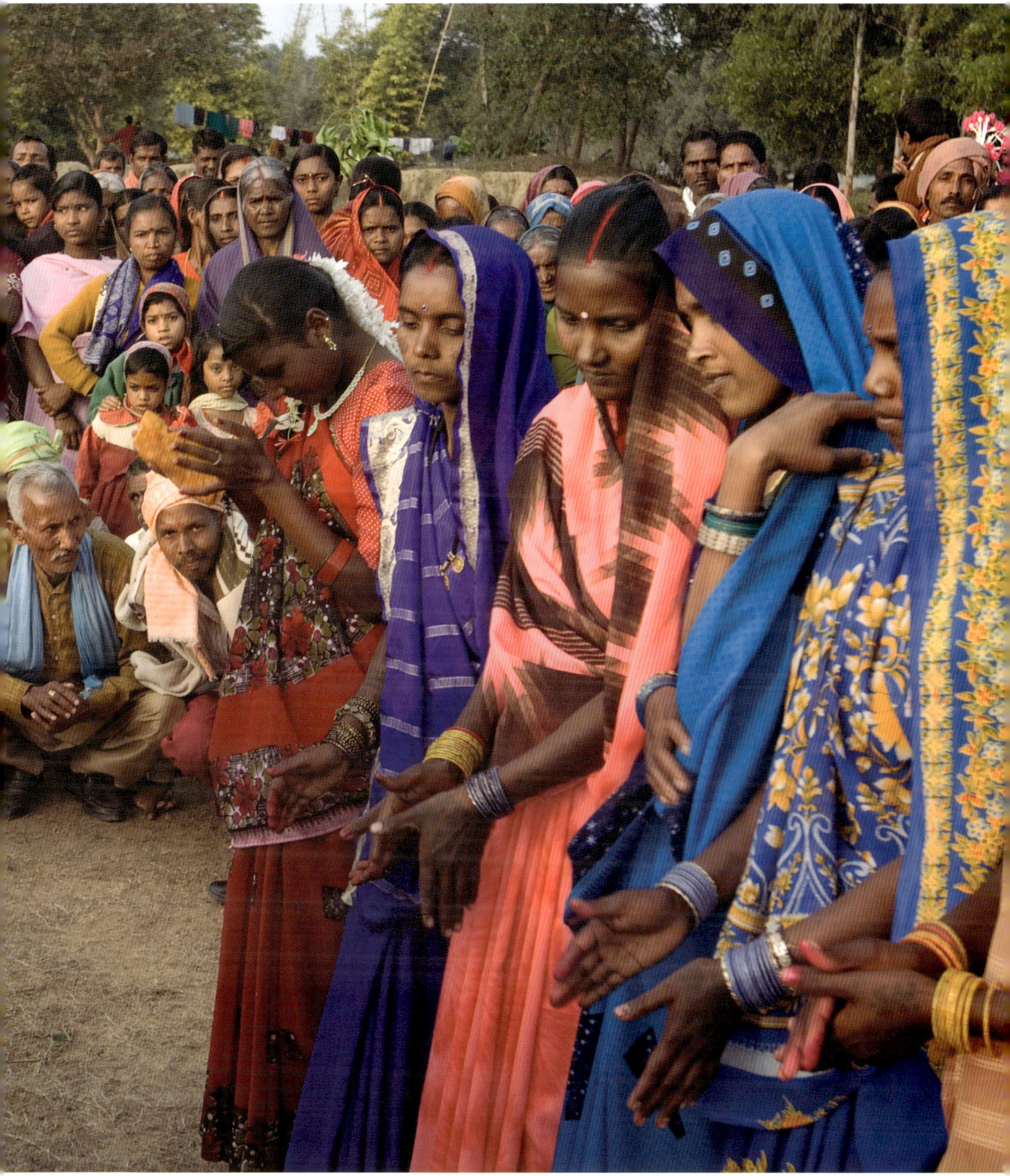

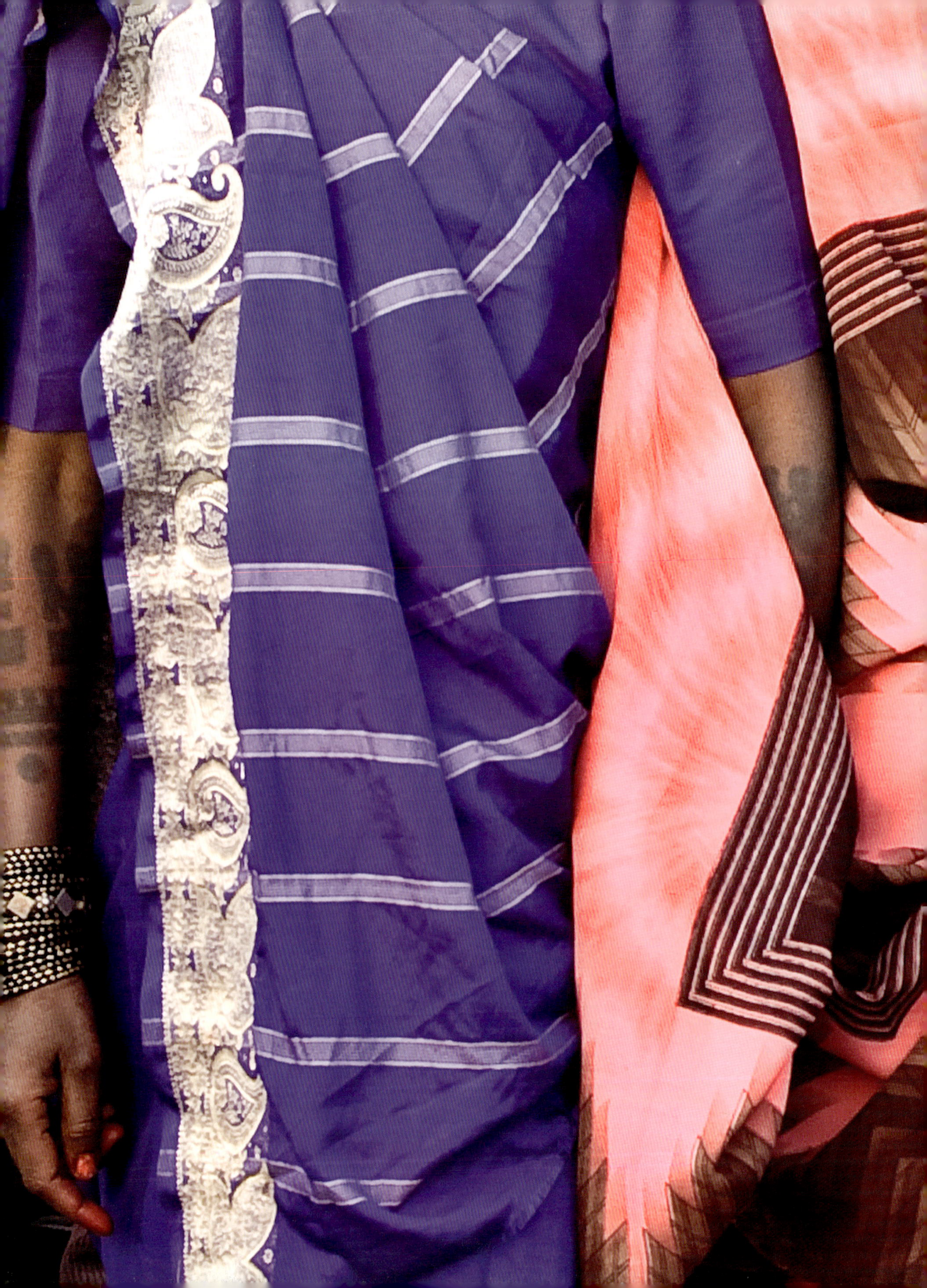

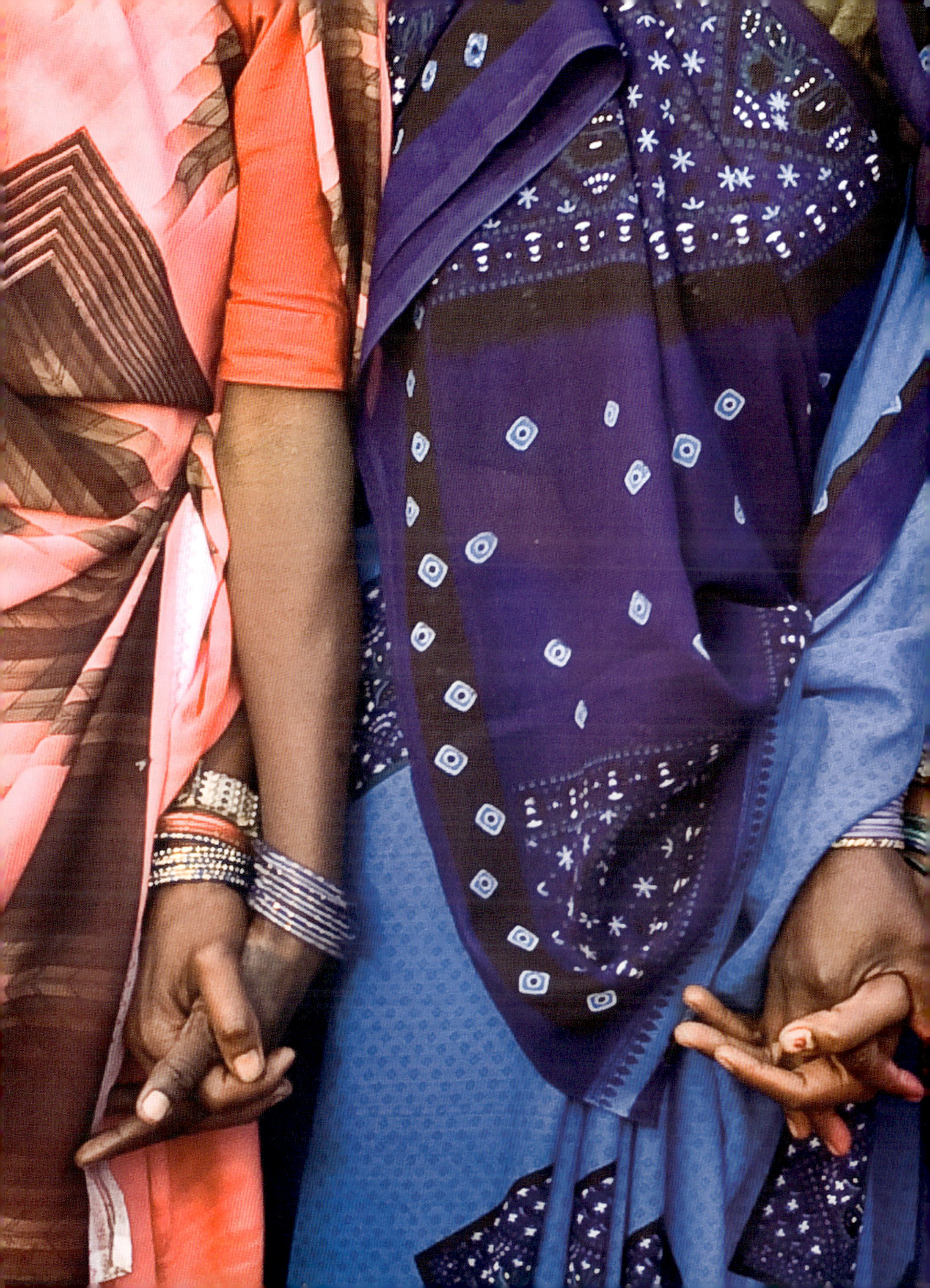

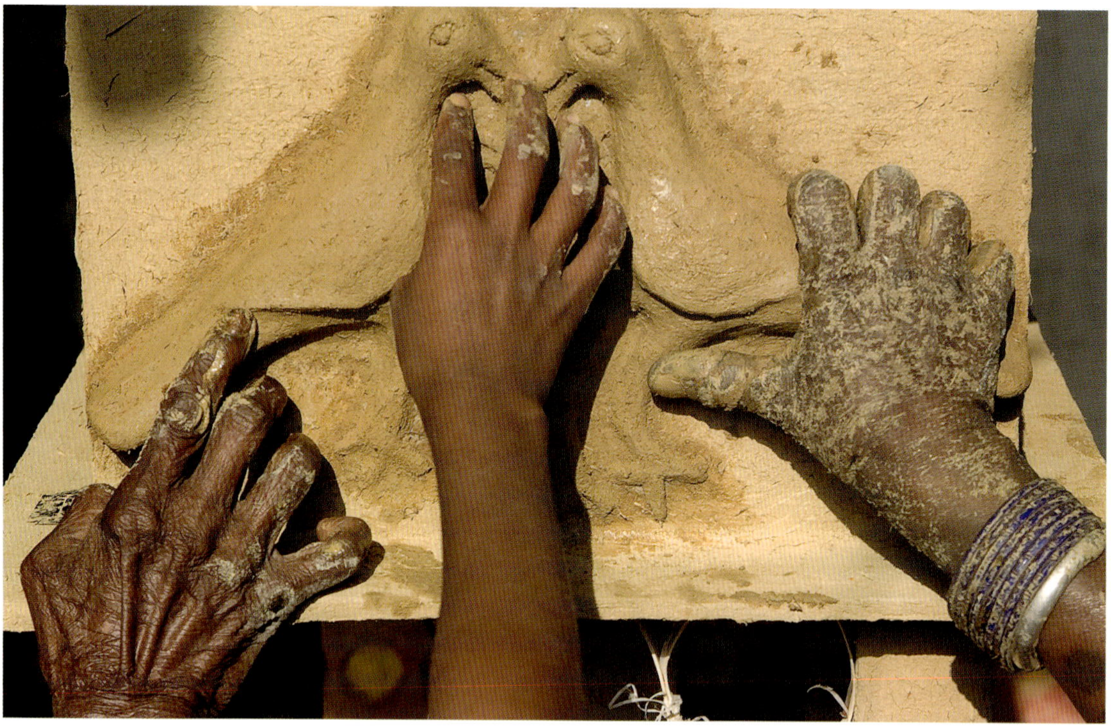

And then the women snaked out from the crowd... They were all dressed in their finest silk and synthetic saris: bright pink, yellow, red, orange, green and blue, with the ends covering their heads. Each of the thirteen women had her arms around the one next to her. Accompanied by male drummers and horn players, the women sang a high-pitched song as they shuffled their bare feet back and forth, frontward and backward, undulating around the field. It was beautiful, moving, primordial. Except for the new prints on some of their machine-made saris, they could have been dancers in almost any time in history. After almost an hour, the dancers stopped and regrouped into two lines of six women separated by a corridor about five feet wide. A threshing basket filled with unhusked rice appeared from within the crowd. On its exterior sides were fastened four intricate hangings woven of rice stalks with the rice still clinging to them. Three painted wooden parrots were placed in the center of the basket; then the entire assemblage was blessed in prayer by Daroga Ram and Sonabai and placed upon the head of the thirteenth woman who stood in the

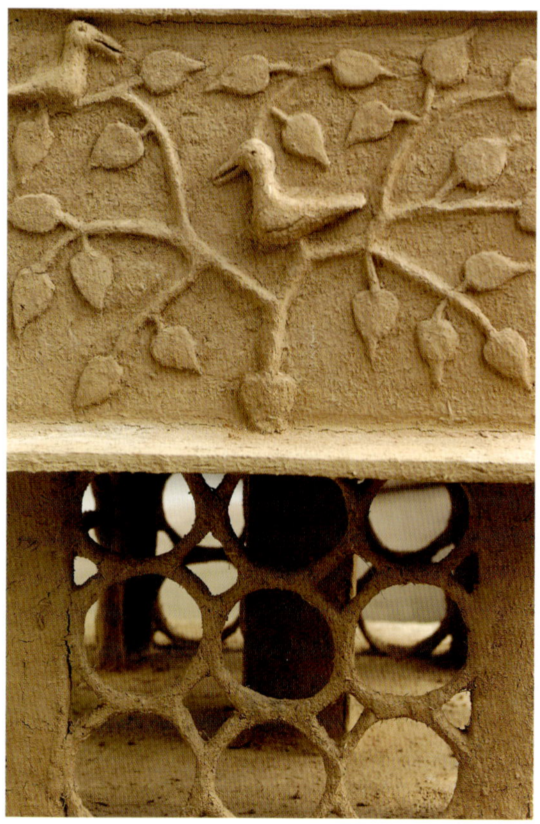

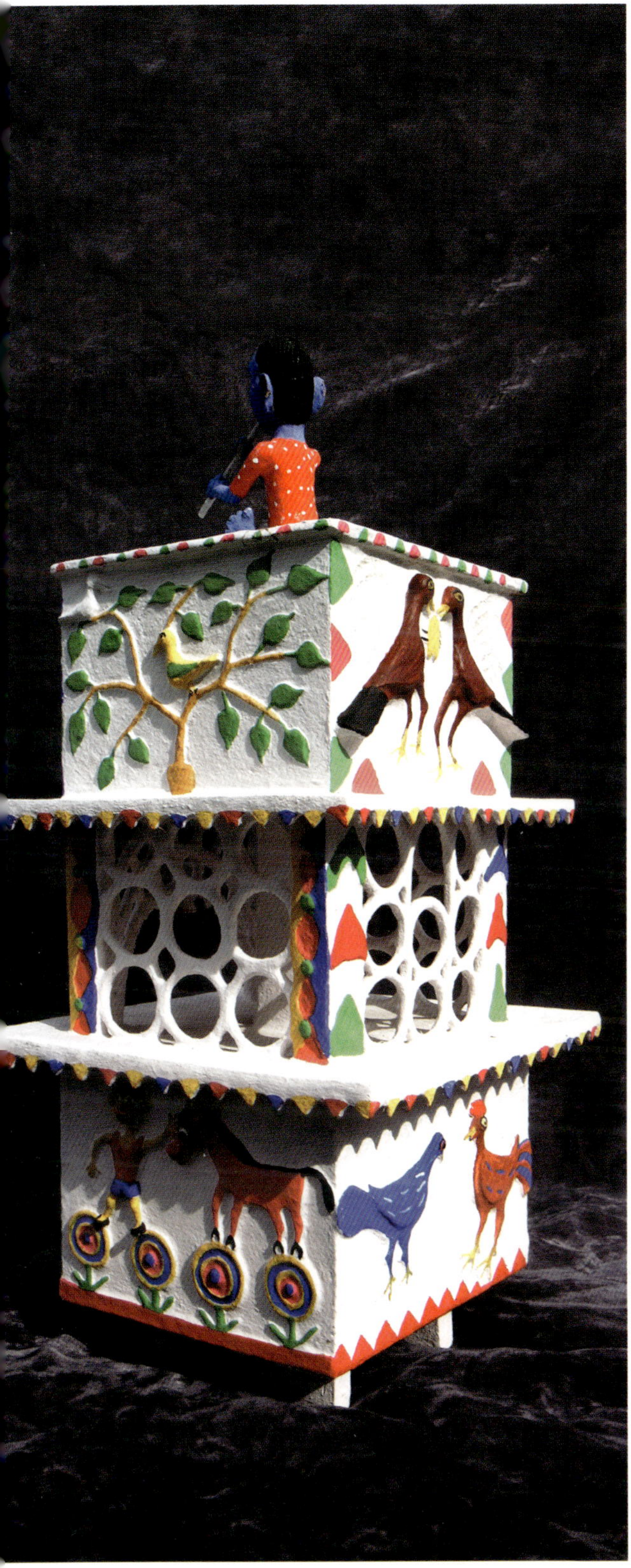

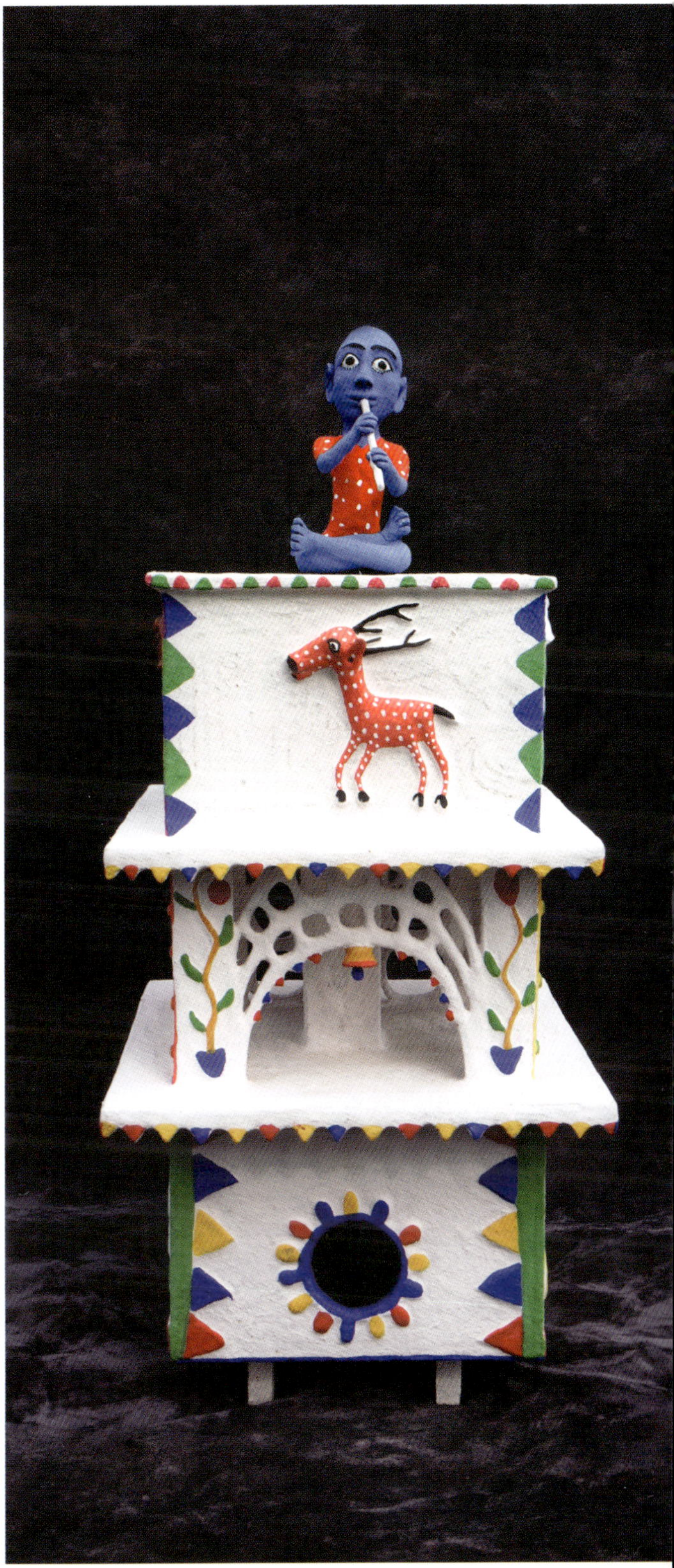

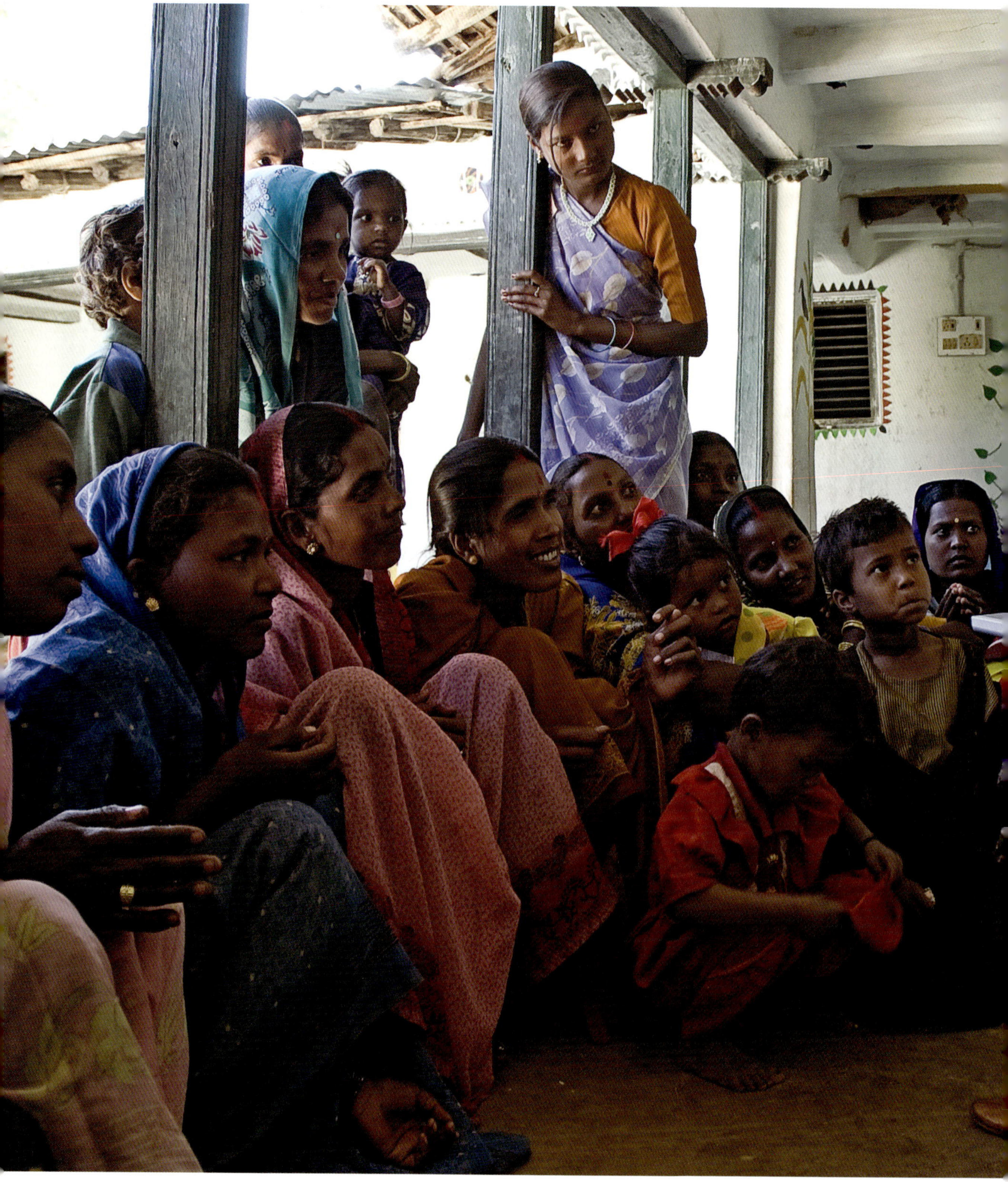

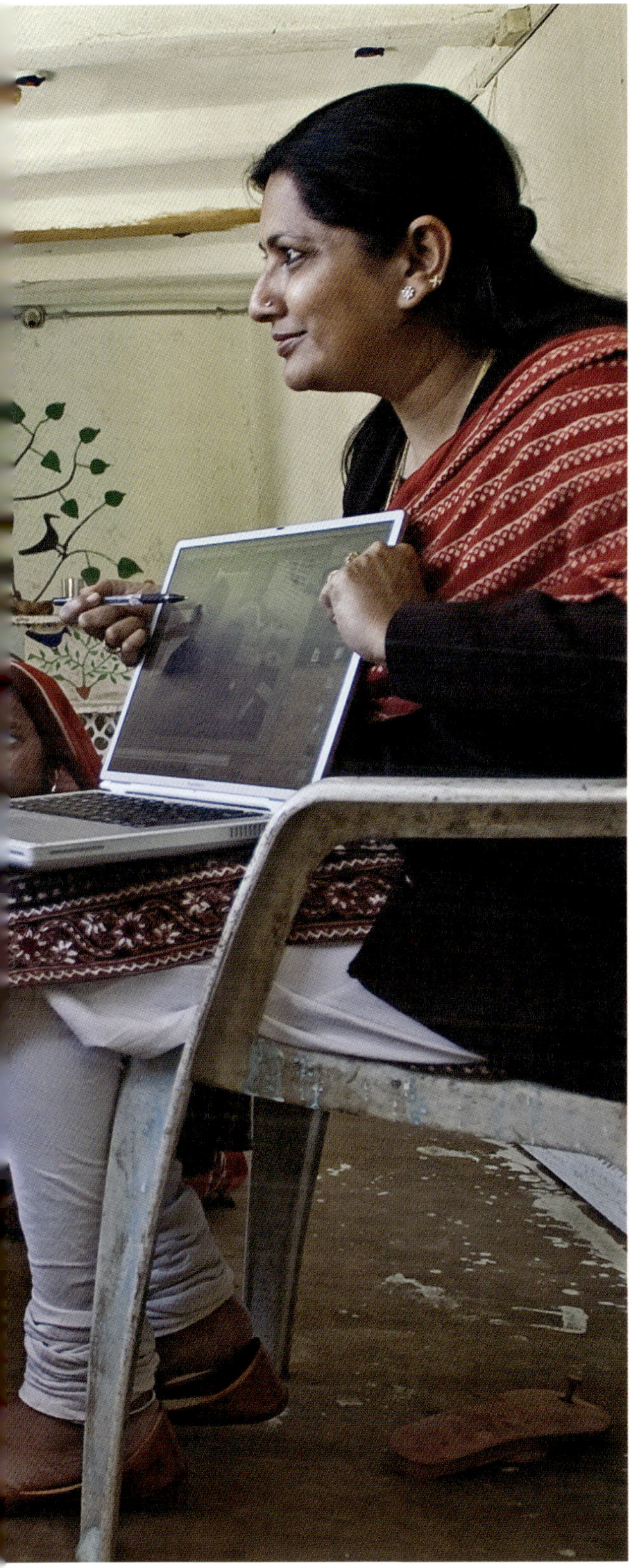

center between the two lines of dancers. The Parrot Dance began as the women in the two lines clapped in unison, laughingly singing out questions to the parrots while stepping side-to-side and back-and-forth. Each question was answered in song on the parrots' behalf by the woman in the center. There were questions about who was going to get married next, who would have how many children, whose husband was good to her, who would have a long life, and so on. No other instruments accompanied the stamping, clapping and singing in this dance. Surrounding the dancers, the entire community was rapt with attention to the nuances of the questions and answers. This dance was clearly represented on the other bas-relief panel where four women dance and clap around a center figure carrying a pot with parrots on her head.

All of us were elated. This re-creation of the harvest dances was a complete success. The villagers obviously enjoyed the unexpected entertainment. The dancers and musicians responded well to our cameras and attention. David and I knew we had captured excellent footage and images: a perfect complement to the sculptures. The dances had begun about one in the afternoon. At dusk, most of the people began to drift back to their homes and their evening farm chores. The women dancers were still so stimulated that they wanted to go on and on. They were all invited back into Sonabai's home and for hours into the night continued to dance in the first big courtyard of the house. In the dim lamp light the bright colors of their saris blended with those of Sonabai's many sculptures on her walls, creating a surreal and beautiful interrelationship. It felt particularly gratifying to sense this strong bond of vibrant community here within this very house that for so many years was the isolated territory of just one lonely woman.

Our work in Puhputra came to an end a couple of days later. Sonabai's family had created for us six excellent sculptures that were well worthy of museum exhibition. While in

Sushmita Tandan displays Stephen's photographs to the women dancers.

Puhputra, I began to envision what such a show might comprise and realized that Sonabai and Daroga Ram's sculptures would be enriched by those of the artists she had influenced. I was able to purchase a total of sixteen other pieces from Bhagat Ram, Atma Das, Sundaribai and Parbatibai. Daroga Ram kindly allowed us to bring all those sculptures to his house and store them in his barn. But each of these twenty-two sculptures was extremely fragile. It was hard to imagine how they could successfully make it to the United States without shattering. During our last few days we commissioned the carpenter to make crates for us and purchased thick bedding foam that Kathleen and I cut to fit each piece. We left for Delhi hoping to find a good shipper who could pick them up and transport them carefully for us.

Leaving Puhputra was difficult. We felt so warmly accepted by the family. We had all worked hard to document Sonabai's family and community and the other artists. We knew we had good material for a book and exhibition but were concerned about whether or not we had enough strong interviews for a full documentary film. Sonabai's increasing dementia meant that it was almost impossible to record anything more than a few words at a time. It was sad to see this great woman deteriorate.

We found an excellent art shipper in Delhi who was able to take two trucks all the way to Puhputra and repack the sculptures there. Three months later they all made it without any breakage to my warehouse in Maine. In editing the film footage, David and I discovered that our apprehensions were correct. David's tapes of the village, the house, the family, the sculpting process and the dance are brilliant, but the interviews are not sufficient to create a saleable documentary. Our diminished budget and Sonabai's decline precluded returning to Puhputra to re-film, so we decided to use David's footage to enhance our exhibition. Over the next years, we worked closely with Duggal Visual Solutions in New York to expand my vision of the show, exploring innovative ways to feature Sonabai's work and the photographs and films far beyond a normal ethnographic exhibition.

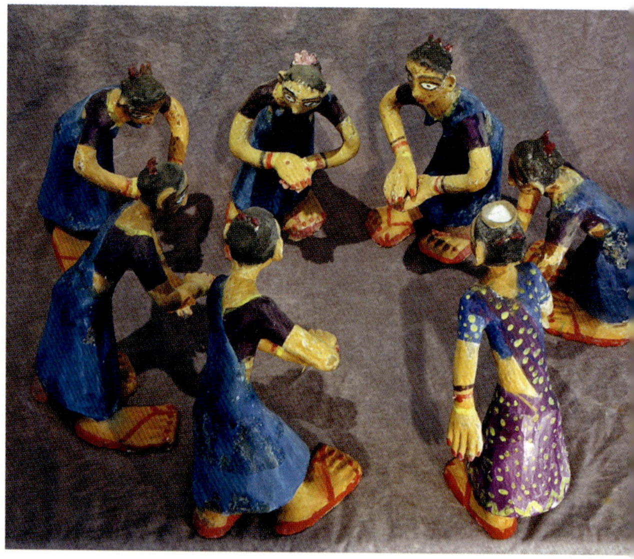

Parbatibai's dancers.

Late in 2005, Kathleen and I returned again to Puhputra for a few days accompanied by two museum curators from Britain, Emma Martin and Nick Gordon. One of my goals was to commission small sculptures from some of the artists as prototypes of objects that might be sold in museum shops during the exhibition's run. I was particularly impressed by the creative productivity of Atma Das and commissioned the birds and small plaques referred to in an earlier chapter. I also arranged for Daroga Ram to create for the exhibition new three-dimensional sculptures of his interpretation of rice cultivation: planting, harvesting and portage. I thought that these would be a good complement to the harvest dance sculptures. Emma commissioned Daroga Ram and Atma Das to make sculptures for the permanent collection of the Liverpool Museum of Art. It was when we visited Parbatibai this time that we first saw her sculptural interpretations of the harvest dance. Parbatibai had been at the community dance we had recorded twenty months before. She was aware that Sonabai and Daroga Ram had sculpted bas-relief panels of the dance that we had purchased and sent back to America. Parbatibai was not certain that we would ever return; she decided to see if she could make her own version of the dancers. When we arrived in her home, she brought out for us two free-standing female dancers, each with her arm around the other, and an accompanying male drummer. They were truly superb and completely unique! I gave Parbatibai enough money so that she would be able to sculpt an entire troupe of male and female dancers and musicians. Parbatibai's sculptures are particularly fragile and prone to break. It would be a miracle if they made it to the U.S. If they did, I knew they would be a center attraction of the growing exhibition. We arranged a second huge shipment from Delhi.

Back in the United States, I was busy working on my book, *Daughters of India,* and finally wrote the chapter on Sonabai that, in 2001, I had traveled with God to research. In 2007, just as the final draft of that book was edited and I was working with my designer on its layout, I heard that Sonabai had died. Babu Mohapatra went to Puhputra and arranged for me to speak to Daroga Ram on the phone not long after she had passed. It was a tearful moment: sad, but no great surprise. Sonabai had been weakening steadily for years.

For four days in March, 2008, Kathleen, Babu and I pitched tents and camped outside Daroga Ram's house. We had come to be with the family with no other expectations, but of course they had created new works of art that I could not resist and I collected a few more for the exhibition. Before we left Maine, and with David Wright's permission, film editor David Berez had helped us create four short films about Puhputra village life, the family, the dance, and Sonabai. I had brought with me a portable digital projector. We white-washed the largest exterior wall of a house nearby that had a large cleared field next to it. We hooked up a thirty-yard extension cord to the house, and Vinod Kumar arranged for a table and speakers. We invited the entire village to arrive at dusk. About seventy-five people initially came, and hundreds more continued to struggle in for the next several hours. By coincidence, the electricity went out in Puhputra as soon as we began the first film. A motor scooter of men buzzed off into the dark to the power station and everyone waited patiently. Twenty minutes later, the electricity returned and we were able to start the film once more. We showed our four films again and again, interspersed with the ubiquitous Indian blackouts that happened another five or six times. The villagers loved to see themselves. They laughed at how the children had grown and at the antics of their friends on camera. They sighed at the loss of beloved elders. They were excited by the dances. Many cried during the film about Sonabai. They might not all understand her art. They might not realize why she has had an impact on the larger world. But Sonabai was a beloved member of their community, one whose singular vision had changed the lives and fortunes of many, and they miss her greatly. So do I.

ACKNOWLEDGEMENTS

Helene, my wife, has been my constant unwavering support and encouragement during this long, eight-year project.

Without the consistent intelligence, insight, creativity, perseverance and flexibility of my assistant, Kathleen Brown, this book and its accompanying museum exhibition could not have materialized.

Babu (Maheswar) Mohapatra has helped us gather this material and work closely with Sonabai, her family, the artists she influenced and their communities. His remarkable abilities are inspiring.

David Wright accompanied us to Puhputra in 2001, volunteering his superb skills as a filmmaker to record footage that is an invaluable record and that greatly enhances this book and our exhibition. Sushmita and Triansha (Shunia) Tandan joined us on that trip and helped to open doors of communication. The dedication of talented filmmaker/editor David Berez is exemplified by his arduous travel to Puhputra in 2006 in order to meet Sonabai and her family. His perceptions greatly inform the production of the film included in this book, as do his filmed interviews of Leslie Umberger and me. Filmmaker Jeffrey Wolf's vision helped craft the film, while he also interviewed Ms. Umberger off-camera. The film is enhanced by the recorded interviews of Dr. Jyotindra Jain, Minhazz Majumdar and Sushmita Tandan, directed by Veenu Pasricha and V. Raja Manikantan.

Minhazz Majumdar visited Puhputra and worked with me to set up initial workshops to try and develop a viable economic outlet for these remote village artists.

Jyoti Bhatt generously shared with me his experiences and photographs recorded in the first visit of outsiders to Sonabai's home in 1983.

Dr. Jyotindra Jain's documentation of Indian folk arts and crafts is unparalleled. My initial inspiration to travel to Puhputra and document Sonabai was in direct response to Dr. Jain's pioneering work with Sonabai and his encouragement that she be recognized for her contemporary artistic merit.

My American publicist, Jeany Wolf, encouraged my collection and production of this material at every step. In order to closely align *Sonabai: Another Way of Seeing*'s design to my earlier publications, Joseph Guglietti created an initial template. Inspired by those first pages, Paulomi Shah adapted and transformed them with her own personal love of the material and her remarkable gifts for design. Joan Phaup thoughtfully and skillfully edited the manuscript, while the input of Mallika Sarabhai and publisher Bipin Shah greatly enhanced the entire production.

Sonabai: Another Way of Seeing is also an exhibition that opens in late July 2009, at Mingei International Museum. Jose Vargas of Duggal Visual Solutions in New York has worked closely with Kathleen Brown and me for four years to develop its innovative design. Rob Sidner, the Director of the Mingei, and his superb staff including Terri Bryson, Martha Ehringer, Jerry Maloney, Alison Rossi and Amy Schindler, have been invaluable in helping me to form this material. Many talented others have contributed to the creation of the exhibition, including Karen Lukas.

Finally, the most important credit goes to the artists themselves. Sonabai, Daroga Ram and Rajenbai Rajawar, Buddhi Ram Rajawar, Sundaribai Rajawar, Bhagat Ram Rajawar, Atma Das Manikpuri, and Parbatibai Sarthi have all created superb original works of art that are the mainstay of both book and exhibition. Without their open willingness to be interviewed, photographed and filmed by all of us, outsiders to their community, the production of this material would not have been possible.

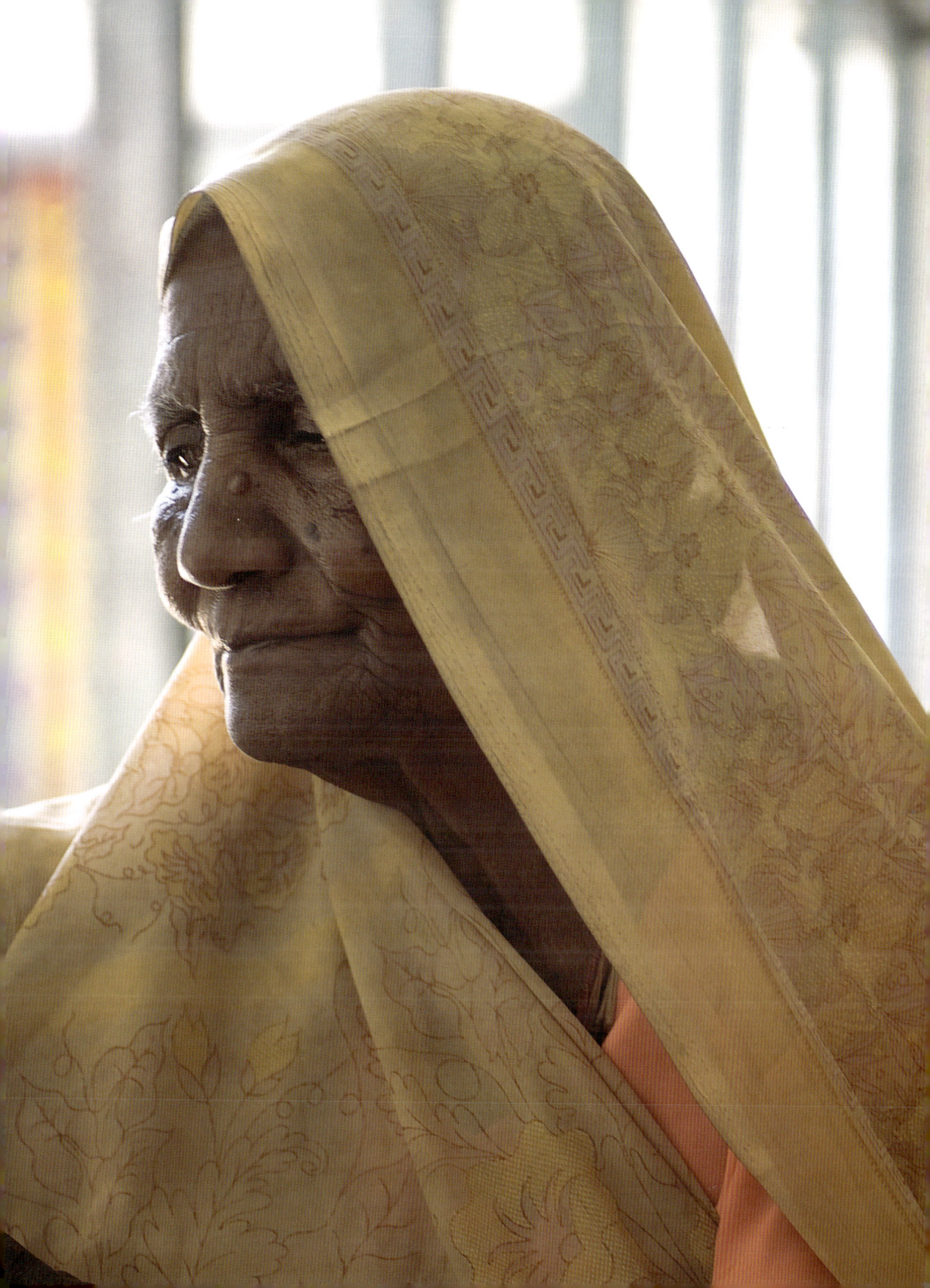

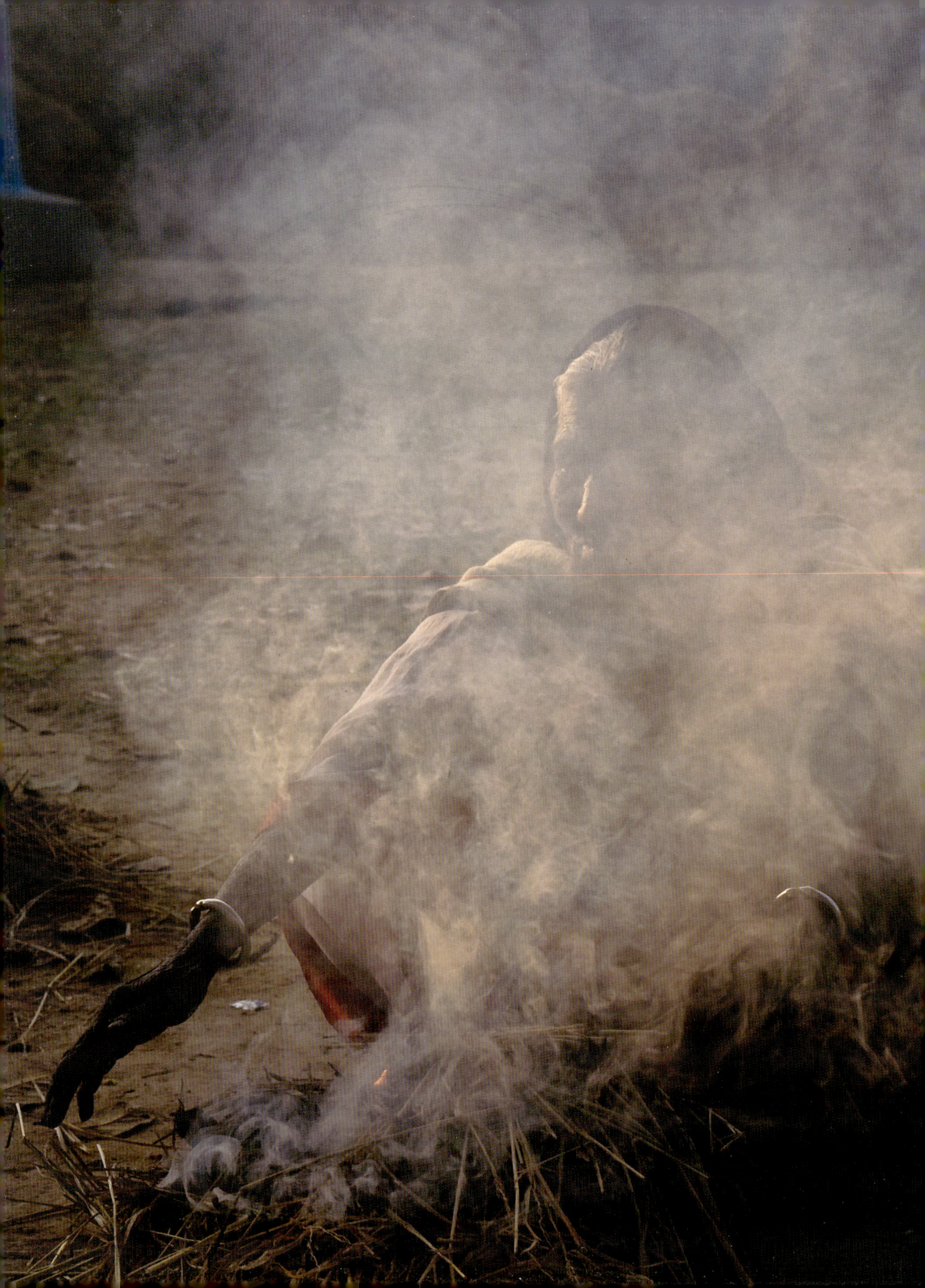